T0340181

Roots of Brazilian Relative
Economic Backwardness

Roots of Brazilian Relative Economic Backwardness

Alexandre Rands Barros

AMSTERDAM • BOSTON • HEIDELBERG • LONDON
NEW YORK • OXFORD • PARIS • SAN DIEGO
SAN FRANCISCO • SINGAPORE • SYDNEY • TOKYO
Academic Press is an imprint of Elsevier

Academic Press is an imprint of Elsevier
125 London Wall, London EC2Y 5AS, United Kingdom
525 B Street, Suite 1800, San Diego, CA 92101-4495, United States
50 Hampshire Street, 5th Floor, Cambridge, MA 02139, United States
The Boulevard, Langford Lane, Kidlington, Oxford OX5 1GB, United Kingdom

Library of Congress Cataloging-in-Publication Data
A catalog record for this book is available from the Library of Congress

British Library Cataloguing-in-Publication Data
A catalogue record for this book is available from the British Library

ISBN: 978-0-12-809756-4

For information on all Academic Press publications
visit our website at https://www.elsevier.com/

Working together
to grow libraries in
developing countries

www.elsevier.com • www.bookaid.org

Publisher: Nikki Levy
Acquisition Editor: Scott J. Bentley
Editorial Project Manager: Susan Ikeda
Production Project Manager: Jason Mitchell
Designer: Mark Rogers

Typeset by TNQ Books and Journals

Dedication

To Tales, my son, and his mother, Analice

Contents

13. Social Conflicts and Human Capital Accumulation in the Period of Search for National Identity

14. Conclusion

Chapter 1

Introduction

Chapter Outline

1.1 INTRODUCTION

Brazil is still included among developing countries, as its per capita GDP (gross domestic product), when corrected for purchasing power parity, ranked at 74 among 178 with available data in the World Bank sample for 2010.[1] Its per capita GDP in 2010 was half that of Portugal, the poorest Western European country by this measure. Even other Latin American countries such as Uruguay, Argentina, and Chile had per capita GDP higher than that of Brazil in 2010, although they are also considered as developing countries.

Why such a huge economy presents this poor development score is still an open question which needs further studies, especially after recent advances in growth and development theories. How did one of the most profitable colonies of the modern era[2] end up as a poor country in the early 21st century? Answering this would be an important contribution to a huge literature that addresses a similar question in a more general form: why have some countries developed so much more than others?[3]

There are some recent hypotheses raised in the literature that address this problem in general frameworks. Examples are the geographical hypothesis put forward by authors such as Diamond (1997), Olsson and Hibbs (2005),

---

1. Data is for 2010, taken from the World Bank website.
2. See Furtado (1959, Chapter 11).
3. For a recent survey of this literature see Spolaore and Wacziarg (2013).

Acemoglu et al. (2001), and Ashraf and Galor (2011, 2013), and the institutional approach proposed by authors such as Acemoglu et al. (2005), Acemoglu and Robinson (2012), North (1990), and Engerman and Sokoloff (1997). While the former group of studies stresses that geographical features such as suitability for agricultural development or European settlements are major determinants of development, the latter argues that the nature of the established institutions accounts for the diversity of performance.

Although these hypotheses can be very enlightening to understand the historical achievements of a specific country, they can miss many particularities that can be relevant to understanding of its current situation. Thus such approaches have to be enriched with studies that focus on the particular circumstances of specific countries and combine the results with their general conclusions. This book fits in this group of necessary approaches when integrated with the literature.

Although this book presents many historical data for the whole Brazilian history, starting with the Portuguese colonial era, its goal is not to present a general economic history of Brazil, as done by others such as Baer (2008). It focuses on the necessary arguments to support a particular hypothesis to explain Brazilian relative backwardness when compared to currently developed countries.

Thus instead of giving a general idea of Brazil, as is common in introductions of these types of books, this introductory chapter only presents some general comments on the structure of the arguments of the book, which are forwarded in Section 1.2, and a summary of the major hypothesis that is thoroughly discussed over the subsequent chapters. Finally, this chapter puts forward some comments on key assumptions behind the economic models underlying the arguments, and on the analytical method that guides the construction of the ideas found in the book.

1.2 STRUCTURE OF THE ARGUMENTS OF THE BOOK

The book starts from the common idea that there are proximate and fundamental causes of growth and development. While the former are related to factors of production accumulations, relative prices of some goods and services, and the evolution of economic policies, the latter are the determinants of all these proximate causes. For example, it has been common recently to point to human and physical capital accumulations as the major proximate causes of growth, while the nature of institutions is seen as the fundamental or ultimate cause of growth.[4] This initial concept motivated a discussion of both types of determinants of development and Brazilian relative backwardness. The proximate determinants are the focus of the first eight chapters, while the last four

---

4. See for example Acemoglu and Robinson (2012) and Acemoglu et al. (2014).

chapters give an analysis of the fundamental determinants of Brazilian failure to have similar per capita GDP to currently developed countries.

The book relies on three types of arguments. First, there is data analysis focusing on basic statistics to identify trends and relative performances. These statistics are already available in their final shape. They are organized here to unveil relationships or strengthen arguments. The data is an object of simple analysis and is often used to illustrate particular arguments. There is no sophisticated statistical analysis; rather, the econometric estimations are very simple, as opposed to the excessive rigor that is common nowadays. Normally they are not used to prove hypotheses, but only to illustrate arguments and their consequences. Thus this book should be seen more as an essay that proposes hypotheses and illustrates them, rather than giving rigorous proof. This allowed the object of analysis to be broader—any more rigorous proof of hypotheses would have to narrow the subject of study.

The second type of argument also relies on data analysis, but some statistical data is built here from previously existing data. Long time series on human capital and per capita GDP in the 19th century are examples. Such series or data are generated to support the hypothesis forwarded in this book. Nevertheless, there is no reliance on sophisticated statistical methods in such estimations, and some of this generated data should be seen rather as educated guesses. These numbers, however, are instruments of analysis as they give some idea of the magnitude of the question under analysis. My idea is that this method is a step forward when compared to the alternative of pure qualitative analysis. Therefore, the numbers found in this book should be seen only as educated guesses that give us more precision in the understanding of the problem under focus.

The book also uses some theoretical developments that are important to put together its hypothesis. The models introduced are also very simple, so they do not transform the text into an excessively technical book. The models are developed only to the point at which their relevant contribution to the book is reached. Hence one should not seek very rigorous and sophisticated general equilibrium theoretical models here, as this is not the aim of this book. Nevertheless, I did not hesitate to draw on mathematical presentation of arguments when they are seen as better instruments to present ideas.

For comparison, some benchmark countries were chosen. They are developed countries, as the focus is on why Brazil has not become one of them. The idea is not to identify why Brazil became a backward country with particular features, so that comparison with other poor countries would be meaningless. It is also not the goal to understand why South Korea, Taiwan, or other countries managed to catch up with the developed club, while Brazil did not. Hence countries that are late starters and caught up in the 20th century were not included in the sample of benchmark countries either.

The benchmark countries included are the ex-European colonies that succeeded, namely the United States, Canada, Australia, and New Zealand, which were called the Western Offshoots by Maddison; the Southern European Periphery, which comprises Portugal, Spain, and Greece; and the Northern European Periphery, formed by Norway, Sweden, Finland, and Switzerland. All countries at the core of initial European industrial development and those that were already very much developed in the 15th century were left out of the sample, as they were part of a common development process which started before Brazil was even colonized by Portugal. Countries such as Britain, France, Germany, Italy, Belgium, the Netherlands, and Austria belong to this group.

From a theoretical standpoint, the underlying foundations of the book combine an economic hypothesis built from neoclassical orthodox mainstream economic arguments with a Marxist political interpretation. The former, however, does not bring in distorted conclusions generated by oversimplistic assumptions. For instance, assumptions such as that of no flow of factors of production through countries' borders, and that there is only one good in the economy, were not used here. Thus ideas such as that there is a long-term convergence of per capita income among nations, as often found in some recent historical analyses, is not taken into account here. Similarly, some deterministic relationships in Marxist political theory were also disregarded, such as that the evolution of productive forces will necessarily disentangle structural changes or revolutions.

1.3 SUMMARY OF THE MAJOR HYPOTHESES

The book has two major hypotheses. One, covered in Chapters 2–9, focuses on the proximate causes of Brazilian long-term growth and relative development, relying on both theoretical and empirical analyses. The second hypothesis tries to explain the fundamental or ultimate causes of Brazilian relative development, and is covered in Chapters 10–13. Although dealt with in different sets of chapters, the empirical material included in the first part of the book helps the arguments advanced in the second part.

An idea that was commonly relied upon by both hypotheses states that Brazil was populated by people with very different ethnic origins. Natives, although subjected to huge decimation over the 500 years since colonization, still had an important role in the social and even ethnic formation of modern Brazil. Africans, mainly brought in as slaves, also had a share in current Brazilian social and ethnic composition. Europeans, mainly from Portugal but also from other countries, such as Italians, Spanish, and Germans, are another important part of Brazilian social and ethnic building, forming around half of current Brazilian ethnic composition. Even Japanese and Arabs generated important migrating flows to Brazil and played some role in shaping current local society. Certainly, all these people carried their cultures and values to Brazil, helping to shape the current culture within the country. This generated the enormous cultural diversity and even tolerance that is an integral component of modern Brazilian society.

All these people had very different skill levels when they entered Brazilian society. Local natives were in 1500 around 10,000−13,000 years behind Europeans, as they were still in the Neolithic era. Africans were something around 1000 years behind when compared to Europeans, although they had a large range of skill levels. These facts molded not only technologies employed in the country but also many features of social organization, such as class relations, urban and rural spatial distribution, the many forms of social interactions, values, and norms, the institutional framework, family structure, and so on.

1.3.1 The Proximate Cause of Brazilian Relative Backwardness

Given these preconditions, there was a search for laws arising from a general equilibrium in economic theory that could more properly fit the Brazilian economy. It should be an equilibrium that would include the whole world and would look at Brazil only as one small part. This approach is obvious given the fact that Brazilian initial colonization had as a basic goal to produce goods that could be traded internationally. Therefore, a world general equilibrium model with many goods, many factors of production, and many countries was analyzed in a search for constraints to the possible equilibrium that could help shape the Brazilian economy.

This model brought some important initial conclusions. First, there is a stable equilibrium in the world economy in which each country has different relative availability of the many factors of production, determining its specialization in world trade. If there is a change in the relative availability of factors of production, the economic specializations are redefined. Thus it is not international trade specialization that determines factor of production availability, but the other way around. This simple idea is already a departure from some theories that place the origin of Brazilian relative backwardness in its primary commodity specialization, such as those proposed by Furtado (1959) and Leff (1997).

Of course these results hold under another important theoretical conclusion, which is that arbitrage in goods and factors of production markets level off world prices for each factor of production. Therefore, there is a tendency to an international equilibrium in which per capita GDP within each country is basically determined by the per capita availability of the many factors of production within this same country, as the income per unit extracted from these factors is very similar in all countries. Thus the relative factor of production accumulations within each country are not determined by relative differences in the return to these factors, as suggested, for example, in the convergence literature.[5] It should be noted that these theories of convergence

---

5. For a recent restatement of the convergence hypothesis see Barro (2012). See also Barro and Sala-i-Martin (1992).

extract their conclusions from models in which there is no international migration of factors of production and only one good is produced, which are not the reality nowadays, nor have been over the last 500 years.

The international general equilibrium model that underlies one of the major hypotheses of this book also shows that there are many possible equilibria when there is free migration of all factors of production across countries' borders. Therefore, if a country has a higher concentration of human capital, it tends to have a higher per capita GDP, as the physical capital availability adjusts through international flow. Furthermore, it is argued that international migration of human capital is more sluggish than that of physical capital, as a consequence of the other social relationships involved in individual motivations for such adventures. This makes the human capital concentration in one country the major determinant of its relative per capita GDP, although the availability of natural resources can also play some role.[6] Hence the major search for the determinants of Brazilian relative backwardness becomes a search for the origins of its low relative per capita availability of human capital.

Another theoretical conclusion was important to understand the long-term dynamics of Brazilian relative backwardness and current low relative per capita stock of human capital: families tend to reproduce their relative proportions of human capital over generations if there is no public policy to change it. Hence human capital disparities among nations tend to be perpetuated over time. Thus the composition of Brazilian society over its history, with low average relative per capita human capital when compared to that found in European countries and Western Offshoots, condemned the country to its current relative backwardness.

The first part of the book uses much historical data and information to persuade the reader that a society was built in Brazil that had much lower per capita human capital, and this led to its economic specialization in the world market. Furthermore, it is argued that there were no motivations among the social agents to change this poor relative per capita human capital. This point, however, is further developed in the second part of the book.

1.3.2 The Ultimate Cause of Brazilian Relative Backwardness

The second part of the book is dedicated to trying to understand why there was no public policy to overcome the relatively low average stock of per capita human capital in the country by providing quality education for the poorest social segments. The hypothesis forwarded is that public policies and institutions are built from the social conflicts among groups with different

---

6. The latter is the major determinant of the relative per capita GDP of countries such as Qatar, the United Arab Emirates, Kuwait, and Saudi Arabia.

interests. The dynamic evolutions of these conflicts are the major determinants of these policies, including those on education.

After this theoretical view, the book introduces the idea that the ethnic and cultural diversity of the low-income strata that composed the majority of Brazilian population led to low class consciousness and, consequently, low organization to demand better access to public education of some quality. The new immigrants who arrived through inflows of foreigners in the second half of the 19th and first half of the 20th centuries did not align with this former social group in support of demands for basic public education. Their higher human capital and income soon after their arrival gave them higher returns from public investments in higher education. Hence their social and political alliance in what concerns public education was mainly with the elites and state bureaucracy, rather than with the poorest social segments. These particularities of local class struggle dynamics relegated the majority of the Brazilian population to a low human capital level, and the country to its current relative backwardness.

1.4 ADDITIONAL COMMENTS ON ASSUMPTIONS AND ANALYTICAL METHOD

Many explanations of Brazilian relative backwardness rely on very different assumptions from those introduced explicitly or implicitly in the underlying models of the hypotheses previously summarized. The idea of free trade is one of them. Everybody, including myself, knows that there are many frictional barriers to trade, which could be natural, such as transport costs, risks involved, and asymmetric information, or artificial, such as tariffs, quotas, and so on. What the book is saying is not that they do not exist, but that they are not relevant to changing the determined equilibrium qualitatively. To think that artificial barriers such as tariffs and quotas were relevant to change the market equilibrium substantially is to lose completely the notion of proportion. If the Brazilian government cannot have effective control of its frontiers in the early 21st century, why should one think that it would do so in the early 20th century?

Another important and realistic assumption introduced is that there is free international factor of production migration, so their prices converge to the same value in all countries. Certainly there are many barriers to factor of production flow through countries' borders and nobody would think they do not exist. When labor and its embodied human capital is the factor in question, these restrictions are even higher. Nevertheless, there is empirical data confirming that these migrations have always existed, and had such intensity that they were sufficient to constrain excessive price disparities. Furthermore, changes in international trade specializations also discipline the divergence of factor prices, as assured by the factor price equalization theorem stated by Samuelson (1948). Together, these two economic adjustments suffice to make the assumption of full arbitrage in the markets for factors of production a better approximation of reality than the idea that such arbitrage does not exist.

Another important assumption made throughout this book is that agents are rational and selfish, so the private interest of their families takes priority over the interest of a nation or country. Therefore, the approach of this book is rooted in the methodological individualism. According to Arrow:

> *The Starting point for the individualist paradigm is the simple fact that all social interactions are after all interactions among individuals. The individual in the economy or in the society is like the atom in chemistry; whatever happens can ultimately be described exhaustively in terms of the individuals involved. Of course, the individuals do not act separately. They respond to each other, but each acts within a range limited by the behavior of others as well as by constraints personal to the individuals, such as his/her ability or wealth.*

Arrow (1994, p. 3).

Although this is a strong assumption, it is well known to be not fully correct. Even orthodox economists such as Kenneth Arrow admit that this is not the case. Individuals often take into account the welfare of others in their actions, and many of the conclusions drawn from supposedly methodological individualism assumptions implicitly introduce the idea that not all economic phenomena are fully reduced to the output of individual actions.[7] This justifies the reliance on political theories to explain Brazilian relative backwardness in a broader way.

Another important methodological approach found throughout this book relies on a suggestion made by Lucas (1980). Before assuming that orthodox theory does not explain a particular phenomenon straightforwardly, and using unorthodox subterfuges, the idea is to build upon this theory and find a solution, instead of easily giving up on its ability to explain the phenomenon. This methodological approach departs from that followed by Furtado (1959) and most other studies on this subject. In what concerns the fundamental causes of relative backwardness, however, economic theory does not present any relevant established hypothesis, but only the idea that institutions are important. There is not really a reasonable theory underneath the assertion that institutions are the major determinant of development, hence this was not considered as a mainstream theory, but only as a mere ideology.

---

7. See Arrow (1994) for a discussion of this subject.

Chapter 2

Historical Origins of Brazilian Relative Backwardness

Chapter Outline

2.1 INTRODUCTION

A central issue in understanding Brazilian relative backwardness is identifying when the country lagged behind those considered as potential benchmarks, such as the United States, Canada, Australia, and New Zealand, all old European colonies like Brazil. This chapter presents some data that can help in this identification. Comparisons are also extended to some European countries, particularly two peripheries within this continent in the early expansion of capitalism: the Southern Periphery, composed by Portugal, Spain, and Greece; and the Northern European Periphery composed by Finland, Sweden, Switzerland, and Norway. Therefore, altogether, data and analysis cover 11 countries in addition to Brazil.

Data comes from the Maddison Project (Maddison, 2011; Bolt and van Zanden, 2013). Figures for population are all from Maddison (2011), while data for per capita GDP (gross domestic product) up to 1820 is from Bolt and van Zanden (2013). Of course this data has serious limitations, as it was only recently calculated and it is always difficult to estimate aggregate variables for a period so long ago. Nevertheless, it can shed some light upon the beginning of Brazilian relative backwardness. This is a crucial step to understanding the causes of Brazilian poor long-term performance.

The next section benchmarks Brazil against other countries in specific periods for which data is available. It organizes the data in a way that the major periods in which there was further loss of relative development can be easily identified. Section 2.3 brings an alternative decomposition of the historical sources of relative backwardness, which can unveil the role of initial

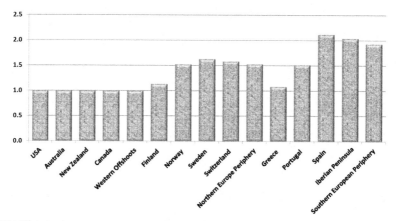

FIGURE 2.1 Proportion of per capita GDP in selected countries or groups to Brazilian GDP, 1500 (%). *Calculated from data by Maddison, A., 2011. Historical Statistics of the World Economy: 1-2008 AD. Maddison Project and Bolt, J., van Zanden J.L., 2013. The First Update of the Maddison Project: Re-estimating Growth Before 1820. Maddison Project Working Paper 4.*

differences of per capita GDP in 1500, when Brazilian colonial history begins. Section 2.4 puts together our major conclusions.

2.2 LONG-TERM DATA ON PER CAPITA GDP GROWTH: FIRST EXERCISE

Before Portuguese colonizers arrived in Brazil, the indigenous population had development standards equivalent to those of the Neolithic era. Hunting and fishing provided most of the necessary food, although there were some very rudimentary agricultural practices. There was no writing and even basic arithmetic notions were unknown.

This low technological development level generated a very egalitarian standard of living, but at very low levels, as productivity was quite low. Maddison (2011) evaluated that this low productivity generated a per capita GDP corresponding to US$400.00 per year in international US dollars of 2005. This value is the same in his estimates for all countries when they were at their maximum potential backwardness. This would cover most of the Americas.[1]

While the Brazilian population had this standard of living in 1500, European societies had already generated better standards of living, even on its periphery. Fig. 2.1 compares yearly per capita GDP according to estimations by Maddison (2011) and Bolt and van Zanden (2013). While Brazil, the United

---

1. Aztecs who were settled in what today is mainly Mexico already had writing and even money, which implies they had basic notions of arithmetic. See Acemoglu and Robinson (2012, p. 50). Consequently, Maddison's estimation for per capita GDP in Mexico in 1500 was US$425.00, which is already above the minimum absolute standard of living.

States, Australia, New Zealand, and Canada all had the US$400.00 minimum standard of living, all European peripheral countries included already had per capita GDP higher than this value in 1500, so the proportions presented in Fig. 2.1 are all equal to or over 1.0. Nevertheless, it should be stressed that all proportions were lower than 2.20, considering that Spain, the most developed country in our sample that year, had a per capita GDP of 2.11 times the Brazilian one.

Fig. 2.2 repeats the exercise in Fig. 2.1 for the year 2010. For all these geographical areas, the proportion presented is above 2.0 and often above 3.0. A comparison of the results of Figs. 2.1 and 2.2 indicates that all countries or groups included had grown faster than Brazil between 1500 and 2010. Nevertheless, they do not reveal if this happened over the whole period or at some particular moments.

Table 2.1 and Figs. 2.3−2.17 provide indexes of the proportion of per capita GDPs of benchmark countries to that of Brazil for selected years. These indexes were made equal to 100 in the year 1500. Thus the rate of per capita GDP in any of these countries compared to the Brazilian GDP was normalized to 100 in this initial year. The same number used to multiply this value to make it equal to 100 in 1500 was also multiplied by the ratio in the other years in all these figures. An average growth rate for each 10-year interval between consecutive years marked in these figures and table was also included to help data interpretation.

Data in these figures clearly indicates that the 19th century was the one in which the Brazilian economy had the poorest relative performance. Per capita GDP in all benchmark countries grew faster than Brazilian GDP in that century. Furthermore, this difference was the highest among all periods covered

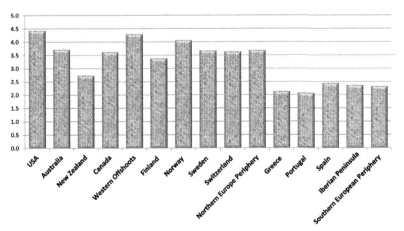

FIGURE 2.2 Proportion of per capita GDP in selected countries or groups to Brazilian GDP, 2010 (%). *Calculated from data by Maddison, A., 2011. Historical Statistics of the World Economy: 1-2008 AD. Maddison Project and Bolt, J., van Zanden J.L., 2013. The First Update of the Maddison Project: Re-estimating Growth Before 1820. Maddison Project Working Paper 4.*

TABLE 2.1 Proportion of Per Capita GDP to Brazilian GDP If the Proportion Was 100 in 1500, and Decennial Per Capita GDP Growth Rate of Benchmark Countries

	United States		Australia		New Zealand		Canada		Western Offshoots		Finland		Norway		Sweden	
	Proportion	Growth	Proportion	Growth	Proportion	Growth	Proportion	Growth	Proportion	Growth	Proportion	Growth	Proportion	Growth	Proportion	Growth
1500	100		100		100		100		100		100		100		100	
1600	93	−0.7	93	−0.7	93	−0.7	93	−0.7	93	−0.7	111	1.0	102	0.2	109	0.9
1700	115	2.1	87	−0.7	87	−0.7	94	0.0	104	1.0	123	1.0	103	0.1	179	5.1
1820	199	4.7	76	−1.2	59	−3.3	132	2.9	191	5.2	101	−1.6	77	−2.4	80	−6.5
1900	577	14.2	566	28.6	607	33.9	411	15.2	567	14.6	208	9.4	174	10.7	181	10.7
2008	443	−2.4	372	−3.8	275	−7.0	363	−1.1	430	−2.5	299	3.4	267	4.0	226	2.1

	Switzerland		Northern Europe Periphery		Greece		Portugal		Spain		Iberian Peninsula		Southern European Periphery	
	Proportion	Growth	Proportion	Growth	Proportion	Growth	Proportion	Growth	Proportion	Growth	Proportion	Growth	Proportion	Growth
1500	100		100		100		100		100		100		100	
1600	111	1.0	109	0.8	104	0.4	180	6.0	99	−0.1	106	0.6	105	0.4
1700	123	1.0	166	4.3	107	0.2	140	−2.4	84	−1.6	90	−1.6	91	−1.4
1820	101	−1.6	82	−5.7	87	−1.7	89	−3.7	70	−1.5	71	−2.0	72	−2.0
1900	527	22.9	182	10.4	161	8.1	121	3.9	119	6.9	116	6.3	117	6.3
2008	230	−7.2	241	2.6	197	1.8	137	1.1	116	−0.3	116	0.0	121	0.3

Calculated from data from Maddison, A., 2011. Historical Statistics of the World Economy: 1-2008 AD. Maddison Project and Bolt, J., van Zanden J.L., 2013. The First Update of the Maddison Project: Re-estimating Growth Before 1820. Maddison Project Working Paper 4.

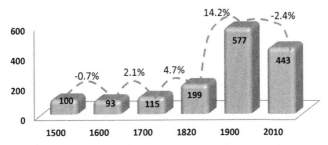

FIGURE 2.3 Index of proportions of per capita GDP, United States to Brazil. 1500 = 100. *Author calculation. Original data from Maddison, A., 2011. Historical Statistics of the World Economy: 1-2008 AD. Maddison Project.*

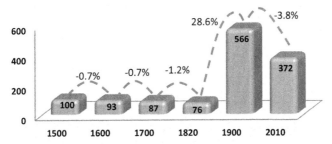

FIGURE 2.4 Index of proportions of per capita GDP, Australia to Brazil. 1500 = 100. *Author calculation. Original data from Maddison, A., 2011. Historical Statistics of the World Economy: 1-2008 AD. Maddison Project.*

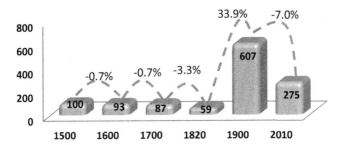

FIGURE 2.5 Index of proportions of per capita GDP, New Zealand to Brazil. 1500 = 100. *Author calculation. Original data from Maddison, A., 2011. Historical Statistics of the World Economy: 1-2008 AD. Maddison Project.*

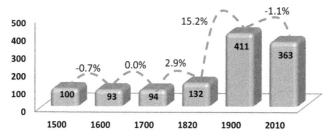

FIGURE 2.6   Index of proportions of per capita GDP, Canada to Brazil. 1500 = 100. *Author calculation. Original data from Maddison, A., 2011. Historical Statistics of the World Economy: 1-2008 AD. Maddison Project.*

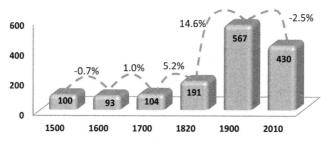

FIGURE 2.7   Index of proportions of per capita GDP, Western Offshoots to Brazil. 1500 = 100. *Author calculation. Original data from Maddison, A., 2011. Historical Statistics of the World Economy: 1-2008 AD. Maddison Project.*

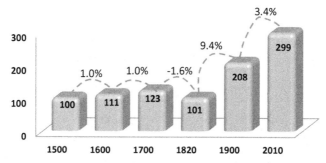

FIGURE 2.8   Index of proportions of per capita GDP, Finland to Brazil. 1500 = 100. *Author calculation. Original data from Maddison, A., 2011. Historical Statistics of the World Economy: 1-2008 AD. Maddison Project.*

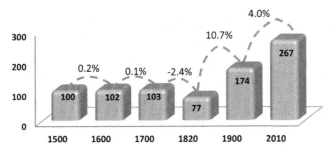

FIGURE 2.9   Index of proportions of per capita GDP, Norway to Brazil. 1500 = 100. *Author calculation. Original data from Maddison, A., 2011. Historical Statistics of the World Economy: 1-2008 AD. Maddison Project.*

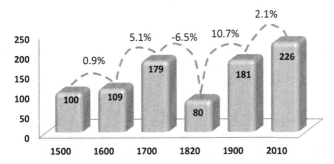

FIGURE 2.10   Index of proportions of per capita GDP, Sweden to Brazil. 1500 = 100. *Author calculation. Original data from Maddison, A., 2011. Historical Statistics of the World Economy: 1-2008 AD. Maddison Project.*

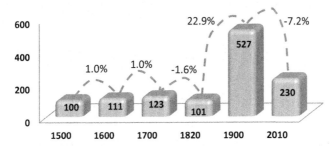

FIGURE 2.11   Index of proportions of per capita GDP, Switzerland to Brazilian. 1500 = 100. *Author calculation. Original data from Maddison, A., 2011. Historical Statistics of the World Economy: 1-2008 AD. Maddison Project.*

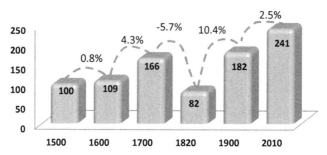

FIGURE 2.12   Index of proportions of per capita GDP, Northern European Periphery to Brazil. 1500 = 100. *Author calculation. Original data from Maddison, A., 2011. Historical Statistics of the World Economy: 1-2008 AD. Maddison Project.*

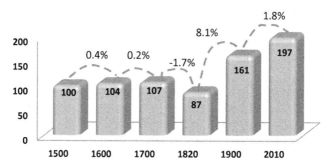

FIGURE 2.13   Index of proportions of per capita GDP, Greece to Brazil. 1500 = 100. *Author calculation. Original data from Maddison, A., 2011. Historical Statistics of the World Economy: 1-2008 AD. Maddison Project.*

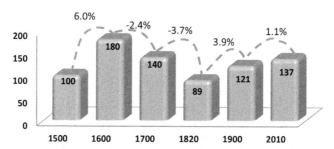

FIGURE 2.14   Index of proportions of per capita GDP, Portugal to Brazil. 1500 = 100. *Author calculation. Original data from Maddison, A., 2011. Historical Statistics of the World Economy: 1-2008 AD. Maddison Project.*

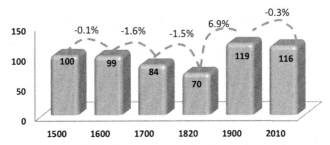

FIGURE 2.15   Index of proportions of per capita GDP, Spain to Brazil. 1500 = 100. *Author calculation. Original data from Maddison, A., 2011. Historical Statistics of the World Economy: 1-2008 AD. Maddison Project.*

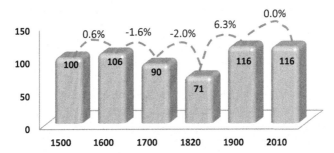

FIGURE 2.16   Index of proportions of per capita GDP, Iberian Peninsula to Brazil. 1500 = 100. *Author calculation. Original data from Maddison, A., 2011. Historical Statistics of the World Economy: 1-2008 AD. Maddison Project.*

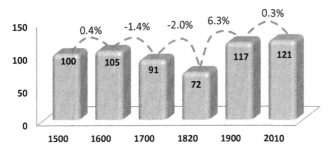

FIGURE 2.17   Index of proportions of per capita GDP, Southern European Periphery to Brazil. 1500 = 100. *Author calculation. Original data from Maddison, A., 2011. Historical Statistics of the World Economy: 1-2008 AD. Maddison Project.*

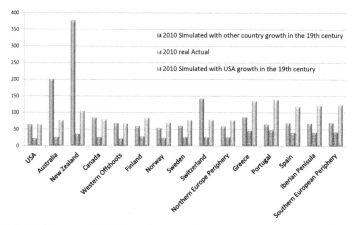

FIGURE 2.18   Proportion (%) of Brazilian to benchmark countries' per capita GDP: actual in 2010 and simulated with 19th-century Brazilian growth rate equal to that of the other country or of the United States. *Original data from Maddison, A., 2011. Historical Statistics of the World Economy: 1-2008 AD. Maddison Project and Bolt, J., van Zanden J.L., 2013. The First Update of the Maddison Project: Re-estimating Growth Before 1820. Maddison Project Working Paper 4.*

and for all countries, with the exception of Portugal, which grew faster between 1500 and 1600. Portugal contracted relative to Brazil in the next two centuries, however, so the 19th century turned out to be the most responsible for Brazilian relative backwardness even with respect to Portugal. Together, this data indicates that the economic performance in the 19th century is the most responsible for Brazilian relative backwardness.

It should be stressed that the figures to generate growth rates and relative per capita GDP for 1900 were corrected to be an average for the five years centered on 1900. The figure from Bolt and van Zanden (2013) for Brazilian per capita GDP this year is such that it is clearly an outlier. Between 1898 and 1902, 1900 is the lowest figure and is clearly out of the trend. Therefore, to avoid overemphasizing the role of the weak performance of the 19th century in Brazilian relative backwardness because of a momentary crisis in Brazil that year, the option was to make this correction.

To assess the extent of the impact of the poor performance of the 19th century in Brazilian relative backwardness, another set of statistics was calculated and is presented in Fig. 2.18 and Table 2.2. The statistics show the proportion of Brazilian per capita GDP to the per capita GDP of benchmark countries had it grown at the same rate as the country under comparison in the 19th century;[2] and grown at the same rate as the United States in that same period. For all other time intervals, growth rates of Brazilian per capita GDP

---

2. It should be noted that, rigorously, the period covered by the statistics for the 19th century is actually between 1820 and 1900.

TABLE 2.2 2010 Proportion of Brazilian Per Capita GDP to That of Selected Countries: Actual, and Simulated with 19th-century Brazilian Growth Equal to That of the Other Country or of the United States

	Actual	Simulated With Other Country's Growth in 19th Century	Simulated With US Growth in 19th Century
United States	22.6	70.4	70.4
Australia	26.9	216.1	83.9
New Zealand	36.4	406.0	113.6
Canada	27.6	92.1	86.0
Western Offshoots	23.3	74.4	72.6
Finland	29.5	65.5	92.1
Norway	24.6	59.7	76.7
Sweden	27.2	66.2	84.8
Switzerland	27.5	154.3	85.7
Northern Europe Periphery	27.1	64.5	84.5
Greece	46.8	93.8	146.0
Portugal	48.2	70.5	150.2
Spain	41.0	75.3	127.7
Iberian Peninsula	42.3	74.3	131.9
Southern European Periphery	43.0	75.7	134.1

Calculated from data by Maddison, A., 2011. Historical Statistics of the World Economy: 1-2008 AD. Maddison Project and Bolt, J., van Zanden J.L., 2013. The First Update of the Maddison Project: Re-estimating Growth Before 1820. Maddison Project Working Paper 4.

were as calculated from data by Maddison (2011) and Bolt and van Zanden (2013). The actual proportion was also included together with these artificially built proportions, allowing a clearer comparison of the impact of the 19th century.

The data in Fig. 2.18 and Table 2.2 shows that Brazilian poor performance in the 19th century alone is responsible for Brazilian relative backwardness only when compared to Australia, New Zealand, and Switzerland. In the two previous centuries Canada and the United States held a lead, but not all that wide. In the particular case of Canada, a similar performance of Brazilian per capita GDP in the 19th century would lead to a proportion of this variable in

2010 equivalent to 89.4% of that of this developed country. European peripheries already had an advantage at the beginning of Brazilian history and continued to do so in the 20th century, although their higher relative development was also built mostly in the 19th century, as comparisons of the first and second columns for each indicate. Therefore, to understand Brazilian relative backwardness, we must assess the reasons for the poor performance of Brazil in the 19th century.

2.3 ALTERNATIVE DECOMPOSITION OF THE HISTORICAL SOURCES OF RELATIVE BACKWARDNESS

The simple method pursued in the previous section to identify the main century in which the economic backwardness of Brazil relative to the benchmark countries emerged is slightly extended here to find a measure of the role of each period and the initial differences, altogether. This method can be derived from the simple growth equation:

$$Y_f = Y_0 \prod_{i=1}^{n} (1 + g_i)^{p_i} \qquad (2.1)$$

where Y_f and Y_0 are the per capita GDP in the last and initial periods, respectively; g_i is the yearly growth rate of per capita GDP in period i; and p_i is the number of years in that same period. There are n periods between the initial and the last period.

If we divide Eq. (2.1) for any benchmark country by the Brazilian one, and take a natural logarithm, the result is:

$$\ln\left(\frac{Y_f}{Y_{Bf}}\right) = \ln\left(\frac{Y_0}{Y_{B0}}\right) + \sum_{i=1}^{n} p_i \ln\left(\frac{1 + g_i}{1 + g_{Bi}}\right) \qquad (2.2)$$

where B was introduced in the subscripts to identify variables defined for Brazil. If the two sides of Eq. (2.2) are divided by the term in the left side, the two sides are equal to one. Therefore, each term in the right side can be viewed as a proportion of the term in the left side that is explained by the proportion of growth rates in that particular period, or the initial state, in what concerns the first term in the right side.

It should be noted that the initial proportion can also be seen as the proportion between the growth rates from the original moment in which all countries had the same per capita GDP to the first period, which is year 1500. Therefore, Eq. (2.2) represents a full decomposition of the proportions of GDP in growth rates for particular periods.

The proportion between per capita GDP in particular countries and Brazilian GDP was decomposed by this method in the role of the initial proportion and that of growth rates for specific periods. This decomposition appears in Table 2.3 and Figs. 2.19−2.29. It confirms the prominent role of the 19th

TABLE 2.3 Decomposition of Each Period's Role (%) in Brazilian Backwardness Relative to Other Countries

Period	United States	Australia	New Zealand	Canada	Western Offshoots	Finland	Norway	Sweden	Switzerland	Northern Europe Periphery
0–1500	0.0	0.0	0.0	0.0	0.0	10.3	30.1	37.4	35.4	32.5
1500–1600	−4.5	−5.2	−6.7	−5.3	−4.6	8.4	1.3	6.8	8.0	6.4
1600–1700	13.8	−5.3	−6.9	0.2	7.1	8.3	0.9	38.0	7.8	32.4
1700–1820	37.0	−10.6	−39.4	26.9	41.8	−15.9	−20.9	−62.1	−15.1	−54.0
1820–1900	71.5	153.1	231.5	87.9	74.7	59.2	58.0	62.7	127.9	60.8
1900–1950	−0.6	−18.6	−18.0	4.6	−1.5	6.4	14.5	24.2	−33.2	19.6
1950–2010	−17.1	−13.4	−60.5	−14.3	−17.5	23.4	16.1	−7.0	−30.9	2.3
Total	100.0	100.0	100.0	100.0	100.0	100.0	100.0	100.0	100.0	100.0

Period	Greece	Portugal	Spain	Iberian Peninsula	Southern Europe Periphery
0–1500	10.4	56.9	83.8	82.7	77.8
1500–1600	5.6	80.1	−1.6	6.7	5.3
1600–1700	2.9	−33.9	−18.1	−18.7	−16.5
1700–1820	−27.3	−61.9	−20.6	−27.6	−28.2
1820–1900	81.8	42.1	60.0	57.0	58.2
1900–1950	−55.6	−53.0	−73.4	−70.0	−68.4
1950–2010	82.1	69.7	69.8	70.0	71.7
Total	100.0	100.0	100.0	100.0	100.0

Calculated from data from Maddison, A., 2011. Historical Statistics of the World Economy: 1-2008 AD. Maddison Project.

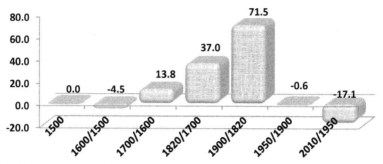

FIGURE 2.19 Decomposition of each period's role in Brazilian relative backwardness when compared to the United States. *Original data from Maddison, A., 2011. Historical Statistics of the World Economy: 1-2008 AD. Maddison Project and Bolt, J., van Zanden J.L., 2013. The First Update of the Maddison Project: Re-estimating Growth Before 1820. Maddison Project Working Paper 4.*

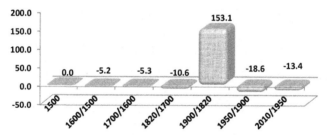

FIGURE 2.20 Decomposition of each period's role in Brazilian relative backwardness when compared to Australia. *Original data from Maddison, A., 2011. Historical Statistics of the World Economy: 1-2008 AD. Maddison Project and Bolt, J., van Zanden J.L., 2013. The First Update of the Maddison Project: Re-estimating Growth Before 1820. Maddison Project Working Paper 4.*

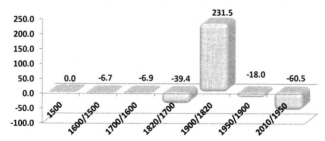

FIGURE 2.21 Decomposition of each period's role in Brazilian relative backwardness when compared to New Zealand. *Original data from Maddison, A., 2011. Historical Statistics of the World Economy: 1-2008 AD. Maddison Project and Bolt, J., van Zanden J.L., 2013. The First Update of the Maddison Project: Re-estimating Growth Before 1820. Maddison Project Working Paper 4.*

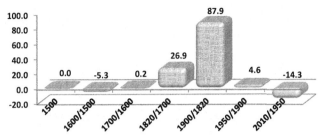

FIGURE 2.22 Decomposition of each period's role in Brazilian relative backwardness when compared to Canada. *Original data from Maddison, A., 2011. Historical Statistics of the World Economy: 1-2008 AD. Maddison Project and Bolt, J., van Zanden J.L., 2013. The First Update of the Maddison Project: Re-estimating Growth Before 1820. Maddison Project Working Paper 4.*

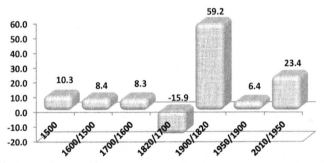

FIGURE 2.23 Decomposition of each period's role in Brazilian relative backwardness when compared to Finland. *Original data from Maddison, A., 2011. Historical Statistics of the World Economy: 1-2008 AD. Maddison Project and Bolt, J., van Zanden J.L., 2013. The First Update of the Maddison Project: Re-estimating Growth Before 1820. Maddison Project Working Paper 4.*

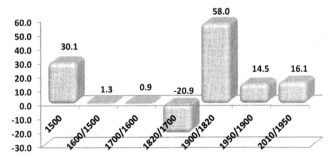

FIGURE 2.24 Decomposition of each period's role in Brazilian relative backwardness when compared to Norway. *Original data from Maddison, A., 2011. Historical Statistics of the World Economy: 1-2008 AD. Maddison Project and Bolt, J., van Zanden J.L., 2013. The First Update of the Maddison Project: Re-estimating Growth Before 1820. Maddison Project Working Paper 4.*

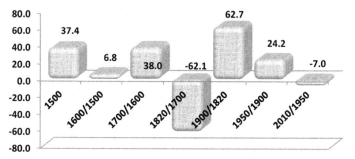

FIGURE 2.25   Decomposition of each period's role in Brazilian relative backwardness when compared to Sweden. *Original data from Maddison, A., 2011. Historical Statistics of the World Economy: 1-2008 AD. Maddison Project and Bolt, J., van Zanden J.L., 2013. The First Update of the Maddison Project: Re-estimating Growth Before 1820. Maddison Project Working Paper 4.*

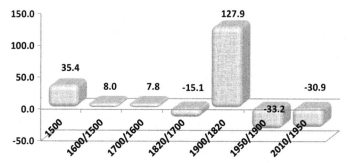

FIGURE 2.26   Decomposition of each period's role in Brazilian relative backwardness when compared to Switzerland. *Original data from Maddison, A., 2011. Historical Statistics of the World Economy: 1-2008 AD. Maddison Project and Bolt, J., van Zanden J.L., 2013. The First Update of the Maddison Project: Re-estimating Growth Before 1820. Maddison Project Working Paper 4.*

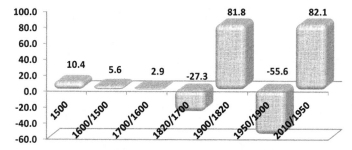

FIGURE 2.27   Decomposition of each period's role in Brazilian relative backwardness when compared to Greece. *Original data from Maddison, A., 2011. Historical Statistics of the World Economy: 1-2008 AD. Maddison Project and Bolt, J., van Zanden J.L., 2013. The First Update of the Maddison Project: Re-estimating Growth Before 1820. Maddison Project Working Paper 4.*

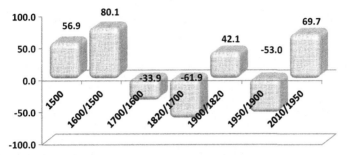

FIGURE 2.28   Decomposition of each period's role in Brazilian relative backwardness when compared to Portugal. *Original data from Maddison, A., 2011. Historical Statistics of the World Economy: 1-2008 AD. Maddison Project and Bolt, J., van Zanden J.L., 2013. The First Update of the Maddison Project: Re-estimating Growth Before 1820. Maddison Project Working Paper 4.*

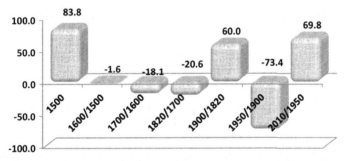

FIGURE 2.29   Decomposition of each period's role in Brazilian relative backwardness when compared to Spain. *Original data from Maddison, A., 2011. Historical Statistics of the World Economy: 1-2008 AD. Maddison Project and Bolt, J., van Zanden J.L., 2013. The First Update of the Maddison Project: Re-estimating Growth Before 1820. Maddison Project Working Paper 4.*

century in Brazilian relative backwardness. For Australia and New Zealand, the 19th century was the determinant. Canada and the United States already clearly outperformed Brazil in the previous century. The Northern European Periphery started from a higher development level in 1500, but also had the 19th century as the major determinant of its relative performance. Norway and Finland had a relevant relative performance in the second half of the 20th century. Likewise, in the case of the European Southern Periphery, the milestone was the 19th century, although in that case one cannot mitigate the importance of the second half of the 20th century. Portugal and Spain also had the initial period as a key to explain current relative development, and for Portugal in particular the 16th century was the most important, although all its advantage built up to the year 1600 was lost until 1820 and recovered again in the 19th century and especially in the second half of the 20th century.

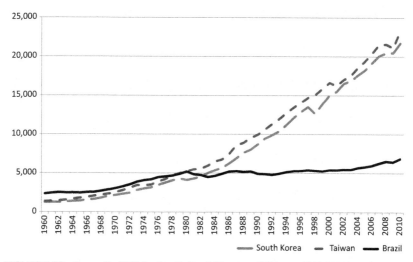

FIGURE 2.30   Per capita GDP for Brazil, South Korea, and Taiwan, 1965–2010. *Original data from Maddison, A., 2011. Historical Statistics of the World Economy: 1-2008 AD. Maddison Project and Bolt, J., van Zanden J.L., 2013. The First Update of the Maddison Project: Re-estimating Growth Before 1820. Maddison Project Working Paper 4.*

All these statistics confirm the leading role of the 19th century in Brazilian relative backwardness, although they indicate that the Southern European Periphery had the initial period and the second half of the 20th century as key periods in explaining its currently higher level of development relative to Brazil. These statistics put into a better perspective the role of this century with respect to other centuries and the initial conditions, which are often implicitly taken as the major determinant of Brazilian relative backwardness, at least in comparison with European countries. It should be noted that performing well in the 19th and 20th centuries could be sufficient to overcome any initial relative backwardness, as the histories of the United States, Canada, Australia, and New Zealand indicate and the previous data can confirm.

2.4 CONCLUSIONS

Brazil has not always been a country with lower per capita GDP than the set of benchmark developed countries analyzed here. In 1820 its per capita GDP was higher than that of Australia, New Zealand, and Greece. Finland, Norway, and even Canada had per capita GDPs not much higher than Brazil. Nevertheless, all these countries managed to grow faster than Brazil in the 19th century, and all built an advantage that was not overcome in the 20th century.

Despite having a reasonable economic performance throughout the 20th century, Brazil did not manage to catch up and recover the relative loss of the previous century. Actually, its development level fell relative to the Northern and Southern European Peripheries. Therefore it ended up as a relatively very backward country in the first decade of the 21st century.

Other countries such as Taiwan and South Korea, whose yearly per capita GDP is shown with that of Brazil in Fig. 2.30, were able to catch up in the 50 years between 1960 and 2010 with many developed countries, such as Spain, Portugal, Greece, New Zealand, and even France, the United Kingdom, and Germany. Therefore it is possible to catch up and Brazil is not condemned to being a relatively poor country. Further knowledge of the reasons why Brazil lagged behind in the 19th century and was not able to catch up in the 20th century can help to define strategies that will speed up the convergence of Brazilian per capita GDP with that of developed countries. This is the focus of the next chapters.

Chapter 3

A Simple Model of World Equilibrium With International Trade and No Restriction on Factor Mobility

3.1 INTRODUCTION

Chapter 2 showed that Brazil lagged behind the benchmark countries mainly in the 19th century, when they grew faster than Brazil and built the gap that was more or less maintained in the 20th century, especially when compared to Western Offshoots (Canada, the United States, Australia, and New Zealand) and the Northern European Periphery (Norway, Finland, Sweden, and Switzerland). The Southern European Periphery was already more developed at the beginning of the 16th century, and through oscillations in relative performance managed to widen the development gap in the second half of the 20th century.

This data left two questions unanswered. Why did Brazil perform so poorly in relative terms in the 19th century? And why it did not catch up in the 20th century as some countries did, such as South Korea and Taiwan? Before dealing with these questions, some major theoretical foundations of the hypothesis proposed in the next chapters must be introduced. This chapter outlines some of these theoretical foundations. In particular, it shows that in a world with free trade and free flow of most factors of production, the determination of relative economic specialization in goods with different human capital intensities is exogenous to market forces. This conclusion plays a major role in the forthcoming hypothesis to explain Brazilian relative backwardness and helps the critique of other important hypotheses still popular among Brazilian economists.

The chapter relies mainly on mathematical arguments, so readers less interested in technical details of economic theory or less trained in mathematical methods in economics could jump from this introduction directly to the conclusions of the chapter, as reading the whole chapter can be quite discouraging. Moreover, the content of the chapter is not essential for the understanding of this book.

The next section sets up microfoundations of a world model with no transaction costs or restrictions to free trade (all goods are tradable), perfect mobility of all factors of production, full information and arbitrage in all markets, and constant return to scale in all production functions. Section 3.3 sketches the equilibrium in this model, and Section 3.4 discusses what happens with equilibrium and relative per capita GDP (gross domestic product) and income when this world is split up into countries. Section 3.5 summarizes the major conclusions of the chapter.

3.2 MODEL SETUP IN THE WORLD ECONOMY WITH MANY GOODS AND MANY FACTORS OF PRODUCTION

A first theoretical hypothesis necessary to understand Brazilian relative backwardness is that there is more than one possible equilibrium in the world economy when there are many goods, many factors of production, free trade among countries, free flow of factors of production, and many countries in the world. This relationship implies that different countries can have distinct per capita GDP and these potential equilibria are stable, so there are no endogenous forces working to displace them.

In the real world, there are several goods and services demanded by the model necessary to reach this conclusion. There are also several factors of production, although they can all be synthetically represented by four groups: physical capital, labor, human capital, and natural resources. A free flow of factors of production is not a correct assumption, although physical capital can easily move across country borders. Human capital and labor could also flow reasonably freely among countries in the 19th century, although their migrations were subject to restrictions in the 20th century. Natural resources, however, do not flow across borders, so it is reasonable to assume that at least one factor of production is not free to flow among countries—as a simplifying assumption, this case will be ruled out. Therefore, a model that considers the existence of many goods and factors of production certainly can quite accurately represent the real world. Free flow of all factors of production, however, is a more questionable assumption, although it is perhaps a better assumption than that often introduced in Heckscher—Ohlin-type models,[1] which is that there is no factor mobility.

3.2.1 Demand for Each Good in the Economy

The world economy has many consumers. Each one faces a utility function, which is a combination of a constant elasticity of substitution and a Cobb—Douglas function. This can be defined as:

$$U_j = \left[\sum_{i=1}^{m} C_{ij}^{\frac{\theta-1}{\theta}} \right]^{\frac{\gamma\theta}{\theta-1}} S_j^{1-\gamma}$$

where C_{ij} is the consumption of good i by consumer j, measured in units of this good. S_j is the saving amount of this individual j, which is measured in monetary units. The Greek letters are parameters, such that $\theta > 1$ and $0 < \gamma < 1$. The first restriction ensures that utility rises with the consumption of each good, and the second restriction makes the utility function linearly homogeneous in S_j and a measure of aggregated consumption.

This utility function imposes that there are m goods in the economy. Nevertheless, contrary to a pure Cobb—Douglas utility function, there is no need that $C_{ij} > 0$ for all goods and all consumers. $C_{ij} = 0$ for some goods but not all is a possible solution for this consumer. The number of goods m will be taken as exogenous, given the state of technology and human needs. This is only a simplifying assumption in the model.

This consumer maximizes this utility function subject to a budget constraint that can be defined as:

$$Y_j = S_j + \sum_{i=1}^{m} P_i C_{ij} \tag{3.1}$$

where Y_j is the income of this consumer and P_i is the price of good i, both measured in monetary units. The other variables are as previously defined. This budget constraint assumes that there is no government, as no share of the individual income goes to pay taxes. This is another simplifying assumption to keep the model as simple as possible to focus on its goals.

A first-order condition for the maximization of the utility function subject to the budget constraint expressed in Eq. (3.1) generates:

$$P_i(1 - \gamma) \left[\sum_{i=1}^{m} C_{ij}^{\frac{\theta-1}{\theta}} \right] = \gamma C_{ij}^{-\frac{1}{\theta}} S_j \tag{3.2}$$

---

1. See for example Leamer (1995) and Feenstra (2004, Chapter 2).

Multiplying both sides of Eq. (3.2) by C_{ij} yields:

$$P_i(1 - \gamma)C_{ij}\left[\sum_{i=1}^{m} C_{ij}^{\frac{\theta-1}{\theta}}\right] = \gamma C_{ij}^{\frac{\theta-1}{\theta}} S_j \tag{3.2'}$$

Summing up both sides of Eq. (3.2') for all goods i generates:

$$\left(\frac{1-\gamma}{\gamma}\right)\sum_{i=1}^{m} P_i C_{ij} = S_j \tag{3.3}$$

Combining Eq. (3.3) with the budget constraint represented in Eq. (3.1):

$$Y_j = \left(\frac{1}{\gamma}\right)\sum_{i=1}^{m} P_i C_{ij} \tag{3.4}$$

and

$$S_j = (1 - \gamma)Y_j \tag{3.5}$$

From Eq. (3.5) it is possible to define a total demand by this consumer as:

$$D_j = Y_j - (1 - \gamma)Y_j = \gamma Y_j \tag{3.6}$$

A combination of Eq. (3.5) with Eq. (3.2) can define C_{ij} as a function of the other variables in the model and its parameters. Multiplying both sides of this result by P_i and using some algebra manipulation yields:

$$P_i C_{ij} = (\gamma Y_j)^{\theta}\left[\sum_{i=1}^{m} C_{ij}^{\frac{\theta-1}{\theta}}\right]^{-\theta} P_i^{1-\theta} \tag{3.7}$$

Summing up both sides for all goods:

$$\sum_{i=1}^{m} P_i C_{ij} = (\gamma Y_j)^{\theta}\left[\sum_{i=1}^{m} C_{ij}^{\frac{\theta-1}{\theta}}\right]^{-\theta}\sum_{i=1}^{m} P_i^{1-\theta} \tag{3.8}$$

Combining Eqs. (3.2), (3.4), and (3.8) yields:

$$C_{ij} = (\gamma Y_j)\left[\sum_{i=1}^{m} P_i^{1-\theta}\right]^{-1} P_i^{-\theta} \tag{3.9}$$

At this moment a definition of a price index is made as a nonweighted geometric mean:

$$P = \left[\left(\frac{1}{m}\right)\sum_{i=1}^{m} P_i^{1-\theta}\right]^{\frac{1}{1-\theta}} \tag{3.10}$$

Combining this definition in Eq. (3.10) with Eq. (3.9) yields:

$$C_{ij} = \gamma Y_j \left(\frac{P_i}{P}\right)^{-\theta} (mP)^{-1} \tag{3.11}$$

This is the demand of individual j for good i. If this individual is a representative one and there are n individuals in the world economy, spread among all countries, the total demand for this good Q_i can be seen as the sum of the demand for all these individuals, which is:

$$Q_i = \sum_{j=1}^{n} C_{ij} = \gamma \left(\frac{P_i}{P}\right)^{-\theta} (mP)^{-1} \sum_{j=1}^{n} Y_j \tag{3.12}$$

It should be noted that the price paid by all individuals is the same, regardless of the country. This is a consequence of some assumptions introduced: free trade with no transaction costs; and full information and perfect arbitrage in all goods markets.

By defining total aggregated demand in the economy as the sum of all individual demands as expressed in Eq. (3.6) and introducing the concept of real total aggregated demand as this sum divided by the price index defined in Eq. (3.10), it is possible to express this variable as:

$$\overline{Y} = \frac{\gamma}{P} \sum_{j=1}^{n} Y_j \tag{3.13}$$

Substitution of Eq. (3.13) into Eq. (3.12) yields:

$$Q_i = \frac{\overline{Y}}{m} \left(\frac{P_i}{P}\right)^{-\theta} \tag{3.14}$$

This is the demand for each good in the world economy. It is worth highlighting that no emphasis is placed on the location of the consumer. For the moment the consumer could live in any country, depending on other determinants of spatial location that are discussed later.

3.2.2 Production of Each Good in the World Economy

Each firm in this economy produces a specific good, which is not a perfect substitute of any other. This is why the demand for all of them is as defined in the last subsection. A firm faces a standard Cobb–Douglas production function, which can be expressed as:

$$Z_i = A_i \prod_{j=1}^{v} F_j^{\delta_{ij}} \tag{3.15}$$

where Z_i is its output, A_i is a productivity index, and F_j is the amount of factor of production j employed in production. There are v factors of production in this economy, which all have to be employed in producing all goods in the economy. The Greek letters δ_{ij} are parameters representing the elasticity of production of good i with respect to the quantity of factor j. By assumption:

$$\sum_{j=1}^{v} \delta_{ij} = 1 \qquad (3.16)$$

This condition makes the production function linearly homogeneous, so it has constant return to scale. Multiplication of all factors of production by a constant also multiplies the output by this same constant.

This firm faces a profit function, which can be defined as:

$$\pi_i = P_i A_i \prod_{j=1}^{v} F_j^{\delta_{ij}} - \sum_{j=1}^{v} w_j F_j \qquad (3.17)$$

where w_j is the rate of return of factor of production j, which is referred to as the factor price hereafter—a nomenclature more in line with the international trade literature. P_i is the price of good i and π_i is the profit of firm i. Solving its demand function, as represented in Eq. (3.14), for P_i and substituting back into Eq. (3.17):

$$\pi_i = \left(\frac{\overline{Y}}{m}\right)^{\frac{1}{\theta}} P \left(A_i \prod_{j=1}^{v} F_j^{\delta_{ij}} \right)^{\frac{\theta-1}{\theta}} - \sum_{j=1}^{v} w_j F_j \qquad (3.17')$$

If this firm maximizes profits, the first-order condition for its profit maximization yields:

$$\delta_{ij} \left(\frac{\theta-1}{\theta}\right) \left(\frac{\overline{Y}}{m}\right)^{\frac{1}{\theta}} \left(A_i \prod_{j=1}^{v} F_j^{\delta_{ij}} \right)^{\frac{\theta-1}{\theta}} = \left(\frac{w_j}{P}\right) F_j \qquad (3.18)$$

There are v equations like this for each firm, one for each factor of production it employs. Therefore there are vm (v times m) equations like this for the whole world. It is worth noting that these equations do not have the price of the good sold as one of their variables, as the relationship between price and quantity sold by the firm was substituted out from the profit function. Nevertheless, the price index P is included to introduce the role of real return to the factor of production as one of the determinants of its amount employed in the production of each good.

It is also worth noting that firms are not supposed to be equal; thus δ_{aj} is not necessarily equal to δ_{bj} for different firms a and b, even if the factor of production j is the same. Actually, it is supposed that some differences exist, especially for the factor of production of basic labor, which is proportional to population.

Another important feature of production decisions as presented here is that no relationship of any firm to any particular country is yet determined. For the moment, any firm could be in any country and can move freely among countries, as there is no immobile factor of production in this economy. Furthermore, as there are no transaction costs or any other restrictions to trade, all firms sell their output in any country for the same price. These simple arguments indicate that there is indeterminacy on location of firms in this model.

3.3 GENERAL EQUILIBRIUM

As a simplifying assumption it is supposed that there is no accumulation or depreciation of any factor of production. Therefore there is no reason for consumers to save, so $\gamma = 1$ and $S_j = 0$ for whatever j. This brings the focus to the static version of the model and the features of its equilibrium. No dynamics of adjustment to this equilibrium are object of analysis here. The focus is only on the equilibrium itself.

If the amount of each factor of production is determined worldwide, it is possible to define a set of equations such as:

$$\overline{F_j} = \sum_{i=1}^{m} F_{ij} \tag{3.19}$$

This equation says that the total given amount of each factor of production j, $\overline{F_j}$, is equal to the sum of all amounts of this factor employed by the m firms in the economy. Although each F_{ij} is determined endogenously, the sum of all of them is given. There are v equations like this in the world economy, one for each factor of production.

All factors of production in this economy have a price (or return) for their employment, as they contribute to the output of the firm and their owners will be interested in their use only if they get some positive return. Furthermore, they will search for the best return to their factors. As, by assumption, the factors are the same within each type and there is full information, arbitrage will ensure that their prices are exactly the same for all those of the same kind, otherwise those with lower return would bid for the positions of those with higher return. In other words, perfect competition is assumed to hold in the factors market. Therefore there are only v prices of factors of production in this economy, represented by w_j in Eqs. (3.17) and (3.18), so there are v of these w_js.

Given the assumptions introduced hitherto, no difference of factors of production among countries or any restrictions on their mobility exist. Consequently, their prices are the same in all countries and there are only the v prices of factors of production in the whole world. It should be noted that, unlike the Heckscher—Ohlin model in which factor price equalization is a theorem to be proved and only works under some special conditions,[2] perfect

---

2. See for example Takayama (1982), Jones and Scheinkman (1977), and Chang (1979). See also Samuelson (1948, 1949) for the original presentation of this theorem.

TABLE 3.1 Number of Variables of Each Type in the Model

Variables	Quantities
1. Individual incomes (Y_j)	n
2. Demand for each type of good (Q_i)	m
3. Output of firms (Z_i)	m
4. Amounts of factors of production of each type employed by each firm (F_{ij})	mv
5. Prices of goods (P_i)	m
6. Prices of factors of production (w_j)	v
7. Price index	1
8. Aggregated real income	1

international factor mobility ensures that this factor price equalization always exists.[3]

The general equilibrium of this model has to determine the demand for each of the m goods in this economy, which are represented by Q_i in Section 3.2.1; the price of each of these m goods, represented by P_i; the Z_i quantities produced of the m goods in the economy; all the F_{ij}, which are the amounts of each factor of production employed by the m firms and mv in the total; all the factor prices w_j, which are v under the full arbitrage conditions defined earlier; and all the n individual incomes, defined as Y_j in Section 3.2.1, which are n in total. In addition to these endogenous variables, there is also a price index P, defined in Eq. (3.10), and a total real income $\overline{Y}$, defined in Eq. (3.13). Table 3.1 gives a synthesis of all endogenous variables in the model listed to this point.

To determine these variables, there are so far the m production functions, one for each good; the m demand functions represented by Eq. (3.14); the mv first-order conditions for profit maximization, one for each of the v factors of production within each of the m firms, which are represented by Eq. (3.18); the v world general equilibrium totals of each factor of production, represented by Eq. (3.19); and the definitions of the price index P in Eq. (3.10) and the aggregated total income, which appears in Eq. (3.13). These equations are listed in Table 3.2 with their respective amounts.

A simple count of equations and endogenous variables indicates that there are some missing equations in the set summarized in the preceding paragraph

---

3. The Heckscher–Ohlin model has factor immobility as one of its key assumptions.

TABLE 3.2 Number of Equations of Each Type in the Model

Equations	Quantities
1. Production functions	m
2. First-order conditions for profit maximization of individual firms	mv
3. Demand functions for each good	m
4. World general equilibrium totals of each factor of production	v
5. Price index definition	1
6. Aggregated real income definition	1

and Table 3.2. One missing set of variables is the condition that, in equilibrium, supply of each good is equal to its demand. Therefore:

$$Z_i = Q_i \tag{3.20}$$

There are m equations like this, one for each good in the economy. The matching between equations and variables indicates that there are still n missing equations which are necessary to determine individual incomes. They are a set of equations that define the individual incomes from the property of factors of production and share of companies by individuals. Accordingly:

$$Y_s = \sum_{j=1}^{v} w_j F_{sj} + \sum_{i=1}^{m} \rho_{si}\pi_i \tag{3.21}$$

where F_{sj} now is the amount of factor of production of type j belonging to agent s, and ρ_{si} is the share of firm i belonging to individual s. In this model all F_{sj} and ρ_{si} are exogenous. So each of these equations determines the income of consumer s as a function of the market returns to the factors of production and the profit of the firms. There are n equations like this, one for each consumer.

The inclusion of $\pi_i s$ again disrupted the balance between equations and endogenous variables, as they start to appear in the determination of other endogenous variables through Eq. (3.21) and are endogenously determined by the behavior of agents. Thus the set of v equations represented by Eq. (3.17) has to be brought into the system of equations to make the number of equations equal to the number of variables.[4]

---

4. It is worth noting that for each factor of production there is an equation such as Eq. (3.19), as all variables $\overline{F}_j$ defined by this set of v equations are exogenous and do not count to the balance between equations and endogenous variables. Nevertheless, by construction, all the v equations in this set are always true.

The model as it is described here can have a unique solution for all endogenous variables. All firms would produce the most profitable amount of goods for them and consumers would maximize their utilities. All factors of production would be allocated in production and would get the highest possible return to their employment. The equations mentioned in Table 3.2, in addition to all those represented by the definitions in Eqs. (3.17) and (3.21), are sufficient to determine the world equilibrium.

The complex task of finding an equation for each endogenous variable as a function of exogenous variables and parameters is not pursued here, as it is of no interest for the purposes of this chapter and book. Nevertheless, the relevant discussions emerging from the analysis of this equilibrium are presented in the next section.

3.4 DECOMPOSING THE WORLD INTO COUNTRIES

Assuming no transaction costs or any other restriction to trade among countries, in addition to perfect factor of production mobility, allowed the world to be treated as only one country and there is no concern with countries in the equilibrium analysis. Full information for all agents and perfect arbitrage in all markets for factors of production ensured that all firms pay the same price for any given factor of production. This is the initial setup to deal with countries. The same assumptions of no transaction costs, full information, and perfect factor of production mobility are held throughout the analysis.

To understand the concept of a country in such an economy, it is necessary to divide the factors of production into two types: those that are embodied in their owners and those that can be physically separated from them. Human capital and labor are among the former type, while physical capital and natural resources are among the latter. Even if any of these factors of production are split into smaller categories, such as type of physical capital and type of human capital, these distinctions still persist.

Under such assumptions and concepts, a country can be defined as a subset of individuals who own a subset of each type of factor of production and share of firms and live in a determined territorial space. Furthermore, some firms operate in this territory and hire a large share of the embodied factors of production of the individuals living within its borders.[5] It is well documented that many workers cross borders of their countries to work in others, even if they still live in their home country (where they do not work). In most cases, however, this behavior employs a minority of the embodied factors of production, as supposed in the definition here.

---

5. A small share of these individuals may find employment for their embodied factors of production in neighboring countries.

The total income of a country Y_c, under this concept can be represented as:

$$Y_c = \sum_c Y_j \tag{3.22}$$

where Y_j is the income of resident j, and the residents are all those included in the subset of individuals c, which includes all individuals living in that country. It is worth noting that no restriction on the number of countries is introduced. The only restriction is that all individuals live in one and only one country, so the total of individuals in the world is equal to the sum of the total individuals in each country.

It is worth noting that if all individuals within this world are ranked by their income, a country can have individuals sorted randomly in all percentiles of this rank. It can also have individuals mainly in a few percentiles that can generate a bias in its average individual income, either upward or downward. For example, a country can have a larger share of individuals with income over the world average such that its average per capita income is above the world average.

It is worth stressing that average per capita income over or under the world mean arises from the composition of the resident population of a country. If there are firms working in that country so that all factors of production are fully employed, as the equilibrium suggests, there is no reason for any of these individuals to migrate to other countries. The world economy could be in equilibrium with some countries with average per capita income over its mean and others with this variable under the world mean, and no arbitrage opportunity would exist. Therefore in this model, with perfect mobility of factors of production, full information, and no transaction costs, it is possible to have equilibria with uneven per capita income among countries and no arbitrage that could generate convergence of per capita income would arise. Some of these assumptions have to be violated to generate instability in equilibria and convergence.[6]

In the same way, the total output of a country, Z_{cT}, may be defined as:

$$PZ_{cT} = \sum_{i=1}^{m_c} P_i Z_i \tag{3.23}$$

where m_c is the number of firms within the country. If units of each good are redefined so that $P_i = 1$ for all them:

$$Z_{cT} = \sum_{i=1}^{m_c} Z_i \tag{3.23'}$$

Obviously, $P = 1$ under this redefinition of units of all goods.

---

6. Growth models that generate convergence, such as that predicted by Barro and Sala-i-Martin (1992, 2003, Chapter 11), normally assumes that there is no factor mobility. As a consequence, factor prices are not the same across countries.

Let us take a factor of production L to be proportional to the number of individuals, such as labor in most economic models. This proportion is taken to be such that the total of this factor of production in a country L_{cT} is equal to its population. Therefore, from Eqs. (3.15) and (3.18):

$$Z_i = \left[\left(\frac{\theta}{\theta - 1} \right) \left(\frac{1}{\delta_{iL}} \right) \left(\frac{m}{\overline{Y}} \right)^{\frac{1}{\theta}} w_L L_i \right]^{\frac{\theta}{\theta-1}} \tag{3.24}$$

where the redefinitions of units are also introduced so that $P = 1$. Substituting this result in Eq. (3.23'):

$$Z_{cT} = \left[\left(\frac{\theta}{\theta - 1} \right) \left(\frac{m}{\overline{Y}} \right)^{\frac{1}{\theta}} w_L \right]^{\frac{\theta}{\theta-1}} \sum_{i=1}^{m_c} \left(\frac{L_i}{\delta_{iL}} \right)^{\frac{\theta}{\theta-1}} \tag{3.25}$$

Defining z_{cT} (small letter) as the per capita output:

$$z_{cT} = \left(\frac{Z_{cT}}{L_{cT}} \right) = \left[\left(\frac{\theta}{\theta - 1} \right) \left(\frac{m}{\overline{Y}} \right)^{\frac{1}{\theta}} w_L \right]^{\frac{\theta}{\theta-1}} L_{cT}^{\frac{1}{\theta-1}} \sum_{i=1}^{m_c} \left(\frac{\ell_i}{\delta_{iL}} \right)^{\frac{\theta}{\theta-1}} \tag{3.26}$$

where ℓ_i is the proportion of labor (the factor of production proportional to population) to the total population of the country.

It is important to stress that arbitrage among countries due to perfect factor of production mobility ensures that w_L is the same in all countries. $\overline{Y}$ and m are variables defined for the whole world and so are the same for all countries. Nevertheless, Eq. (3.26) implies that the higher the population of a country, the higher tends to be its per capita output. This result, however, is conditional on the number of firms within this country, which is represented by m_c in Eq. (3.26). If the number of firms increases when population increases, which is a reasonable assumption, this relationship between per capita output and total population can be eliminated.

Eq. (3.26) reveals that, for a given country, the higher the concentration of employment (ℓ_i) in firms with lower labor intensity (lower δ_{jL}), the higher will be its per capita output. As $\sum_{j=1}^{v} \delta_{ij} = 1$, sectors with lower δ_j, tend to have relatively higher human and/or physical capital intensities, although this can also happen because of a high natural resource intensity. However, on average it is reasonable to assume that lower labor intensity is associated with higher human and/or physical capital intensities. Therefore countries that specialize in human capital-intensive goods tend to have higher per capita output.[7]

Now suppose all persons are distributed among countries following an exogenous rule or randomly. Every person initially placed in a country carries

---

7. Kuwait and other Arab countries with high concentration of their production in sectors with high intensity of natural resources, oil reserves in their case, are examples of countries in which low intensity of labor was actually associated with high intensity in natural resources in their specialization.

with them all their factors of production, both embodied and disembodied. Given this initial distribution of persons and factors of production, firms enter into this fictitious world with their managers choosing their locations rationally. Rigorously, they would be distributed randomly, as there is no cost for factor price movements. After their random choice of locations they would create incentives for movements of factors of production so that the spatial distribution of the latter adjusts to the needs of the former. Nevertheless, if there is a minimum cost to move people around, firms would rationally set up where there is availability of the embodied factors of production they need in their productive processes. Then they buy the disembodied factors of production from wherever they are available. Therefore, the spatial distribution of production would be determined by the distribution of the population and their embodied factors of production.

Given that labor is the standard to measure per capita output, human capital is the obvious candidate to be the embodied factor of production that is exogenously distributed spatially, as people could consider other nonmarket determinants in choosing their places to live. Therefore, under the conclusions of the previous paragraphs, the given spatial distribution of human capital tends to determine relative per capita output among countries in this world equilibrium model.

The spatial distribution of firms would adjust to the human capital spatial distribution, with those employing proportionally more of this factor of production concentrating on those countries with higher relative availability of this factor. This is why countries with higher availability of human capital are those with higher concentrations of total production in firms that employ relatively more human capital.

Given that the spatial distribution of firms reaches its equilibrium at a point at which all factors of production are employed in the place they are settled, there is no market mechanism that would push the economy out of this equilibrium to any other. Thus no migration of any factor of production would exist. Only when changes in technology or preferences of consumers occur does a new adjustment movement take place. The simplest way these adjustments take place is through migration of those factors that are easier to move. In modern economies, capital is this factor of production, although some labor or human capital movements across borders also happen.

3.5 CONCLUSIONS

This chapter presents a model summarizing some of the major setups upon which the hypothesis to explain Brazilian relative backwardness is based. The model is an obvious simplification of reality with some radical assumptions that are clearly incorrect in the real world, such as full information, no transaction costs, and perfect factor of production mobility. Nevertheless, this is considered to be a better approximation of reality, and as such to be a better backstage to explain reality, than hypotheses that agents do not have information to make rational decisions, there is no trade because of high transaction costs, or there is no mobility of factors of production, as assumed in the Heckscher—Ohlin model.

The major conclusions emerging from this model relevant to the forthcoming developments in this book are that it is possible to have full arbitrage in all factors of production markets and still have per capita income and output differences among countries; if a worldwide equilibrium emerges with uneven per capita outputs among countries, there is no endogenous force pushing for convergence in these outputs, as all markets for factors of production will be in equilibrium; and in a world with the features of this model there are many possible equilibria, as the absence of transaction costs ensures that any firm, with all its suppliers of embodied factors of production, could migrate from one country to another and the new world equilibrium will be as stable as the previous one. This movement of firms could alter the relative per capita output among countries, but it would not affect the relative income of the many consumers.

To simplify the exposition, it is assumed that there are no savings and investment in this model. It is reasonable to think that if there were population growth and savings which are equal to investment in equilibrium, some firms in this economy would be producing capital goods. These capital goods would be incorporated in the economy either in new firms or in expansion of currently existing ones. There is no relationship in the model that determines the country in which the new firms would set up, or which firms of which countries would expand. Of course, demand evolution would determine the firms and any bias in country destination of these new investments, given the spatial distribution of population and its features, including human capital availability. Nevertheless, if demand expands in the same proportion for all goods, population and other factors of production supply grow in the same proportion as capital, and the number of firms grows at this same common rate, investments would be directed for all countries in the same proportion in which capital goods are already distributed. Therefore no change in relative per capita output would emerge.

Human capital expansion, in particular, has a specific expansion rationale that is discussed in Chapter 5, thus its potential expansion on a world level and distribution among countries is not further discussed here. Nevertheless, one of the major conclusions of this chapter is that the higher the proportion of human capital to labor in a country, the higher tends to be per capita GDP in this country.

Chapter 4

Some Empirical Evidence on the Sources of Brazilian Current Relative Backwardness

Chapter Outline

4.1 INTRODUCTION

Chapter 3 made very clear that under free trade with no transaction costs, perfect factors of production mobility, and full information, a country will have a lower per capita output only if it reaches an equilibrium in which the proportion of some other factors of production to labor, which is proportional to population, is lower than that in the country of reference. These other factors of production have to be relatively more abundant in countries with higher per capita output, while labor has to be relatively more abundant within the poorer country.

Economists normally divide the factors of production into labor, physical capital, human capital, and natural resources. These broad categories are used throughout this chapter. Investigation begins with identifying the factor of production whose supply is proportionally lower in Brazil than in the benchmark countries. This search is the major target of this chapter, to advance identification of the sources of Brazilian relative backwardness.

The chapter is organized as follows. The next section introduces some basic arithmetic of development, which sets up the basic concepts underlying the subsequent empirical investigations. Sections 4.3—4.5 rely on international data to compare Brazilian relative availability of human capital, physical capital, and natural resources, respectively. Data include the benchmark countries of Chapter 2, but extend the sample to other countries whose data are also available. This extension helps create an international standard on the relationship between per capita GDP (gross domestic product) and the availability of particular factors of production. These standards are created by simple linear functions relating the two variables, per capita GDP, and the factor of production availability indicator. Section 4.6 extends the initial analysis of the previous sections, drawing on a more rigorous development accounting method, in line with recent literature on this subject, to search for the role of relative availability of factors of production in Brazilian relative backwardness. Section 4.7 summarizes the major conclusions of the chapter and introduces additional comments on the results of Section 4.6, comparing them with those found in similar studies in the literature.

4.2 SOME BASIC DEVELOPMENT ARITHMETIC

The developments in this chapter start with a simple Cobb—Douglas production function for the whole country, which is defined as:

$$Y_i = A_i K_i^\alpha N_i^\delta (h_i L_i)^{1-\alpha-\delta} \tag{4.1}$$

where Y_i is output, K_i is stock of physical capital, and h_i is the per capita stock of human capital. L_i is the amount of labor employed and N_i is the natural resource availability. The subscript i indicates that the variable refers to country i and Greek letters are parameters, such that $0 < \alpha < 1$ and $0 < \delta < 1$.

There are many aggregation problems when one goes from production functions for individual firms, such as those used in Chapter 3, to the country ones expressed in Eq. (4.1). They are of different natures, and range from those that are difficult to aggregate, for example skills with different intensities in the same and different professions, to the unique measure of the stock of physical capital, which is composed of different capital goods.[1] This is not object of discussion here, however, as it is a theoretical problem that is outside the scope of this book.

---

1. This difficulty in aggregating physical capital in only one measure was the subject of an intense controversy on the theory of capital. For the original contributions that created the controversy see Robinson (1953—1954) and Sraffa (1960). For surveys see Harcourt (1972) and Stiglitz (1974).

It should be noted, though, that the individual production functions of the last chapter are all homogeneous in the first degree, as is the aggregated Cobb—Douglas production function expressed in Eq. (4.1). Therefore, if the aggregation problem of variables is bypassed, it is reasonably consistent with developments in Chapter 3 to rely on an aggregated production function such as the one expressed in Eq. (4.1). It is worth noting that the parameters of this function should vary among countries, as their production structures, or sectoral distribution of total output, are not the same.

If L, the amount of labor employed, is a proportion of P, population, such that $L = vP$, dividing both sides of Eq. (4.1) by L and substituting this last relationship yields:

$$y_i = A_i' k_i^{\alpha} n_i^{\delta} h_i^{1-\alpha-\delta} \qquad (4.1')$$

where small letters represent the capital letter divided by P, so that, for example, $k_i = (K_i/P_i)$. Furthermore, $A_i' = v^{1-\alpha-\delta} A_i$. Under such notation, per capita output of a country could differ from the one of others if the value for at least one of the variables on the right side of Eq. (4.1') is different; and at least one parameter in Eq. (4.1') differs. Thus this chapter starts focusing more closely on these differences, given the existing data.

4.3 HUMAN CAPITAL AVAILABILITY DIFFERENCES

As previously mentioned, there is a measurement difficulty for human capital, as different types of skills are aggregated in only one variable. Nevertheless, it is normally assumed that human capital, whichever way it is measured, is positively correlated with schooling years and quality of education.[2] Therefore, the higher the average number of years of schooling and the quality of education within a country, the higher tends to be its average per capita human capital.

Average schooling years is a variable available for many countries, although again there are some comparison problems, as this measurement in years does not imply the same amount of schooling within a year in all countries. For example, students can have an average of four daily hours of schooling in one country, but up to six or even eight daily schooling hours in others. Furthermore, the number of schooling days within a year can vary from country to country. Thus this international measure is very imprecise, although still useful.

---

2. The relationship between human capital and schooling years is an old one; it was particularly stressed by Mincer (1958, 1974), and has been very much stressed lately—see for example Bils and Klenow (2000) and Caselli (2005). The relationship between quality of education and human capital has also been stressed recently by many researchers—see for example Card and Krueger (1992, 1996).

The major indicator of quality of education within countries is the student scores in international exams. The PISA (Programme for International Student Assessment) measure is the most widely used, as it covers a reasonable sample of countries and has been perfected over recent years. Its obvious shortcoming as a measure of quality of education is that it unveils scores for students currently in school, not those for professionals in the labor market, thus the scores do not measure the quality of education of the current labor force in a country.

Nevertheless, it is reasonable to assume that current quality of education is strongly correlated with past quality of education, as a major determinant of the current quality is teachers' intellectual abilities, which were determined by the previous quality of education. Of course, this correlation is not immediate, as the social groups from which teachers are selected can strongly affect the correlation. But it is reasonable to assume that quality of education evolves slowly, and this correlation is strong. Therefore, despite the obvious imperfections, current students' scores on international tests can be seen as a reasonable indicator of quality of education.

It is worth stressing that any indicator of quality of education is very incomplete as a proxy of per capita human capital, as two countries with the same quality of education can generate completely different per capita human capital in the future if the school coverage is different. For example, if in one country only 50% of children of schooling age go to school while in another country 90% do so, it is obvious that there is a higher accumulation of per capita human capital in the latter country. Furthermore, it is not possible to rule out that the internal distribution of quality among individuals also has important consequences for the average stock of per capita human capital, as stressed, for example, by Jones (2008). Therefore, this measure has to be used with caution, although the quality of education is important in building human capital.

Figs. 4.1 and 4.2 show the dispersion of the two indicators of human capital, schooling years in 2010 and average scores on the PISA 2012.[3] The sample includes all countries for which there are statistics from Penn World Table 8.0 for per capita GDP,[4] Barro and Lee (2013) for schooling years, and OECD (2013) for PISA data. It is possible that some countries are in one of these databases and not in another. Notably, Qatar and Macao were in all datasets, but were excluded from the sample because they were outliers with very high per capita GDP and no correspondent developments in other factors of production. Their inclusion would distort the parameters of the tendency line that sets world standards for the relationships captured by these figures.

---

3. Nonweighted mean for reading, math, and science scores.
4. See Feenstra et al. (2013).

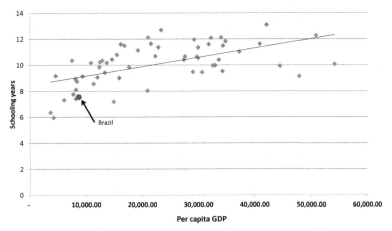

FIGURE 4.1   Relationship between average schooling years and per capita GDP in the countries studied. *Feenstra, R.C., Inklaar, R., Timmer, M.P., 2013. The Next Generation of the Penn World Table. Available for download at: www.ggdc.net/pwt; Barro, R., Lee, J.W., April, 2013. Educational Attainment for Total Population, 1950–2010. Available for download at www.barrolee.com/data/yrsch.htm.*

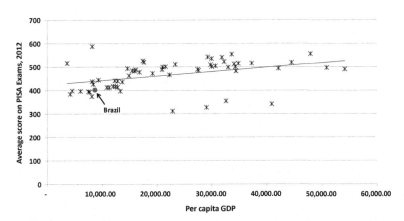

FIGURE 4.2   Relationship between average score on PISA 2012 and per capita GDP in the countries studied. *OECD, 2013. PISA 2012 Results: What Students Know and Can Do, Paris: OECD. Available for download at: www.oecd.org/pisa/keyfidings/pisa-2012-results; Feenstra, R.C., Inklaar, R., Timmer, M.P., 2013. The Next Generation of the Penn World Table. Available for download at: www.ggdc.net/pwt.*

The tendency lines drawn on these two figures give a world average standard for the relationships of the two human capital proxies and per capita GDP. They are obtained by simple linear regressions of the variable in the vertical axis as a function of that in the horizontal axis plus a constant. Their inclusion can give an idea of the current Brazilian position when compared to the world standard in the availability of these factors of production or their proxies. Therefore, per capita GDP is in the horizontal axis in all these figures. The position of the Brazilian value relating to the proxy when compared to the tendency line gives an idea of the surplus (if above the line) or shortcoming (if below the line) in availability of this proxy versus the world standard.

In both figures, Brazilian proxies for human capital are below the world standard or its expected value given the country's per capita GDP. They both indicate that Brazil has a deficit of human capital for a country with its per capita GDP. It means that in Eq. (4.1) the per capita human capital h contributed negatively to its per capita GDP when compared to the world standards. No proportion of the deficit of these proxies should be inferred from the figures, as the data are very raw and the functions $h = f(s)$ and $h = g(q)$, where s and q are schooling and score in PISA respectively, are not well established. Furthermore, it is possible there is some bias in estimations of the tendency lines, which are the basis for the definition of the so-called world standards.

4.4 PHYSICAL CAPITAL AVAILABILITY DIFFERENCES

A similar analysis as the one undertaken in Section 4.3 for the two proxies for human capital was also pursued for the physical stock of capital. Penn World Table 8.0 has data for the stock of physical capital, so a dispersion graphic including per capita figures for GDP and stock of capital was built (Fig. 4.3).

Before proceeding to analyze this figure, it should be stressed that the measure of this variable also has some aggregation problems. In particular, it

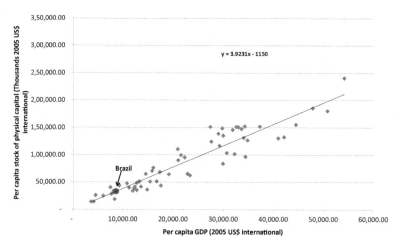

FIGURE 4.3   Relationship between per capita stock of capital and GDP, 2012. *Feenstra, R.C., Inklaar, R., Timmer, M.P., 2013. The Next Generation of the Penn World Table. Available for download at: www.ggdc.net/pwt.*

takes into account local relative prices of different equipment, for example. Nevertheless, the relative prices of two exactly equal pieces of equipment, when compared to a given bundle of commodities whose prices define the price index, can be different in two distinct countries, as local taxes and other transaction costs can differ. Therefore, when added together to create a measure of total capital, they easily generate a different value in the two countries, although they are exactly the same by assumption.

Furthermore, physical capital includes both public and private stocks, and the former share is not negligible. As the former is not decided by market incentives, much of this capital equipment can have very low rates of return. Consequently, the market prices actually could be much lower than the building costs. Nevertheless, their aggregation prices are determined by their costs, as they come from the investment share in GDP. When such distortion exists, the stock of physical capital would be overestimated. Despite these problems, the existing data on physical capital stocks are widely used in the literature, and this tradition is followed here. It can certainly give a fair idea of relative availability of physical capital between Brazil and the other countries in the sample, despite all the possible distortions.

Brazilian relative availability of physical capital is fair when compared to what would be expected given its per capita GDP and average world standards, as it is slightly over the value of the tendency line drawn in Fig. 4.3 for its per capita GDP. Thus this first approach to the problem indicates that there was no relative shortage of physical capital in Brazil in 2011. At a first glance, physical capital relative availability could not be blamed for the low relative per capita GDP in Brazil when compared to more developed countries.

4.5 NATURAL RESOURCES

If there were aggregation problems for the three proxies for availability of human and physical factors of production mentioned earlier, this difficulty is even greater for natural resources. There are large varieties of them and they are difficult to price, as many are currently reserves still not in use. For instance, a rigorous measurement of relative availability of natural resources should consider the relative productivity of lands in the many countries, which is difficult to make as their technologies of exploitation are often very different. Thus it becomes difficult to disentangle the effects of technologies from the quality of lands.

The transport infrastructure can also make a large difference in the measure of stock of natural resources. A new road, for example, can change the economic potential of lands at its margins. If they were almost nonexploitable before as the transport costs could erode all the potentially generated profits, they can become valuable after the road is built. Growth of a nearby city can also change the value of lands, as their economic exploitation can become profitable because of the proximity of a larger market. All these possibilities make it very difficult to create estimates of the stock of natural resources that are comparable internationally.

Nevertheless, the World Bank (1997) estimated the value of the stock of natural resources for a set of countries in 1994, calling it natural capital. The experts of the Bank used the present value for the future flow of income that could be obtained from lands, in both pasture and agricultural production, and the value of known mineral reserves estimated from present values of their expected flow of extraction. More details on the methodology can be found in World Bank (1997). The World Bank sample of countries and the one used here in previous exercises only have 38 countries in common, but they can be compared with the per capita GDP, as done with the previous proxies for availability of factors of production.

Fig. 4.4 plots the per capita stock of this natural capital (in natural logarithms) against per capita GDP, in an exercise similar to those in previous sections. The data indicate that Brazil has an excess availability of this factor of production when compared to what would be expected for this country given the world average standard and its per capita GDP. Thus the data indicate that Brazil does not have any relative shortage of this factor of production, and its relative backwardness can hardly be explained by the absence of this factor.

As this measure of natural capital is complicated to elaborate and is still on the first estimates, another proxy for natural resources was used to do a similar exercise: per capita value of rents from the use of natural resources in each

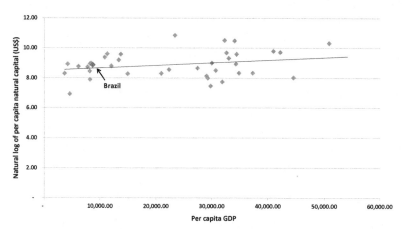

FIGURE 4.4   Relationship between per capita GDP (X axis, 2011) and World Bank natural logarithm of natural capital (Y axis, 1994). *World Bank, 1997. Expanding the Measure of Wealth: Indicators of Environmentally Sustainable Development, Washington: World Bank, pp. 34–38; Feenstra, R.C., Inklaar, R., Timmer, M.P., 2013. The Next Generation of the Penn World Table. Available for download at: www.ggdc.net/pwt.*

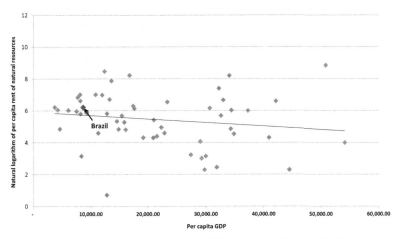

FIGURE 4.5 Relationship between per capita GDP (X axis, 2011) and World Bank natural logarithm of per capita rent of natural resources (Y axis, 2011). *Feenstra, R.C., Inklaar, R., Timmer, M.P., 2013. The Next Generation of the Penn World Table. Available for download at: www.ggdc.net/pwt; World Bank, 2013. World Economic Indicators, Washington: World Bank.*

country. This variable is less appropriate than the measure of the stock of natural capital, as local price distortions can change the relationship between economic availability of natural resources and the income generated. However, it is one more indicator and is available for a larger sample. These data are presented in Fig. 4.5, plotted against per capita GDP, in a similar exercise as that for the stock of natural capital. The data are from World Bank Economic Indicators (2013), and the method to build these data are found in World Bank (2011).

In this case the apparent relationship between the proxy for natural capital and per capita GDP is negative. Such a result is often found in the relationship between per capita GDP growth and abundance of natural resources[5]; if this is true for growth, it could also emerge in the relationship in Fig. 4.5. Data in Fig. 4.4 challenge this result with statistics that are probably more reliable as an estimation of the stock of natural capital. Nevertheless, the relationship between the two proxies is still apparently positive, as shown in Fig. 4.6.

The relevance of Fig. 4.5 for this study is that again Brazil has a relative abundance of natural resources when its per capita GDP and an average world relationship are taken into account. Thus the data indicate that any shortage of natural resources is not a constraint on Brazilian relative development, as already inferred from data in Fig. 4.4.

---

5. See for example Ranis (1991), Sachs and Warner (1995), and Ding and Field (2004).

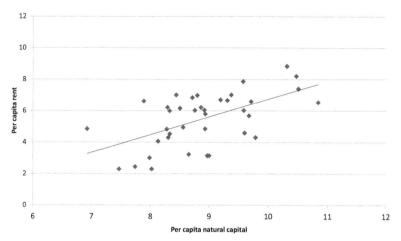

FIGURE 4.6   Relationship between natural capital (X axis, 1994) and natural logarithm of per capita rent of natural resources (Y axis, 2011). *World Bank, 1997. Expanding the Measure of Wealth: Indicators of Environmentally Sustainable Development, Washington: World Bank; World Bank, 2013. World Economic Indicators, Washington: World Bank.*

4.6 EXPLORING FURTHER THE POTENTIAL ROLE OF THE MANY FACTORS OF PRODUCTION IN BRAZILIAN RELATIVE BACKWARDNESS

The last three sections show that the only factor of production in which Brazil seems to have lower availability than the expected level for its current development is human capital. Relative availability of the others seems to be fair, given the world average standards. Nevertheless, the previous exercises are excessively simplistic and subject to distortions, as they do not consider the role of functional forms, estimation bias of the world standard, and other potential caveats to generate conclusions. This section puts forward some development accounting to shed light on the potential role of the availability of each factor of production in Brazilian relative backwardness.

4.6.1 Estimating Variables and Parameters of the Relevant Production Functions

The exercise starts with Eq. (4.1′). Both y and k are known in this equation, as Penn World Table 8.0 has data for these two variables for the set of countries included in the sample used in the last sections. Thus h, n, A', and the coefficients α and δ are the unknowns of this equation. If their values are found, the whole equation would be specified for each country and a simple decomposition of per capita GDP would be available; hence the relative role of each factor of production and the coefficients for the relative backwardness for each particular country could be estimated. Therefore, the first challenge is to estimate these variables and coefficients.

The physical capital marginal condition for profit maximization from a Cobb–Douglas production function is:

$$\frac{\partial y_i}{\partial k_i} = \alpha A_i' k_i^{\alpha-1} h_i^{1-\alpha-\delta} n_i^{\delta} = \alpha \frac{y_i}{k_i} = r \tag{4.2}$$

where r is the rate of return to physical capital. If all firms reach this equilibrium individually, this relationship would also hold for the aggregated values, and consequently:

$$\alpha = \frac{rk_i}{y_i} \tag{4.2'}$$

In words, the parameter α is equal to the share of capital in total GDP. There are estimations for the share of capital in the US total GDP: it has been reasonably stable at 33% for a long period.[6] Given the figures for y and k in the United States in 2011, this share implies an annual rate of return to capital equal to 10.4909%. If the hypothesis of arbitrage in the capital markets around the world is introduced, this rate of return and the figures for k and y for all countries in the sample could generate the individual figures for α.

The World Bank figures for rents arising from exploitation of natural resources, which were used in Figs. 4.5 and 4.6, together with this equilibrium rate of return for US stock of capital can be used to generate a value of the stock of natural capital in each country. To reach these figures, it is necessary to assume that the expected rent flow is permanent in forthcoming years, forever, and that the value of these reserves is generated in a market that arbitrates with the world market for physical capital. In this case the present value of the infinity flow of future rents, when discounted by the rate of return mentioned, would give the value for the stock of natural capital. Therefore, n also becomes known in Eq. (4.1′).

A similar procedure as the one to obtain α can also be used to obtain δ. The marginal condition for profit maximization in this case is for n, the natural capital in the World Bank language. This would yield:

$$\frac{\partial y_i}{\partial n_i} = \delta A_i' k_i^{\alpha} h_i^{1-\alpha-\delta} n_i^{\delta-1} = \delta \frac{y_i}{n_i} = r_n \tag{4.3}$$

---

6. For a detailed analysis see Gollin (2002). The value used in the text is from Gollin (2002, p. 470, adjustment 3). For examples of other research using similar values see Bils and Klenow (2000), Caselli (2005) and Hsieh and Klenow (2010).

where r_n is the return obtained on a unit of natural resources. This equation yields:

$$\delta = \frac{r_n n_i}{y_i} \qquad (4.3')$$

The rent on natural resources $r_n n_i$ is known from World Bank data, and y_i is available from the Penn World Tables. Therefore δ is promptly estimable and becomes a known coefficient for each country in the sample. Thus the variables still missing at the moment are h and A'.

To estimate h, it is necessary to rely on the marginal condition with respect to h for profit maximization:

$$\frac{\partial y_i}{\partial h_i} = (1 - \alpha - \delta) A_i' k_i^{\alpha} h_i^{-\alpha - \delta} n_i^{\delta} = (1 - \alpha - \delta) \frac{y_i}{h_i} = r_h \qquad (4.4)$$

This equation generates:

$$(1 - \alpha - \delta) = \frac{r_h h_i}{y_i} \qquad (4.4')$$

Therefore the share of human capital in total per capita GDP is already known, as are α and δ. This share multiplied by y_i gives the annual income accruing to per capita human capital. If it is assumed as an approximation that the generated flow of income is eternal, the present value of this future flow generates the value of the current stock of human capital. The return rate to physical capital could be used in this case as well, under the assumption of full arbitrage among markets.

This method could generate a value for the stock of human capital in all countries in the sample. Thus the problem of transforming proxies for quality of education indication (PISA average score) and extent of education (schooling years) is overcome by this method. Nevertheless, it is useful to check the relationship of this estimated value for the stock of human capital and the two other proxies. Table 4.1 gives an ordinary least square (OLS) estimation of this stock of human capital and the two proxies whose data are presented in the previous sections. It can be seen that this estimated equation (all variables in natural logarithms) has a reasonable explanatory power ($R^2 = 0.6163$), and the two proxies are positively correlated with the dependent variable. It should be mentioned that the coefficients themselves are not of much relevance, as their unbiased estimation demands an independence of the two proxies from the dependent variable that is not necessarily correct in this case.

The only variable still unknown in Eq. (4.1') is the coefficient A'. It can be obtained by simple algebraic manipulation of Eq. (4.1'), as all its parameters and other variables are already known. Consequently, this was the procedure used to obtain A' as a residual. Table 4.2 shows the values for all variables and

TABLE 4.1 OLS Estimated Equation for Calculated Human Capital (2011) as a Function of Average Schooling Years (2010) and PISA Average Score (2012)

Variables/Statistics	Coefficient	t Statistics	p Value
Constant	−13.29868	−2.58454	0.00975
PISA average score	3.34854	3.21008	0.00133
Average schooling years	1.83696	2.74237	0.00610
R^2	0.6163		
Sample size	54		

Note: All variables are in natural logarithms. Estimated t statistics relied on the Eicker–White method for correction for heteroskedasticity.
Feenstra, R.C., Inklaar, R., Timmer, M.P., 2013. The Next Generation of the Penn World Table. Available for download at: www.ggdc.net/pwt; World Bank, 2013. World Economic Indicators, Washington: World Bank; OECD, 2013. PISA 2012 Results: What Students Know and Can Do, Paris: OECD. Available for download at: www.oecd.org/pisa/keyfidings/pisa-2012-results.

coefficients for the benchmark countries in Chapter 2. Table 4A.1 shows these same statistics for a sample of other countries.

Data in Table 4.2 indicate that Brazilian per capita physical and human capital stocks are much lower than those of all benchmark countries. This is also true for per capita GDP, as seen in Chapter 2, but comparisons of natural capital do not give a clear rule for all benchmark countries. These results suggest that gaps in domestic supplies of human and physical capital are already strong candidates to explain Brazilian relative backwardness when its per capita GDP is compared to that of benchmark countries. The next subsection deals in more detail with this hypothesis.

4.6.2 Method for Decomposition of Per Capita GDP Differences

The data just generated can be used to build a decomposition of per capita GDP differences between Brazil and other countries. The method starts with Eq. (4.1') and takes natural logarithms on both sides, yielding:

$$\ln y_i = \ln A_i' + \alpha_i \ln k_i + \delta_i \ln n_i + (1 - \alpha_i - \delta_i)\ln h_i \qquad (4.5)$$

Note that the parameters of the production function, α and δ, are now indexed for countries. As was seen before, they are not the same for all countries, as the proportion represented in Eqs. (4.2')−(4.4') varies among them. Thus a first source of difference of Brazilian per capita GDP compared to the other benchmark countries arises from the production function itself.

TABLE 4.2 Estimated Variables for the Sample of Benchmark Countries, Given the Method Described in the Text

Country	y	k	N	H	A'	A	δ	$(1 - \alpha - \delta)$
Greece	22.3143	95.3960	1.4791	128.1325	0.20	0.45	0.01	0.55
Australia	34.0617	131.3094	38.5268	175.1275	0.26	040	0.11	0.49
Brazil	8.6585	33.0182	5.2198	49.4903	0.23	0.40	0.06	0.54
Canada	32.2666	101.5506	17.3208	210.3086	0.22	0.33	0.05	0.62
Finland	32.6028	151.1346	3.0919	173.2926	0.21	0.49	0.01	0.50
New Zealand	23.3606	62.3010	7.2795	169.9191	0.20	0.28	0.03	0.69
Norway	50.8427	180.3978	72.5705	263.5846	0.26	0.37	0.14	0.49
Portugal	20.9464	110.4003	7763	97.8500	0.20	0.55	0.00	0.44
Spain	27.4229	151.0051	2668	121.7060	0.20	0.58	0.00	0.42
Sweden	34.4048	96.6021	4.3323	251.2845	0.19	0.29	0.01	0.69
Switzerland	44.5085	155.3380	1045	297.0275	0.19	0.37	0.00	0.63
United States	42.1402	132.5551	7.6945	289.6672	0.20	0.33	0.02	0.65

Note: y, k, n, and h are per capita GDP and stocks of physical, natural, and human capitals, respectively. They are all figures for 2011, measured in chained purchasing power parity of US dollars in 2005. A' is the productivity parameter and α, δ, and $(1 - \alpha - \delta)$ are the parameters of Eq. (4.1').
Estimations by the author with data from Feenstra, R.C., Inklaar, R., Timmer, M.P., 2013. The Next Generation of the Penn World Table. Available for download at: www.ggdc.net/pwt; World Bank, 2013. World Economic Indicators, Washington: World Bank.

In particular, coefficients α and δ can be different from those of other countries. Nevertheless, it is possible to estimate a surrogate per capita GDP for each country, which is built from the stocks of factors of production existing in each country but with the Brazilian parameters. Therefore, it is possible to define:

$$\ln y_i^* = \ln A_i' + \alpha_b \ln k_i + \delta_b \ln n_i + (1 - \alpha_b - \delta_b)\ln h_i \qquad (4.6)$$

where y^* is the surrogate per capita GDP for country i, and α_b and δ_b are the parameters from the Brazilian production function. Given this concept, it is possible to define:

$$\ln y_i - \ln y_b = \left(\ln y_i - \ln y_i^*\right) + \left(\ln y_i^* - \ln y_b\right) \qquad (4.7)$$

where y_b is Brazilian per capita GDP and y_i is this same variable for country i. The first term in the right side of this equation can be considered to be the *structural differences of the two economies*, as such differences lead to different values for the average parameters for individual firms within the country when all sectors are represented with only one production function. The second term in Eq. (4.7) represents the factors plus productivity differences, which will be further decomposed. Substituting Eqs. (4.5) and (4.6) in this second term, it is possible to obtain:

$$\ln y_i - \ln y_b = \left(\ln y_i - \ln y_i^*\right) + (\ln A_i - \ln A_b) + \alpha_b(\ln k_i - \ln k_b) \\ + \delta_b(\ln n_i - \ln n_b) + (1 - \alpha_b - \delta_b)(\ln h_i - \ln h_b) \qquad (4.8)$$

If both sides of Eq. (4.8) are divided by $\ln y_i - \ln y_b$, the result is:

$$1 = \frac{\left(\ln y_i - \ln y_i^*\right)}{\ln y_i - \ln y_b} + \frac{(\ln A_i - \ln A_b)}{\ln y_i - \ln y_b} + \frac{\alpha_b(\ln k_i - \ln k_b)}{\ln y_i - \ln y_b} \\ + \frac{\delta_b(\ln n_i - \ln n_b)}{\ln y_i - \ln y_b} + \frac{(1 - \alpha_b - \delta_b)(\ln h_i - \ln h_b)}{\ln y_i - \ln y_b} \qquad (4.8')$$

Each term on the right side of Eq. (4.8') has a particular meaning. They can be considered as shares of the role of alternative sources of proportional differences between per capita GDP of countries i and b (Brazil). These concepts are more precisely specified in Table 4.3.

In a simpler way, it can be said that Eq. (4.8') decomposes the proportional differences in total per capita GDP in five components. One arises from structural differences in the production function, which appear because of distinct specializations in the world market. This can be called the first difference proposed by ECLA, the United Nations Economic Commission for Latin America,[7] and is represented in the first term of the right-hand side of

---

7. ECLA is the United Nations Economic Commission for Latin America. Under the leadership of Raul Prebisch it developed theories explaining the development level differences among nations, relying heavily on the hypothesis that they had different specializations on the world market.

TABLE 4.3 Meaning of Each Term of Eq. (4.8)

Term	Meaning
$\dfrac{(\ln y_i - \ln y_i^*)}{\ln y_i - \ln y_b}$	Share of the role of structural differences of the two economies in total proportional difference in per capita GDP.
$\dfrac{(\ln A_i - \ln A_b)}{\ln y_i - \ln y_b}$	Share of the role of the proportional differences in total factor productivity in the total proportional difference in per capita GDP.
$\dfrac{\alpha_b (\ln k_i - \ln k_b)}{\ln y_i - \ln y_b}$	Share of the role of the proportional differences in the stock of physical capital in the total proportional difference in per capita GDP.
$\dfrac{\delta_b (\ln n_i - \ln n_b)}{\ln y_i - \ln y_b}$	Share of the role of the proportional differences in natural resource availability in the total proportional difference in per capita GDP.
$\dfrac{(1 - \alpha_b - \delta_b)(\ln h_i - \ln h_b)}{\ln y_i - \ln y_b}$	Share of the role of the proportional differences in the stock of human capital in the total proportional difference in per capita GDP.

Eq. (4.8′). A second component emerges from differences in total factor productivity (TFP), and appears because of institutional and social capital differences, as well as domestic spatial distribution and cultural determinants of production. As all the variables are in per capita terms, this term also captures the role of differences in the proportion of employment to total population.

The third component introduces the role of proportional differences in the stock of physical capital, and can be considered as the traditional neoclassical determinant of international income disparities. The fourth component captures the role of proportional differences in the known stocks of what the World Bank called natural capital, and the last component introduces the role of the proportional differences of the stock of human capital in the per capita GDP differences.

4.6.3 Figures Comparing Brazil to the Benchmark Countries

The decomposition presented in Eq. (4.8′) and Table 4.3 can be made with the data given in Section 4.6.1. It generates the figures appearing in Fig. 4.7 and Table 4.4. It can be seen that the source of differences in per capita GDP lies mainly in human and physical capitals. Human capital is more relevant for all countries except Portugal and Spain, but it is still the second most relevant component even in these two countries. Recent investments in infrastructure from the European Union in the last decades probably explain this special role of physical capital in these countries. It should be noted that physical capital

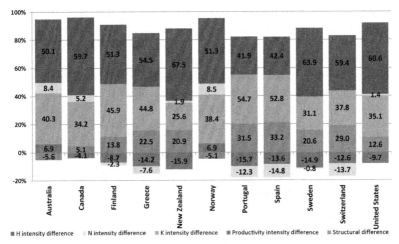

FIGURE 4.7 Proportion of each component in total proportional difference of per capita GDP of the country to Brazilian GDP.

TABLE 4.4 Proportion of Each Component in Total Proportional Difference of Per Capita GDP of the Country to Brazilian GDP

Country	Structural	Total Factor Productivity Intensity	Physical Capital Intensity	Natural Capital Intensity	Human Capital Intensity
Australia	−5.6	6.9	40.3	8.4	50.1
Canada	5.1	−4.1	34.2	5.2	59.7
Finland	13.8	−8.7	45.9	−2.3	51.3
Greece	22.5	−14.2	44.8	−7.6	54.5
New Zealand	20.9	−15.9	25.6	1.9	67.5
Norway	−5.1	6.9	38.4	8.5	51.3
Portugal	31.5	−15.7	54.7	−12.3	41.9
Spain	33.2	−13.6	52.8	−14.8	42.4
Sweden	20.6	−14.9	31.1	−0.8	63.9
Switzerland	29.0	−12.6	37.8	−13.7	59.4
United States	12.6	−9.7	35.1	1.4	60.6

Author calculation from data by Feenstra, R.C., Inklaar, R., Timmer, M.P., 2013. The Next Generation of the Penn World Table. Available for download at: www.ggdc.net/pwt; World Bank, 2013. World Economic Indicators, Washington: World Bank.

availability is the second most relevant component for all countries but Portugal and Spain. Thus human and physical capital availabilities are the major sources of per capita GDP differences, and their roles together account for over 90% of differences with all countries.

Before focusing closely on these figures, it is important to stress that "development accounting does not uncover the ultimate reasons why some countries are much richer than others: only the proximate ones. Like growth accounting, it has nothing to say on the causes of low factor accumulation, or low levels of efficiency. Indeed, the most likely scenario is that the same ultimate causes explain both. Furthermore, it has nothing to say on the way factor accumulation and efficiency influence each other, as they most probably do. Instead, it should be understood as a diagnostic tool, just as medical tests can tell one whether or not he is suffering from a certain ailment, but cannot reveal the causes of it" (Caselli, 2005).

Francesco Caselli expresses very appropriately the limits of development accounting as used here. There is no causality relationship from the components of Table 4.4 and differences of per capita GDP, and there is no explanation as to why Brazilian availabilities of human and physical capitals are lower than those of the benchmark countries. Thus it is not possible to say that low accumulations of human and/or physical capital are the ultimate causes of Brazilian relative backwardness; rather, the causes of the low stock building of these factors of production are what explain Brazilian relative backwardness. Furthermore, these causes can be the same as those that justify the non-negligible role of structural differences in the total per capita GDP differences, as seen in Table 4.4.

Before concluding this section, a striking result arising from the statistics shown in Table 4.4 and Fig. 4.7 should be commented upon. The data indicate that in 9 out of 11 benchmarking countries the TFP was lower than in Brazil. The estimated TFPs with the method used here, which appear in Table 4.2, are such that there is a weak negative relationship between per capita GDP and TFP. Most studies have reached different conclusions.

The major reason for this apparently odd conclusion is that the use of schooling years as the major source to determine the stock of human capital shrinks its dispersion and consequently leaves a reasonable share of its effect to the estimated TFP, which is always left as a residual. As more developed countries have higher stocks of human capital, the consequence is that the relationship becomes positive. The method of this chapter does not face this problem, as its calculation of human capital better captures its dispersion among countries.

Nonetheless, other reasons presented in the literature could justify a positive relationship between TFP and per capita GDP. Hsieh and Klenow (2010) stress the potential role of misallocation of inputs across firms and industries as an important determinant of differences in TFP. According to them, poorer countries would be less efficient in such an allocation. Other studies stressing the role of institutions in determining development argue that better institutions in more developed countries justify such a positive relationship between per capita GDP and TFP.

Caselli (2005), on the other hand, argues that poorer countries could be more efficient in physical capital allocation, as it is a relatively scarce factor of production in these countries.[8] The same argument also extends to human capital. Thus for a given amount of factors of production, relative scarcity could generate extra effort in their efficient allocation, and the total output could be higher in a developing country. If all human beings are rational, this would be an expected outcome and is in line with what was reached in the estimations shown here.

It should also be stressed that most productive processes are causes of many risks and negative externalities for the environment and people's health and welfare, although they also generate welfare-improving goods and services. The poorer a country is, the less the population is satiated with the major welfare-improving goals of production processes, thus the people become more tolerant of the negative externalities. As a consequence, firms in more developed countries spend a larger share of their productive effort on restricting negative externalities than they do in poorer countries. Under such a reasonable hypothesis, the final result could be that TFP is negatively correlated with per capita GDP, as found in the estimates proposed in this chapter. Therefore, although the found correlation is contrary to that reached in most research in the literature, it is plausible given the basic assumptions of economic theory, and is in line with what other studies have reached through different methods.

4.7 CONCLUSIONS

The data used in this chapter show that Brazil has a relative shortage of human capital when its per capita GDP is taken into account. All other factors of production are domestically supplied at a fair level for a developing country with its per capita GDP, although stocks of physical capital are under the level reached by richer countries if per capita GDP is not taken into account.

A more rigorous methodological development unveils that Brazil lags behind the sample of benchmarking countries mainly because of its relative shortage of physical and human capitals. Natural resources, TFP, and structural differences play some role in explaining Brazilian relative backwardness when compared to some countries, but they are not as important as human capital, firstly, and physical capital, secondly. Thus it is in the causes of the relative

---

8. This conclusion is reached when he replaces a Cobb–Douglas by a CES production function in his development accounting.

availability of these two major factors of production that the sources of Brazilian relative backwardness must be sought, and the next chapters continue this investigation.

To reach these conclusions the chapter departed from traditional development accounting literature, which relies on schooling years, some measure of quality of education, and returns to schooling to build estimates of human capital for particular countries.[9] Instead, two assumptions were introduced: there is arbitrage among capital markets, including physical, natural, and human capitals, across countries; and societies have instruments to replicate current stock of human capital forever. Particularly the former is a key assumption underlying all the arguments of this book. Additionally, different from most other studies, the decomposition of development accounting introduced one more factor of production, natural resources. Under the assumption that there is arbitrage among capital markets, it is possible to include this factor of production and still identify the parameters and levels of these factors for all countries in the sample.

The results reached in this development accounting differ from some recent studies that identify disparities in TFP as a major source of per capita GDP gaps between developed and developing countries.[10] In the particular case of Brazil, human and physical capital availabilities are the major causes of the relative backwardness of the country. This result arises because of a basic difference. In the exercises in this chapter production functions coefficients were supposed to vary across countries, while the return to physical capital was supposed to be the same as a consequence of arbitrage. Other development and growth accounting exercises assume that production functions are similar across countries, while the physical capital return rate is not the same in all countries, unlike what would be predicted by economic theory.

Although physical and human capitals both play important roles on the composition of per capita GDP disparity between Brazil and the benchmark countries, they can both be built through market incentives, endogenously. In this case, the ultimate causes of Brazilian relative backwardness would generate differences in the stocks of these two types of capital. Future chapters extend the research to identify these causes and try to relate them with human and physical capital accumulations.

---

9. See for example Hall and Jones (1999), Caselli (2005), Bils and Klenow (2000), Arezki and Cherif (2010), Hsieh and Klenow (2010), and Ferreira et al. (2013).
10. See for example Caselli (2005), King and Levine (1994), Klenow and Rodriguez-Clare (1997), Prescott (1998), Hall and Jones (1999), and Hsieh and Klenow (2010).

APPENDIX

TABLE 4A.1 Estimated Variables for Additional Sample of Countries, Given the Method Described in the Text

Country	Y	k	n	h	A'	α	δ	(1 − α − δ)
Albania	7,513.0	40,406.8	4,064.0	30,417.8	0.23	0.56	0.05	0.38
Argentina	13,322.8	50,987.7	8,612.9	75,367.1	0.24	0.40	0.06	0.54
Austria	34,287.6	152,193.5	1,345.2	191,613.4	0.20	0.47	0.00	0.53
Belgium	29,785.6	148,287.1	104.7	149,755.6	0.20	0.52	0.00	0.48
Chile	13,690.2	41,397.7	27,629.5	70,815.8	0.27	0.32	0.19	0.49
China	8,189.4	34,177.9	7,839.6	40,647.8	0.25	0.44	0.09	0.47
Colombia	7,728.7	28,347.7	9,866.7	40,210.4	0.26	0.38	0.12	0.49
Costa Rica	8,367.9	18,566.6	245.8	67,370.5	0.17	0.23	0.00	0.76
Croatia	15,896.8	70,381.0	2,053.5	87,607.5	0.21	0.46	0.01	0.52

Continued

TABLE 4A.1 Estimated Variables for Additional Sample of Countries, Given the Method Described in the Text—cont'd

Country	Y	k	n	h	A'	α	δ	(1 − α − δ)
Czech Republic	21,036.8	90,064.6	2,356.8	119,690.6	0.21	0.45	0.01	0.54
Denmark	32,998.5	150,617.1	8,264.7	172,859.1	0.22	0.48	0.02	0.50
France	30,000.2	135,054.9	245.7	166,494.5	0.20	0.47	0.00	0.53
Germany	34,833.3	126,648.5	982.5	225,949.0	0.20	0.38	0.00	0.62
Hungary	16,152.9	76,069.6	1,290.3	84,783.3	0.21	0.49	0.01	0.50
Indonesia	4,216.7	13,810.5	4,440.2	24,711.0	0.25	0.34	0.10	0.56
Ireland	40,951.4	130,517.0	779.4	286,313.6	0.19	0.33	0.00	0.66
Israel	22,870.9	64,897.4	1,047.0	168,125.3	0.18	0.30	0.00	0.70
Italy	29,050.8	138,542.6	616.6	152,270.8	0.20	0.50	0.00	0.50
Japan	31,866.7	145,710.9	121.9	174,502.6	0.20	0.48	0.00	0.52
Jordan	4,577.4	25,804.1	1,334.0	18,364.4	0.22	0.59	0.03	0.38
Korea	29,271.5	116,517.3	214.1	179,334.0	0.20	0.42	0.00	0.58
Latvia	14,629.3	64,666.9	2,180.4	80,445.6	0.21	0.46	0.01	0.52
Lithuania	15,490.4	50,731.7	3,066.2	104,025.6	0.20	0.34	0.02	0.64
Luxembourg	54,168.2	240,924.2	573.9	303,728.8	0.20	0.47	0.00	0.53
Malaysia	10,836.6	47,342.1	11,707.5	50,115.5	0.26	0.46	0.10	0.44
Mexico	12,005.6	33,723.5	11,409.5	77,772.7	0.23	0.29	0.09	0.62

	y	k	n	h	A'	α	δ	$(1-\alpha-\delta)$
Netherlands	37,278.3	151,633.9	4,218.0	220,857.9	0.21	0.43	0.01	0.56
Peru	8,139.8	30,771.7	11,671.8	40,056.7	0.27	0.40	0.14	0.47
Poland	17,635.1	43,535.0	4,846.0	132,785.4	0.19	0.26	0.03	0.71
Romania	12,846.9	48,291.8	3,530.8	78,415.7	0.22	0.39	0.03	0.58
Russia	16,817.1	51,078.9	39,018.6	81,662.5	0.28	0.32	0.22	0.46
Serbia	9,322.4	43,352.0	3,750.2	46,534.0	0.23	0.49	0.04	0.47
Slovak Republic	19,210.1	64,133.0	787.3	130,673.2	0.19	0.35	0.00	0.65
Slovenia	21,574.4	99,335.0	852.1	116,614.8	0.20	0.48	0.00	0.51
Thailand	8,200.1	33,532.7	3,463.4	45,850.2	0.23	0.43	0.04	0.53
Tunisia	6,097.7	24,883.1	4,346.5	32,381.1	0.24	0.43	0.07	0.50
Turkey	14,909.0	36,176.9	1,326.0	115,724.4	0.18	0.25	0.01	0.74
United Kingdom	30,691.0	103,483.5	4,960.4	203,939.5	0.20	0.35	0.02	0.63
Uruguay	11,295.8	39,712.6	1,037.6	74,052.0	0.20	0.37	0.01	0.62
Vietnam	3,658.8	13,742.1	5,257.7	18,093.1	0.27	0.39	0.14	0.47

Note: y, k, n, and h are per capita GDP, and stocks of physical, natural, and human capital, respectively. A' is the productivity parameter and α, δ, and $(1-\alpha-\delta)$ are the parameters of Eq. (4.1').

Estimations by the author with data from Feenstra, R.C., Inklaar, R., Timmer, M.P., 2013. The Next Generation of the Penn World Table. Available for download at: www.ggdc.net/pwt; World Bank, 2013. World Economic Indicators, Washington: World Bank.

Chapter 5

Intergenerational Transmission of Human Capital and Its Role in Physical Capital Accumulation

5.1 INTRODUCTION

Chapter 2 shows that the 19th century was the specific moment at which the largest share of Brazilian current per capita gross domestic product (GDP) gap was built. This could be pointed to as the century in which Brazil lagged behind. Consequently, any hypothesis trying to explain Brazilian relative underdevelopment should account for this relatively poor economic performance in the 19th century and why there was no catching up thereafter.

Chapter 3, building on these initial conclusions, shows that if the world economy works under free trade, perfect mobility of factors of production, monopolistic competition, and full information, any event that creates an unbalanced distribution of some factor of production, other than labor, will generate a stable disparity of per capita GDP among nations which could last forever if no other exogenous events reverse this uneven distribution of this factor, as no arbitrage would lead to factors of production migration that could leverage per capita GDP among nations.

Empirical investigations in Chapter 4 point to the fact that relative lower availability of firstly human capital and secondly physical capital is responsible for the largest share of Brazilian relative backwardness compared to most of the benchmark countries. Total factor productivity differences and natural resource availability play negligible roles in the composition of per capita GDP gaps, while structural differences are a relevant component for comparisons to some countries but of secondary order to most of them. Thus human and physical capital gaps built in the 19th century and the inability to catch up thereafter are the causes of Brazilian relative backwardness.

We can now start to build the hypothesis that particular historical reasons led to the construction in Brazil of a society with relatively low per capita human capital until the 19th century, and particular historical conditions did not lead to catching up in the stock of this factor of production thereafter. This is the inner root of Brazilian relative backwardness. A human capital gap was built, and no market forces led to its reversal. Furthermore, no restrictions on physical capital accumulation played a relevant role in explaining this relatively low development level, as argued by important interpretations of Brazilian underdevelopment such as that forwarded by Furtado (1959). Only the relatively low local supply of human capital built the gap. Market forces adjusted the availability of other factors of production, mainly physical capital, to generate fairly arbitrated rates of return so there were no market incentives to narrow the gap.

To build support for this hypothesis, a first necessary step is to show why once a gap in human capital appears, it persists thereafter, with no market forces working to level it off. An understanding of such persistence is necessary to find out why gaps appearing in the 19th century were not later eroded by market mechanisms. If such behavior is rationally explained, it is possible to stick to the assumption that there are capital flows across countries' borders that lead to an equilibrium in the world economy with per capita GDP disparities like those found nowadays, and particularly why Brazil could lag behind even if there was reasonably free flow of capital in the world economy.

From Chapter 3 it is known that if an original gap was created in the 19th century, equalization of factor of production prices among nations ensures that no market mechanism works to generate migration among countries that could push for any convergence of per capita income. Disparities will persist once they are established and markets are in equilibrium, unless extra market forces could generate any tendency toward convergence through faster accumulation of human capital in countries with relatively low availability, as arbitrage among markets in different countries would not generate such impulses.

There is still one possible way for markets to work to generate convergence, even if human capital is allocated exogenously within nations: the potential market incentives for faster human capital accumulation among families with a lower supply of it. If families with less human capital tended to accumulate it faster than families with more human capital, even if both reach the same marginal return on this factor of production, this would generate a tendency for convergence, as countries with lower income would have more families with less human capital.

This chapter approaches this problem. Particularly, it shows that once the gap in human capital availability among families emerges, market forces tend to replicate this disparity forever. This means that once inequality among per capita output of nations emerges, market forces by themselves will tend to reproduce it thereafter. Only nonmarket interventions can overcome the relative disadvantage imposed on some nations.

The next section discusses intergenerational human capital transmission, focusing on the literature on this subject and some of its conclusions. Section 5.3 presents a model unveiling the logic of rational intergenerational human capital transmission, and Section 5.4 discusses the implications of this model for Brazilian relative backwardness. Section 5.5 comments on free capital mobility, while Section 5.6 summarizes the major conclusions of the chapter.

5.2 INTERGENERATIONAL TRANSMISSION OF HUMAN CAPITAL

There is some empirical research unveiling a positive relationship between education of parents and of their offspring.[1] The longer the period the former spend in school, the longer will tend to be spent there by the latter. The strength of this relationship varies from country to country, and can also change among communities in the same society. Nevertheless, it is always found in reality.

The literature points to three major sources of this relationship. The first is *a causal relationship arising from the domestic environment*. In households in which parents are more educated, children tend to be stimulated to develop cognitive skills through their social interactions. Logical reasoning is demanded more often from children, which forces them to practice and develop such skills. Of course such domestic practice also helps develop other crucial abilities that are usually associated with human capital, such as discipline and focus. The result is that heirs from households with higher education become more competitive in school activities, and as such they tend to progress further in schooling.

A second source of intergenerational transmission of human capital is *genetic*. People with natural higher intellectual abilities tend to transmit this genetic asset to their heirs. With higher biological intellectual abilities, people tend to focus more on its further refinement and development, as they have comparative advantage in this area. It is also assumed that people with higher biological intellectual skills tend to search for partners with similar higher

---

1. See, for example, Hertz et al. (2007), Sacerdote (2002), Nichols and Favreault (2009), and Black et al. (2005). Black and Devereux (2010) is a recent survey on this subject.

intellectual skills. This means that social differences in biological intellectual abilities do not tend to vanish in a society.

The third source of intergenerational transmission of human capital is the *rational tendency* of parents with more qualifications to foster the engagement of their heirs in activities that will further promote their intellectual abilities. They choose better schools and encourage a choice of games and toys that are more reason enhancing. Such behavior also promotes their abilities to develop human capital and makes its acquisition less demanding. The consequence is also that these heirs tend to progress further in human capital building.

The three sources of intergenerational transmission of human capital have different features. The genetic transmission happens with almost no individual effort, while the transmission of cognitive abilities through simple daily relationships also does not involve much effort, although there is some need for personal engagement. The third source, however, involves a rational effort targeting human capital building in the heirs. Together they build a strong transmission relationship, which can be further understood through a simple model of parents' rationality, discussed in the next section.

5.3 MODEL UNVEILING THE LOGIC OF RATIONAL INTERGENERATIONAL HUMAN CAPITAL TRANSMISSION[2]

Suppose a representative consumer's life has two phases. In the first one she/he works and raises her/his child, taking care of his/her education. In the second phase the child works while the consumer is retired. Thus when this consumer takes decisions in the first phase, she/he considers the two phases and faces a Cobb–Douglas-type utility function of the form:

$$U = C_1^\sigma C_2^{1-\sigma} \tag{5.1}$$

where C_1 and C_2 are consumption in the first and second phases, respectively, and $0 < \sigma < 1$ is a parameter. This consumption is measured in the only good in the economy. The consumer does not face any credit constraint and she/he can spend some resources on the human capital building of her/his descendant. These resources are measured in units of the only good in the economy. Therefore, she/he faces a budget constraint that can be represented as:

$$C_1 + (1 + r)^{-1} C_2 + E = Y_1 + (1 + r)^{-1} Y_2 \tag{5.2}$$

where Y_1 and Y_2 are the family net income[3] in the first and second phases,

---

2. The model presented here is a modified version of the model presented by Barros (2011, Appendix 3).
3. These incomes are net of government taxes. Families do not consider these as variables under their control nor associate them with public investment in human capital, as this latter is only a small part of total government expenditure.

respectively, and r is the interest rate. E is the total expenditure on human capital building by the family, also measured in the only good in the economy. This is the source of transmission of human capital which involves personal effort of parents spending resources. It is worth stressing that $E \geq 0$.

The incomes of periods one and two are determined by a wage rate found in the economy, the amount of labor spent, and the human capital of the family member working in that period—the parent in the first period and the heir in the second. These incomes are defined as:

$$Y_1 = wH_PL_P \tag{5.3}$$

and

$$Y_2 = vwH_OL_O \tag{5.4}$$

where w is the basic wage rate, $v = (1 + g_w)$, g_w is the growth rate of the wage rate between generations, H_P and H_O are the human capital of parent and her/his offspring, respectively, and L_P and L_O are the amount of labor spent at work. As there is no disutility of work in the utility function (1), these amounts will always be equal to the total potential supply in each period, so L_P and L_O are exogenously determined.

Human capital in this model is measured as the productive ability of the individual. Thus w, the basic wage rate, covers the whole economy and is the same for all workers, regardless of their skills. Individual incomes differ according to the level of individual human capital, as it is measured here. Therefore a worker with twice the income of another has twice her/his human capital.

While the human capital of the parent H_P is exogenously determined in the family, as it was decided by the previous generation, the human capital of the offspring H_O is endogenously determined. Furthermore, it is determined by the following relationship:

$$H_O = (E + \pi)^\delta H_P^{1-\delta} \tag{5.5}$$

where π is the amount of resources spent by the government on education of a child. δ is a parameter, such that $0 < \delta < 1$. Eq. (5.5) indicates that the offspring's human capital is built by invested resources $(E + \pi)$ and the human capital of the parent, which is H_P. When E increases, everything else being constant, the accumulation of human capital also rises, but at a decreasing amount. This same logic applies to H_P.

Inclusion of H_P in Eq. (5.5) with $(1-\delta) > 0$ incorporates the two other sources of intergenerational human capital transmission in the model—the genetic and social interaction sources discussed in the previous section. As the mechanism of investment was introduced in Eq. (5.2), with $E > 0$ among the expenditure of the family, this model incorporates all three mechanisms introduced in Section 5.2 and proposed by the literature.

Substitution of Eqs. (5.3)–(5.5) in Eq. (5.2) yields:

$$wH_PL_P + (1 + r)^{-1}vwL_OH_P^{1-\delta}(E + \pi)^\delta = C_1 + (1 + r)^{-1}C_2 + E \qquad (5.2')$$

The rational representative consumer will maximize the utility function defined in Eq. (5.1) subject to the budget constraint appearing in Eq. (5.2'). C_1, C_2, and E are the variables under her/his control in this problem. For an interior solution, among other results, this procedure yields:

$$E = \left(v\frac{wL_O\delta}{1 + r}\right)^{\frac{1}{1-\delta}}H_P - \pi \qquad (5.6)$$

Substitution of this result in Eq. (5.5) produces:

$$H_O = \left(\frac{vwL_O\delta}{1 + r}\right)^{\frac{\delta}{1-\delta}}H_P \qquad (5.5')$$

Eq. (5.5') implies that:

$$\frac{H_P}{H_O}\frac{\partial H_O}{\partial H_P} = 1 \qquad (5.7)$$

This means that more educated parents raise more educated heirs, as there is a family effort to maintain human capital stock over generations. Furthermore, a comparison between any two families yields the same proportion between the human capital of parents and that of their offspring. Or, mathematically:

$$\frac{H_{O1}}{H_{O2}} = \frac{H_{P1}}{H_{P2}} \qquad (5.8)$$

so human capital tends to be intergenerationally transmitted, keeping the relative stock among generations.

Eq. (5.6), however, also implies that this relationship will be violated if π, public investment in education, is so high that E, private expenditure, is nonpositive. As such expenses cannot be negative, a society with this situation for all members would end up having convergence of human capital, as heirs would not reproduce the proportion of human capital among their parents. In this case:

$$\frac{H_P}{H_O}\frac{\partial H_O}{\partial H_P} = 1 - \delta < 1 \qquad (5.7')$$

this gives convergence of human capital among families.

The relevant conclusion extracted from this simple model of rational accumulation of human capital over generations is that if public investment in education is below a given level, market incentives perpetuate inequalities in the distribution of this factor of production among families. Individuals born in a family with twice the human capital of another will tend to have this same proportion of human capital relative to the offspring of the other family. Only if public investments reach a given minimum level does this relationship no longer hold.

An additional relevant conclusion can be extracted from Eq. (5.5′). All variables and parameters determining the evolution of human capital between two generations tend to be equal across countries if there is full arbitrage in markets for factors of production. Thus it is reasonable to assume that when there are no public policies on education, the growth rate of the stock of human capital is quite similar between different countries. This simple conclusion is used in the following chapters.

5.4 ADDITIONAL COMMENTS

Eq. (5.5′) indicates that the higher the expectations for the growth rate of wages between generations (v), the higher will be the intergenerational growth rate of human capital. Hence societies with higher mobility, and consequently higher v, will also increase faster their stock of human capital.[4] This simple relationship could be one of the sources of higher growth in the United States in the second half of the 19th century when compared to England and European countries.[5] It is one of the foundations of Brazilian underdevelopment in Buarque's (1936) conception of the low probability of social advancement given existing rules.[6]

It is worth mentioning that $E = 0$ is an equilibrium for a given family only when public expenditure on education is so high that additional investments on education by that family do not bring any gain in utility. Furthermore, Eq. (5.6) implies that two families with different human capital of the parents, H_P, will have different required π to force E to be equal to zero, everything else being the same. Parents with higher H_P will have a higher threshold for π to force $E = 0$. Thus when a government gradually raises per capita public investment on education, it starts crowding out investments by lower-skilled families, only reaching these expenditures by the upper-class families at much higher E.

As a consequence, it is possible to compare the path of human capital between two families, one whose threshold value is reached by government per capita expenditures on education, so $E = 0$ for this family, and another in which this threshold is not reached. These two paths are represented in Fig. 5.1 as continuous lines of the natural logarithm of human capital. For these two

---

4. It should be noted that an assumption of upward bias in expectations of wages for next generations was introduced, as most families envisage the possibility of improving their welfare in the future when mobility is high. The higher the social mobility, the higher will be the average expectations of future income.

5. Long and Ferrie (2013) and Xie and Killewald (2013) give evidence of this higher mobility in the United States when compared to Great Britain in the second half of the 19th century.

6. See Cardoso (2013, pp. 273–277) for a summary of this view.

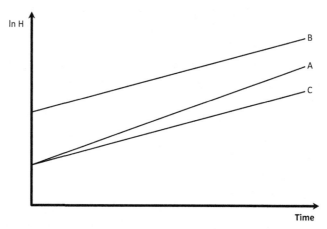

FIGURE 5.1   Time path of natural logarithm of human capital over generations.

families the lines are A and B, respectively.[7] Another line, C, was inserted in this figure to represent the natural logarithm of the path for the poorer family if its threshold value for E was not reached. In this case its growth rate of human capital would be the same as that of the richer family, as indicated by Eq. (5.5′).

It can be seen from Fig. 5.1 that when $E = 0$ for the poorer family (line A), its human capital growth rate rises above that of the richer family. Thus convergence of human capital happens among families, extracted from Eq. (5.7′), with the poorest families increasing their human capital faster across generations than the richest families. If human capital is the engine of growth in this country, as suggested by Lucas's (1988) seminal model, the growth rate in this economy will rise when the poorest family moves from path C to path A. As a consequence of this relationship, when government public expenditure on education is such that it makes $E = 0$ for all families, this levels off human capital accumulation by the upper level in society. Thus human capital accumulation in this society will be higher than it would be otherwise.

In spite of its simplicity, the model presented here can have very important implications to understand Brazilian relative backwardness when placed together with the results unveiled by the previous chapters. If for some reason per capita income disparities arose in the 19th century because of an unbalanced world distribution of families with distinct human capital, this same unequal equilibrium would persist if there was no public investment in

---

7. A natural logarithm was introduced to force these time representations to be straight lines. It is worth stressing that as the model is discrete, only specific dots on lines A, B, and C actually exist.

education in the lower-income countries, such as Brazil, working to reverse this disadvantage in relative availability of human capital of this initial equilibrium. Market forces and capital mobility would not reverse the initial inequality, regardless of their efficiency. The model in Chapter 3 shows that even full capital mobility with no transaction costs and full arbitrage among markets would not reverse such initial disparities.

The 19th century, the era when most of the inequality between Brazilian per capita income and those of the benchmark countries arose, was a period in which public education was less a responsibility of the government and more one of families. Hence the human capital of immigrants to both the United States and Brazil was mostly reproduced among generations. Recent research on human capital building in the United States indicates that there was considerable government effort on education in that century,[8] certainly generated by demands from the local population, even when they were new arrivers. In Brazil, however, the existing studies indicate that such governmental effort was low and mainly restricted to some regions, such as south and southeast Brazil,[9] where immigration resembled the US immigrant composition when continental closer similarities of culture and expectations in the 19th century are considered. Therefore there was more convergence among generations and faster average intergenerational human capital growth in the United States than in Brazil in that century, as predicted by this simple model.

5.5 NOTE ON FREE CAPITAL MOBILITY

The basic explanation for Brazilian relative backwardness forwarded here relies on a simple hypothesis. Migration of physical capital is faster than that of human capital. Thus world prices and production spatial distribution adjust more quickly to the local availabilities of human capital and less to physical capital availability. Despite the existing migration of both types of capital, the faster movement of physical capital when compared to human capital makes the adjustments of production and relative prices of goods to force the former to cross borders more intensive when the economy converges to a new equilibrium after any exogenous shock. As a consequence, countries that for historical reasons end up with higher per capita human capital concentration at some point in time will also tend to have higher per capita physical capital stocks, built through migration if local saving rates are not high enough. The consequence is that they will have higher per capita GDP. Therefore, some comments on capital mobility are important at this stage to give an idea of whether this assumption on physical capital movements is reasonable. This is pursued in this section.

---

8. See Goldin and Katz (2008).
9. Ver Engerman et al. (2009).

There is a huge literature on capital mobility, mainly for the 20th century but also dealing with the 19th century.[10] This literature stresses the existence of changes in capital mobility worldwide over the course of time. The second half of the 19th century is normally taken as the gold age of liberalism and a period in history with higher capital mobility, only matched by recent levels.[11] Nevertheless, the evidence is that in the first half of the 19th century there was also a reasonable flow of capital among countries. Brezis (1995) shows that the British current account registered a sizable export of capital in this period, while it had imported capital from 1740 to 1800. Imlah (1958) also reached the same conclusion on 19th-century capital flows from Britain.

Capital mobility in the 19th century could take the form of loans, direct investments, or flows of precious metals, such as gold. As most countries at that time had a metallic monetary regime, capital flows were easy, as there were no restrictions on trade of these metals. Nevertheless, all such trans-actions had costs and risks that reduced their attraction to private agents, constituting obstacles to perfect capital mobility. Government restrictions on capital mobility, however, were more difficult to impose in that period, as smuggling precious metals was always an option. Thus capital mobility in the 19th century is a good assumption, although there were costs involved in this flow and consequently it was not perfect.

Estimations for the 20th century conclude that there was also high capital mobility in the period before World War I. Between the two world wars there was a fall in capital mobility, but it rose again after World War II to levels similar to those in the second half of the 19th century. Thus there was lower capital mobility[12] in the 20th century only at times of political distress in the world economy, such as the two world wars and the Great Depression.

5.6 SOME CONSEQUENCES FOR BRAZILIAN RELATIVE BACKWARDNESS

The model dealing with human capital accumulation and the comments on capital mobility advance the hypothesis of this book a little further. The idea is that the best approximation for the world economic reality is that it works as a free market where firms, goods, services, and factors of production move freely spatially. Nevertheless, goods, services, firms, and physical capital move faster than human capital, labor, and natural resources. The latter, particularly, barely move, although technological progress can alter the relative relevance

---

10. See Obstfeld and Taylor (2003), Obstfeld (2002), Bordo (2002), and Hoffman (2004).
11. See Obstfeld (2002) and Bordo (2002).
12. These results are presented mainly by Hoffman (2004) for the United States and the United Kingdom, using more sophisticated methods than previous studies, although they do not differ much from results reached by Taylor (1996) for many countries and the summary of several studies by Obstfeld and Taylor (2003).

of their spatial distribution. Thus one can consider that there is also some economic relevant spatial mobility of this factor of production.

Human capital and labor move spatially across country borders, but these movements are slower than that of physical capital. The consequence is that the permanent search for equilibrium in international market relies more on physical capital movements than on human capital movements. Furthermore, human and physical capitals are complementary. When per capita availability of human capital increases, per capita availability of physical capital immediately responds and also increases, adjusting to the optimal level given the level of other factors of production. Fig. 5.2 shows the relationship between stocks of physical and human capitals (in natural logarithms) according to data discussed in Chapter 4. It can be easily seen that these two variables grow together in this cross-section of 60 countries, suggesting this complementarity.

Consequently, a country that for some historical reason ends up with lower per capita stock of human capital will end up with a lower per capita availability of physical capital and lower per capita GDP. Physical capital adjusts to local demand, which is determined by the availability of the other more rigid factors of production, especially human capital. Therefore, the role of physical capital in proportional differences of per capita GDP presented in Chapter 4, Table 4.4 and Fig. 4.7, would shrink considerably if its share, which is determined by the availability of other factors of production, is input in the other factor of production.

Table 5.1 gives a new decomposition of proportional differences of per capita GDP between benchmark countries and Brazil. The method is the same as explained in Chapter 4, Section 4.6.3. The only difference is that it supposed

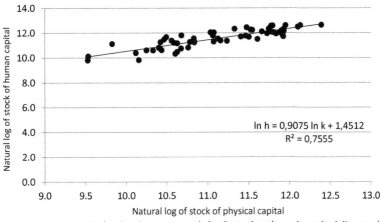

Note: Human capital estimations were made by the author through method discussed in chapter 4. There are 60 countries in the sample.

FIGURE 5.2 Relationship between stocks of physical and human capitals. *Original data is from Feenstra, R.C., Inklaar, R., Timmer, M.P., 2013. The Next Generation of the Penn World Table. Available for download at: www.ggdc.net/pw.*

TABLE 5.1 Proportion of Each Component in Total Proportional Difference of per Capita GDP of a Country to That of Brazil, Decomposing Physical Capital to Its Independent Part and Those Potentially Explained by Human and Natural Capitals (%)

Country	Structural	Total Factor Productivity Intensity	Independent Physical Capital Intensity	Natural Capital Intensity	Human Capital Intensity
Australia	−5.6	6.9	18.5	2.6	77.8
Canada	5.1	−4.1	4.7	1.6	92.8
Finland	13.8	−8.7	16.1	−0.7	79.7
Greece	22.5	−14.2	9.5	−2.4	84.7
New Zealand	20.9	−15.9	−10.6	0.6	104.8
Norway	−5.1	6.9	16.0	2.7	79.7
Portugal	31.5	−15.7	23.2	−3.9	65.1
Spain	33.2	−13.6	19.3	−4.6	65.8
Sweden	20.6	−14.9	−4.9	−0.2	99.3
Switzerland	29.0	−12.6	−4.5	−4.3	92.3
United States	12.6	−9.7	2.6	0.4	94.2

Author's calculation from data by Feenstra, R.C., Inklaar, R., Timmer, M.P., 2013. The Next Generation of the Penn World Table. Available for download at: www.ggdc.net/pwt; World Bank, 2013. World Economic Indicators. World Bank, Washington.

that physical capital is formed by two components: one determined by natural and human capitals, and another that is independent of these two other factors of production. More precisely, physical capital k was decomposed as:

$$k = Vn^{\varphi}h^{\gamma}v \tag{5.9}$$

where k, n, and h are per capita stocks of physical, natural, and human capitals, respectively. V is a constant and v is the deviation from 1 that, together with V, ensures that Eq. (5.9) holds. The Greek letters φ and γ, are parameters. By assumption, n and h are supposed to be independent of k. Therefore φ, γ, V, and v can be estimated by standard econometric methods if the natural logarithm of Eq. (5.9) is taken, as this equation becomes linear after such transformation. Estimations by least absolute deviation of these variables and parameters are shown in Table 5.2. The natural logarithms of V and v are the

TABLE 5.2 Estimation Results of the Natural Logarithm of Eq. (5.9), Using Least Absolute Deviation Method

Variable	Coefficient	t-statistic	p-value
ln V (constant)	3.290188161	3.60200	0.00073618
ln h	0.751620697	10.68096	0.00000000
ln n	−0.098404439	−2.89664	0.00562311

Sample size was 52 countries for which there was full data. All the data is for 2011. Author's estimation based on data from Feenstra, R.C., Inklaar, R., Timmer, M.P., 2013. The Next Generation of the Penn World Table. Available for download at: www.ggdc.net/pwt; World Bank, 2013. World Economic Indicators. World Bank, Washington.

estimated constant and the error terms. They are combined to generate the independent physical capital whose role in total per capita GDP differences appears in Table 5.1.

Results in Table 5.1 indicate that the largest share of proportional differences of per capita GDP between Brazil and the benchmark countries arises from differences in human capital, when this stock in each country is supposed to be insensitive to physical capital availability and all convergence for equilibrium is made through physical capital mobility across country borders, given h and n. This is a strong assumption. Nevertheless, a major hypothesis of this book is that it is a better approximation of reality than to assume there is no factor mobility and arbitrage across country frontiers, as is usual in many explanations of development differences.

Before concluding this section, Table 5.3 and Fig. 5.3 show some statistics for immigrants for selected countries and areas and a rough estimation of the share of foreign owned to total capital in the world. Immigration data is for the proportion of foreign born to total population within the country. As human capital is embodied in people, its international migration demands population migration. This data shows that population movements across country borders are not negligible for most countries and can reach high figures for some, such as Australia, New Zealand, Canada, and Switzerland. Even for the United States, the Euro area and the United Kingdom, these figures have lately reached over 10%. For a comparison of the relevance of these movements, it is worth mentioning some Brazilian statistics for migration among domestic states, which has no restrictions. In 1991, 2000, and 2010 15.4%, 15.8%, and 14.5%, respectively, of the Brazilian population were not resident in their state of origin.[13] This data indicates that the

13. Census data from IBGE.

TABLE 5.3 Share of Foreign Born in Total Population for Selected Countries and Areas (%)

Country/Area	1960	1965	1970	1975	1980	1985	1990	1995	2000	2005	2010
Australia	16.5	18.0	19.6	19.1	19.7	20.0	21.0	21.3	21.0	21.3	21.4
Austria	11.5	10.3	9.1	9.5	9.5	9.6	10.3	12.5	12.4	14.1	15.6
Brazil	1.9	1.6	1.3	1.1	0.9	0.7	0.5	0.5	0.4	0.4	0.4
Canada	15.5	15.4	15.3	15.2	15.5	15.0	16.2	17.2	18.1	19.5	21.1
Switzerland	13.4	15.2	17.7	17.2	16.9	18.6	20.5	20.9	21.8	22.3	22.5
Euro area	3.4	3.9	4.4	4.7	5.0	5.3	6.2	7.5	8.3	9.8	10.9
Spain	0.7	0.9	1.1	1.3	1.6	1.9	2.1	2.6	4.4	10.6	13.8
European Union	3.7	4.2	4.4	4.6	4.7	4.9	5.7	6.7	7.3	8.5	9.4
Finland	0.7	0.7	0.7	0.8	0.8	1.0	1.3	2.0	2.6	3.3	4.2
France	7.5	8.9	10.0	10.3	10.7	10.5	10.1	10.2	10.3	10.3	10.3
United Kingdom	3.2	4.7	5.3	5.6	6.0	6.3	6.5	7.2	8.1	9.7	10.4
Greece	0.6	0.8	1.0	1.4	1.8	3.1	4.1	5.2	6.7	8.8	10.0
High income	5.0	5.3	5.6	5.9	6.5	7.1	7.8	8.7	9.6	10.7	11.5
Republic of Korea	0.5	0.6	0.6	0.8	1.4	1.4	1.3	1.3	1.2	1.2	1.1
Latin America and Caribbean	2.8	2.4	2.0	1.8	1.7	1.5	1.6	1.2	1.2	1.2	1.2
North America	6.9	6.7	6.7	7.3	8.0	8.9	10.0	11.4	12.9	13.9	14.6

Norway	1.7	1.9	2.0	2.5	3.0	3.6	4.6	5.4	6.7	8.0	9.9
New Zealand	14.1	14.7	14.6	16.0	15.1	14.8	15.7	16.2	17.8	20.7	22.0
High income, OECD	4.7	4.9	5.1	5.4	5.7	6.1	6.8	7.8	8.7	9.8	10.5
OECD members	4.4	4.6	4.7	4.8	5.1	5.4	6.0	6.8	7.6	8.4	9.0
Portugal	0.4	0.7	1.2	1.8	2.7	3.5	4.4	5.3	6.2	7.2	8.6
Sweden	4.0	5.1	6.6	7.1	7.5	7.8	9.1	10.3	11.2	12.3	13.9
United States	6.0	5.8	5.8	6.5	7.2	8.2	9.3	10.7	12.3	13.3	13.8
World	2.6	2.5	2.3	2.3	2.3	2.3	3.0	2.9	2.9	3.0	3.1

Data extracted from World Bank, 2013. World Economic Indicators. World Bank, Washington.

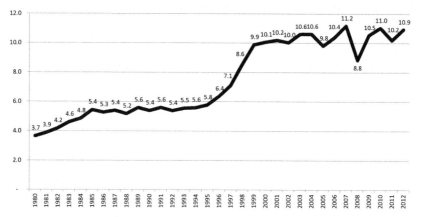

Note: Total foreign owned capital is the sum of foreign direct investment and total external debt.

FIGURE 5.3   Share of foreign-owned capital to its total: world aggregate. *UNCTAD for foreign direct investments and GDP; World Bank Economic Indicators for total external debt. Proportion of physical capital to GDP used was from Feenstra, R.C., Inklaar, R., Timmer, M.P., 2013. The Next Generation of the Penn World Table. Available for download at: www.ggdc.net/pwt.*

hypothesis of free population migration across country borders is a reasonable approximation, although people may prefer to live in their country of origin, as also happens in Brazilian states.

Data from Table 5.3 and Fig. 5.3 together indicates that capital, in its financial form which is mainly used to finance physical capital investments, has a larger share of foreign owned around the world than the share of population living outside their country of origin. If the former variable is an approximation to the share of physical capital that migrated across country borders while the latter is an approximation of human capital migration, this data may be showing that physical capital crosses country borders in a larger proportion, which is a reasonable outcome from the hypothesis forwarded here.

5.7 CONCLUSIONS

This chapter extends the arguments of previous ones, unveiling the rationality for human capital availability and its unequal spatial distribution. A model of intergenerational rational decisionmaking by families is forwarded. In this simple model, two families tend to reproduce their relative human capital inequality through generations unless there is a public policy that explicitly seeks to alter this stable equilibrium. This arises from their rational decisions, when they maximize utility taking into account the options between working, consuming, and investing in human capital. Similar utilities and input—output functions for all families and countries were introduced as assumptions to reach such conclusions. It is also assumed that agents are as rational in rich countries as they are in poor countries, and have similar intergenerational utility functions.

Conclusions from this model help shape the conclusions of the general equilibrium model of Chapter 3. An unequal spatial distribution of human capital in the past, mainly in the 19th century in the case of Brazil, generated a world equilibrium in which per capita GDP inequality fostered by the unbalanced distribution of this factor of production persisted over time. Physical capital world distribution, relying on migration through country borders when necessary to balance savings and the needed investment to ensure full arbitrage, adjusted to this unequal distribution of human capital. This process reproduced the inequality emerging in the past. Brazil, in particular, was locked in by events in its past history that condemned the country to a poorer position than others. The generated equilibrium persisted over history.

To strengthen these arguments, the chapter also quickly reviews the literature on capital mobility, which stresses its relevance on a world scale since the 19th century. Some data on recent stocks of foreign-owned capital and populations living outside their country of birth is used to show that capital and population mobility is an important feature of the world economy. It is worth stressing that when people move across country borders they change the relative human capital availability in the relevant countries, as they always have an amount of this factor of production embodied in them. Figures on Brazilian current interstate population migration are also presented to show that figures for many countries are close to that existing in an area with no restriction to population movements across borders.

Under this new conception of the mechanics of reaching worldwide equilibrium, with major physical capital migration among countries and mainly local reproduction of human capital, although there is some migration of this factor of production but at a lower scale, the decomposition of the sources of Brazilian relative backwardness was recalculated. The assumption that the part of physical capital that can be explained by human and natural capitals is actually determined by these two other factors of production changed the relative role of each component of the inequalities unveiled in Chapter 4.

Human capital, under this hypothesis, accounts for over 75% of the total proportional differences in per capita GDP between Brazil and the benchmark countries. An exception was found for Portugal and Spain, where these figures reached only about 65%. These countries were subject to huge infrastructure investment by the European Union in recent years. This fact certainly strengthened the role of independent physical capital (that is not determined by human and natural capitals) and structural differences in the Brazilian economy.

Developments in this chapter suggest the need for further understanding of the origin of the unbalanced distribution of human capital that emerged in the 19th century when the Brazilian economy is compared to those of benchmark countries. The next chapters deal with this problem.

Chapter 6

Migration Profile and Human Capital Building in Brazil and the United States in the 19th Century

6.1 INTRODUCTION

The 19th century was a period not only of high capital mobility, as stressed in the previous chapter, but also of European mass migration, mainly to the New World in the Americas and Oceania.[1] These two phenomena were stronger in the second half of that century and continued until the First World War. The way Brazil, Argentina, Chile, Uruguay, the United States, Canada, Australia, and New Zealand responded to European mass migration was a key determinant of future development of these countries.

In the second half of the 19th century European countries already had a per capita GDP (gross domestic product) much higher than the world average. In 1820 this per capita figure was US$1396.00, almost double the world average of US$704.00.[2] In 1870 these figures were US$1971.00 and US$876.00, respectively, thus Western European per capita GDP was more than twice the world average that year. In 1913, when per capita GDP was also estimated for the whole world, Western Europe had reached US$3437.00 while the same figure for the whole world was only US$1531.00—a very similar proportion as in 1870.

This higher per capita GDP in Europe was a consequence of higher technological development and especially higher human capital embodied in its population. The European population had incorporated productive processes and social organizations far beyond most of the other regions and countries in the world. Some of these processes and organizations were transported to the colonies and excolonies, together with the inherent abilities they demand, but they were not embodied in all populations of the New World, as many of the local people had other origins and were not necessarily integrated in the same productive systems. The larger the share of the population to whom such values, knowledge, and skills were transmitted, the higher the per capita income of a colony. This would explain, for example, the possibility of some regions in the United States having a higher per capita GDP than that of England, as argued by Lindert and Williamson (2014).

Such transmission was not straightforward. Often the local nonEuropean population worked under lower organizational practices, but were able to generate outputs that could be traded with the more organized and skilled sectors of the economy. As these populations could generate low but sustainable standards of living, they engaged in trade with the sectors and economic systems working under European standards and did not necessarily collapse, as they could offer goods and services at low cost and still survive by maintaining their low standard of living.

---

1. See for example Hatton and Williamson (1992a, 1992b), Abramitzky et al. (2012), Chiswick and Hatton (2003), and O'Rourke (2004).
2. Numbers are from Bolt and van Zanden (2013). European figures are for the 30 countries forming Western Europe. The values are for US$ international, constant PPP at 2005 prices.

Above all, European higher productivity emerged from the application of knowledge and discipline to more complex processes than nonEuropean populations were acquainted with. These skills were not automatically incorporated in the productive processes led and conducted by nonEuropeans in the New World, as their low productivity was often already sufficiently high to generate market values that were welfare improving for both parties in any trade activity. In addition, the lack of domestic development of necessary abilities to allow them to learn these skills and knowledge created a barrier to such learning and absorption of processes. Often the necessary effort or investment to overcome the shortcomings would not yield a present value of the gain, given local return rates, which was sufficiently high for these agents because of associated risk and intertemporal preferences.

Thus European immigration could be a faster way to catch up on knowledge, skills, and discipline. This is why the way each country participated in this population movement was a major determinant of its later economic success. The necessary physical capital to expand productivity, and production itself, could also migrate from somewhere else in the world, as this factor of production faces lower mobility cost. In other words, the assumption that physical capital adjusts almost costlessly and fast to the existing spatial distribution of human capital and natural resources is used in this chapter.

This chapter tries to show that the 19th century was a period in which the United States built a huge stock of human capital by its acceptance of European migration, while Brazil lagged much behind in this. There is no discussion of data for Canada, Australia, and New Zealand, but the hypothesis is that there was the same difference in these countries regarding this migration. Brazil also lost development relative to the other European benchmark countries because these countries generated social structures that promoted human capital building in this period much more intensively than Brazil did. This question is further dealt with in later chapters.

The major instrument of analysis in this chapter is the comparison between Brazil and the United States in what is called here the *predicted surrogated per capita GDP* in specific years. This variable is an average per capita GDP that would prevail if all migrants and their offspring were able to generate individual incomes that were equal to the average they would have in their country of origin. The variable is useful to compare per capita GDP that could be explained only by the inherited or family-built human capital and the actual per capita GDP which prevails within the countries when other local determinants of economic dynamics are considered, such as institutions.

The next section discusses European mass migration, summarizing its causes presented in the literature and unveiling some of its features. Section 6.3 introduces some of the necessary assumptions to build the predicted surrogated per capita GDP, while Section 6.4 presents and discusses the origins of the data and methods to proceed to calculations. Section 6.5 gives the output of the estimations and discusses the results. Section 6.6 discusses the consequences of these results for the major question tackled by this book and summarizes the major conclusions of the chapter.

6.2 EUROPEAN MASS MIGRATION IN THE 19TH CENTURY

In the 19th century there was a sizable migration from Europe to the United States, Australia, New Zealand, and Latin American countries, such as Argentina, Brazil, Uruguay, and Chile. Before this century such migration was restricted to few origins, such as England, Portugal, Spain, and France. In this century there was some diversification, with Germans, Italians, Russians, and Nordic citizens also playing a major role. Altogether, a simple estimation procedure indicates that Western Europe, composed of 30 nations in the Maddison (2011) concept, lost 17% of its population through migration between 1820 and 1900.[3] This was possible because countries like Brazil, the United States, Australia, New Zealand, Argentina, Chile, and Uruguay were opened to European migrants. The United States, however, was the major destination, especially for Northern European emigrants.

It is important to stress that European-born people could return to their home countries if they wished. Thus their migration implied that they could improve their standard of living when reaching their destination, or at least keep it at the same level. Certainly there were many individual frustrations, as well as positive surprises. However, on average improvement probably prevailed, as migrants were rational agents and would not make persistent mistakes. Information on what they would find in their destinations had spread in their countries and regions of origin. Any systematic errors or adverse mismatches between expected and actual standards of living would lead to collapse of migration flows and even their reversal.

Therefore, migration numbers indicate that a reasonable model to explain differences in per capita GDP in the 19th century would include an assumption of free movement of labor across Europe and nations such as Brazil, the United States, Australia, and New Zealand. All these countries had a large share of their population of European origin, who could return to their home countries if that was rational. Furthermore, they accepted European migrants, although there was some regulation. Such regulations were hardly restrictive, however, as the figures for immigration show.[4]

---

3. This number assumes that migration was as estimated by Hatton and Williamson (1998), and population figures are from Maddison (2011).
4. The United States restricted migration from Southern European countries in some periods, and Brazil used positive policies to try to promote migration from Northern European countries such as Austria and Germany.

Such population movements should lead to arbitrage between labor markets. Of course, migration costs, imperfect information, and risk aversion were obstacles to perfect arbitrage, but they certainly restricted differences in income per labor unit when corrected for purchasing power parity (PPP). If the income for a baker or a brewer in Germany was much lower than it was in Brazil or the United States, some German residents would migrate to these excolonies and improve their standard of living; thus some equilibrium between their incomes within the three countries would exist. The Stolper—Samuelson theorem and factor price equalization strength this relationship even further.

6.3 NECESSARY ASSUMPTIONS TO BUILD SURROGATED PER CAPITA GDP

Five basic assumptions underline the estimations of the surrogated predicted per capita GDP in the two countries under focus in this chapter, namely the United States and Brazil.

1. An appropriate index measuring human capital of immigrants moving either to Brazil or the United States would have the same meaning as this same index for the local population of the country of origin of migrants.
2. Families tend to reproduce their human capital in their offspring, as argued in the previous chapter. Thus human capital in a society tends to have full inertia between generations, unless there are public policies or other cooperative decisions to change this tendency.
3. All immigrant communities, independent of their origins, generate the same growth rate of their populations in the destination country, which is equal to the average growth rate of the population in the receptor country. An exception to this rule is for African descendants, as there are periodical estimations of their population in both Brazil and the United States. Therefore the growth rates between the existing estimations were taken as the actual growth rates of their communities.
4. There was free mobility of population among countries in all directions, and the costs of migration were not enough to generate significant differences in the standard of living of someone who migrated to the excolonies, given his/her personal productive attributes.
5. There was perfect capital mobility among countries, so the optimal relationship among physical capital, human capital, labor, and natural resources was reached in short periods, perhaps a few years. This assumption was discussed in the previous chapter when dealing with capital mobility.

Each of these assumptions not previously discussed in the last chapter is further analyzed in this section. Of course, they are all extreme simplifications of the most appropriate hypotheses, but they are good approximations that enable the creation of the predicted surrogated per capita GDP.

6.3.1 Human Capital of Immigrants Is Similar to That of the Population in Their Country of Origin

This hypothesis is quite simplistic and unrealistic in most periods and for the many migration flows. Normally there is some bias in immigration: in some periods it is more attractive for higher-qualified workers to migrate, while in other periods less-qualified workers have more to gain from migration. This depends on the state of the economies in the countries at the two ends of the population flow, and this state changes over the years.

Theories on migration generate models which point to both possible biases in selection of migrants. When motivated by the Roy model (1951) of earnings distribution, research suggests that a negative selection of migrants could arise if the destination country pays a lower return to education. Under this hypothesis, emigrants on average tend to be less qualified than the average population in their original place of residence. Borjas (1987, 1991, 2008) contributes to this approach. Most models, however, suggest that emigrants tend to be more qualified than the population left behind, as their higher abilities, especially entrepreneurship, initiative, and disposition to work, encourage them to seek better opportunities abroad. Chiswick (1999, 2000), for example, relies on human capital models by Becker (1964) and Sjaastad (1962) to reach such a conclusion.

Most studies of recent migration to North America indicate that there is positive selection in qualification of emigrants. Gould and Moav (2010) found such a relationship for Israeli emigration, while Feliciano (2005) and Grogger and Hanson (2008) found that there is a positive selection of skills in emigration from most countries around the world, independently of their relative return to skills, when migrants move to the United States.

Nevertheless, there are very few empirical studies on 19th-century European migration to the Americas. Wegge (1999, 2002, 2009, 2010) studied emigration from Germany to the United States in specific periods and found that it was more concentrated in the middle of the earnings and qualification distribution, with a resulting positive bias on skill, while Abramitzky et al. (2012) studied Norwegian migration from 1850 to 1900 and found a bias for the lower end of qualification. Such studies are not conclusive, as they do not extend their analysis to the whole period nor to all Europeans countries.

Many particular circumstances help determine any skill bias in migration. The high cost of emigration was important. In some periods in the 19th century and in some countries it represented one year of average earnings of migrants. This reduced the ability of poor people to migrate to the New World, as there was no financial support from government or local businesses for European migration in the case of the United States. Europeans moving to Brazil had some financial support from the Brazilian government and local businesses, which helped migration of poorer Europeans to this country.

There were also noneconomic determinants of emigration within some countries and periods, such as political and religious disputes or crop failures that generated scarcity. German and Irish religious disputes are examples of the first type, while Irish famine and agricultural production falls in southern Italy and Minho (a northern Portuguese region) were examples of the second type of noneconomic factors. While political and religious persecutions tended to generate a positive skill bias in emigration, food shortage could generate a negative bias.

Some data on immigrants, such as the fact that they were mainly male and young[5], also has consequences for the bias. Young males in societies with the social values of the 19th century and the rapid transformations in Europe tend to generate a positive skill bias in migration, as migrants tend to be better qualified, although with less experience. These two features affected both destinations, Brazil and the United States.

In spite of all this information on potential sources of bias, there is no clear idea of the comparative human capital between immigrants and the population within their countries of origin during the 19th century. It is known that most Portuguese who migrated to Brazil in that century were from the Minho region and were mainly rural workers. A serious crisis in that region in its rural sector forced these workers to migrate. As this was a relatively poor region in Portugal, as it still is today, probably the human capital embodied in these migrants was lower than the average found in Portuguese citizens in the same period. For the United States, however, there is no clear conclusion on the skill bias of immigration. Therefore, estimations start with the skill-unbiased hypothesis and make some alterations to it.

6.3.2 Families Tend to Reproduce Their Human Capital in Their Offspring

This hypothesis plays a major role in the developments in this chapter. As it is important for the whole argument of this book, it is discussed in detail in Chapter 5, including the elaboration of a model in which this behavior arises from rational decisions of families. Thus no further discussion is pursued here.

The 19th century was a period in which public education was less a responsibility of government and more one of families. Thus the human capital of immigrants to both the United States and Brazil was mostly reproduced across generations. Recent research on human capital building in the United States indicates that there was considerable effort by governments on education in that century.[6] In Brazil, however, the existing studies indicate that such governmental effort was low and mainly restricted to two regions, south and southeast Brazil.[7] Thus there was more convergence among generations in the United States than in Brazil in that century. Nevertheless, estimations of

---

5. Jerome (1926) gives a statistical analysis of immigrants to the United States in the 19th century.
6. See Goldin and Katz (2008).
7. Engerman et al. (2009).

surrogated per capita GDP for the two countries start from the hypothesis that there was the same transmission across generations as postulated by the model in Chapter 5.

6.3.3 Immigrant Communities Generated a Growth Rate of Their Populations Equal to the Average Growth Rate of the Population of the Receptor Country

Although population growth rate is taken as exogenous in most growth models, some take this variable as endogenous.[8] Radical supporters of the exogeneity hypothesis normally argue that cultural, religious, and biological aspects are the major determinants of population growth rate. However, few economic researchers would accept this idea, although they may still think that these aspects possibly would have some role to play.[9]

The growth models incorporating the hypothesis that population growth rate is endogenous normally define the economic incentives that should determine this variable, and are based on Malthus's idea that population growth is determined by age at marriage and coition frequency during marriage, plus mortality rate. Certainly recent developments in contraceptive methods, mainly in the 20th century, changed the role of this original definition, but for the 19th century they are a good starting point.

Starting from rational decisions by families, Becker (1960) introduced the idea of supply and demand of children, considering them as durable goods or a capital investment, to determine the fertility rate. Barro and Becker (1986) extended Becker's analysis and introduced the economic determinants of supply and demand and the resulting population growth rate. All these studies relied on the hypothesis that parents extract utility from their offspring. This by itself generates a propensity to have children. Although more are preferred to fewer, there are costs associated with children. Therefore there is an equilibrium growth rate of families.

Such models lead to some basic determinants of population growth.

1. Labor market conditions, both current and expected developments, which determine current income and its expected future stream, in addition to expected utilities of heirs.
2. Interest rate, which determines intertemporal allocation of resources and current versus future consumption.
3. Consumer preferences with respect to personal consumption and that of descendants, which can have a strong cultural and religious influence.

---

8. Becker et al. (1990) is an example of such models.
9. Malthus (1798) and Becker (1960) are among the economists who first stressed that this set of potential determinants is not sufficient to explain most of the growth rate of the population.

4. Development level of the community and some of its features, such as share of rural population, access to public health services, etc.
5. The level of social protection through a welfare state for retired and unemployed people.
6. Probability of a person falling into unemployment during her/his life.
7. Potential free time to dedicate to leisure, as this would change the utility people extracted from interaction with their descendants.
8. Relative utility extracted from quantity and quality of children, where quality is associated with outcome from more expenditure, especially on human capital building. This is also strongly influenced by the community and perspectives of its labor market.

Only the third of these determinants is more related to the past of immigrants; all the others are heavily determined by the social environment migrants find at their destinations. Thus the hypothesis that the growth rate of the population descending from the various immigrants is the same regardless of their origins is not so distorted. It does not mean there is no recognition that different origins of immigrants could generate different population growth rates, but only that the assumption that they all have the same growth rate is a reasonable approximation.

6.3.4 Free Mobility of Population Among Countries, and Costs of Migration Were Not Enough to Generate Significant Differences in Standard of Living of a Migrant to the Excolonies Given Personal Productive Attributes

This assumption has two parts: there was free migration of population among countries; and the actual costs of migration were not sufficient to generate a high disequilibrium among the income earned by workers with the same attribute in different countries. A condition for the second part to be correct is that the first is true, so each is analyzed separately.

First, research indicates that in the 19th century, between 1820 and 1900, the total European emigrating population reached around 55 million persons.[10] This represents around 17% of the population in the whole continent in 1900, including Russia and all its Asian regions in the measured population.[11] This is a significant share. Furthermore, studies indicate that a considerable number of people who migrated from Europe to the United States returned to Europe some years later. It means that bidirectional flow was possible and existed.

In some periods at the end of the 19th century, the United States placed restrictions on immigration from East and South Europe. This reduced the free flow of people across borders, but the results created only some bias in the origin of

---

10. Data is from Hatton and Williamson (1998).
11. Population data is from Maddison (2011).

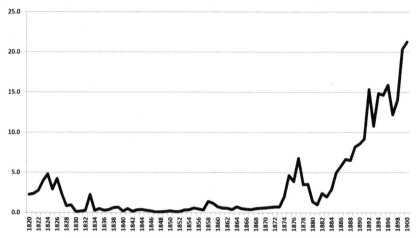

FIGURE 6.1   Share (%) of Portuguese, Spanish, and Russians in total immigrants to the United States in the 19th century. *Dillingham, W., 1911. Statistical Review of Immigration 1820–1910, Government Printing Office, Washington.*

migrants for some periods and had a restricted effect, as indicated by data on immigration of Portuguese, Spanish, and Russian citizens shown in Fig. 6.1.

Brazil did not place any relevant restriction on immigrants, and actually created some incentives for North European and Italian immigrants at the end of the 19th century. Such incentives, which were in financing their transport costs, could help create a bias for these origins, although they also bias downward the expected income and, consequently, education and skills of these migrants. Thus Brazil did not restrict migration, but actually promoted this flow of people.

There were costs of migration for both Brazil and the United States. These costs fell across the 19th century[12] and increased European migration to the Americas. Migration was not totally free, but its costs were sufficiently low to allow a considerable amount of migration. In spite of such restrictions, the amount mentioned earlier was probably sufficient to ensure arbitration between labor markets.[13] This is the hypothesis used in the comparisons made in this chapter.

6.3.5 Perfect Capital Mobility Among Countries

Capital mobility plays a major role in the whole argument of this book, thus it deserved a whole section in the previous chapter and no further discussion is pursued here. It is worth noting that the second half of the 19th century is

12. See Keeling (1999) and Chiswick and Hatton (2003).
13. Hatton and Williamson (1999) give evidence of the power of this population mass migration in arbitration in the labor markets.

normally taken as the golden age of liberalism and a period in history with high capital mobility, only matched by recently reached levels.[14] Additionally, the first half of the 19th century is taken as a period of reasonable flow of capital among countries. This is the point made in Chapter 5 that is most relevant for the purposes of this chapter.

6.4 DATA AND ITS ORIGINS

There are two major sources of data used to calculate the surrogated per capita GDP in the United States: Maddison's (2011) data on population and per capita GDP, with the per capita GDP figures in this dataset updated by Bolt and van Zanden (2013); and Dillingham (1911), which gives data on origins of US migrants. Data from Maddison (2011) and Bolt and van Zanden (2013) was used to obtain per capita GDP from countries of origin of immigrants to the US economy. Brazilian surrogated per capita GDP was built from data by Maddison (2011) for per capita GDP of countries of origin of immigrants and IBGE data on population and immigrants from many origins for Brazil.

The initial hypothesis is that the set of individuals who migrate to a new country has the ability to generate an income that would be equivalent to that embodied in the per capita GDP of the country of origin. Thus British immigrants to the United States would generate an average per capita GDP equal to that they would generate in Britain. It was seen from the discussion of this assumption in the previous section that this is not the case. As US private agents and government did not pay migration costs, there probably was an upward bias in the skills of immigrants to that country. A study by Lindert and Williamson (2014) seems to suggest that this bias existed for British emigration to the United States, at least before the 19th century, while Abramitzky et al. (2012) argue that there was an opposite bias for Norwegian migration. Nonetheless, both these biases are disregarded for the moment.

It is worth noting that this initial hypothesis draws heavily on the idea of free capital and labor mobility among countries. As stressed in the previous section, although this is not fully correct, it is a reasonable approximation of what was found in the 19th century in Europe and the Americas, mainly in its second half. Both Brazil and the United States were on the routes of capital and labor migration over that century.

Thus it is possible to rebuild the US and Brazilian per capita GDP in any particular year if one divides the populations of these countries by origin. If Portuguese immigrants were 10% of the Brazilian population and Africans were 90%, for example, the Brazilian per capita GDP would be a weighted average of Portuguese and African per capita GDP, with 0.1 and 0.9 as weights. Given this simple idea, it is necessary only to decompose Brazilian and US populations by their origins to estimate their per capita GDP in any particular year.

---

14. See Obstfeld (2002) and Bordo (2002).

Mathematically, it means that per capita GDP in country j and year t could be defined as:

$$Y_{jt} = \sum_{i=1}^{n} w_{it} Y_{it} \qquad (6.1)$$

where Y_{jt} is per capita GDP in country j and year t and w_{it} is the share of resident population of country i origin in year t. Y_{it} is directly obtained from Maddison (2011) and updates by Bolt and van Zanden (2013). Therefore it is only necessary to estimate w_{it}.

As any family tends to replicate its human capital in its descendants, as noted in Section 6.2 and the previous chapter, it is possible to see immigrant descendants with the same skills as their forebears and consequently the same ability to generate per capita GDP. Therefore in the decomposition of the American and Brazilian populations it is assumed that descendants are part of the community of their parents. In the previous example, Portuguese and their descendants are included in the same group, as are Africans and their descendants. Dividing the sum of immigrants and their descendants in a particular group by the total population of the country in a particular year gives w_{it}.

Two difficulties appear at this point. The first is how intermarriages are treated in the calculations, and the second is how to estimate the population growth of each national group of immigrants. Beginning with the second question, population growth inside groups of each country of origin was assumed to be the same as population growth for the whole country, Brazil or the United States. Although not fully correct, this hypothesis is a good approximation when the determinants of population growth discussed in the previous section are taken into account.

Intermarriages generate some unpredictability. Freyre (1933) analyzed this fact more extensively in Brazilian colonization. His hypothesis is that women tended to determine the standards of the family in the Brazilian colonial period. It is possible that a similar relationship happened in the United States and extended to the whole history of both countries up to the end of the 19th century. Nevertheless, there were both women and men among immigrants and their descendants. Although the migrant population was not well balanced between genders, it tends to be fairly balanced among descendants. This fact justifies the assumption that intermarriages engender in their heirs skills that are able to generate a per capita GDP equivalent to a weighted average of those of the parents.

If descendants of immigrants are placed in the same category as their parents, the population of the United States or Brazil each year could be decomposed as:

$$P_t = \sum_{i=1}^{n} (1 + p_t) P_{it-1} + M_{it-1} \qquad (6.2)$$

where P_t is total population in year t; P_{it-1} is the population of i origin in year $(t-1)$; p_t is the natural growth rate of the population in the country between the years t and $(t-1)$; and M_{it-1} is the total immigrants from i origin in year $(t-1)$. The natural growth rate of total population was estimated by subtraction of all immigrants in that year from the total population in year t and calculation of the growth rate of this result compared to the total population of the previous year. These concepts imply that w_{it}, which appears in Eq. (6.1), is obtained as:

$$w_{it} = \frac{P_{it}}{P_t} \qquad (6.3)$$

Eqs. (6.1)–(6.3), together with the previous concepts, demand an initial division of the stock of US and Brazilian populations among the many nationalities that composed them for a particular year. The chosen year was 1819, because 1820 is the first year for which there is relevant data for immigration to the United States. Brazilian data on immigration is also scarce before that year.

US figures were built on data from studies of US genealogy by Meyerink and Szucs (1984) which identified the composition of the American population in 1790 by national origin. Table 6.1 shows this data. Campbell and Jung (2002) was the source for total population and indigenous population in 1820.

TABLE 6.1 American Nonindigenous Population in 1790 by Origin

Country of Origin	US Population in 1790
Africa	757,000
England	2,100,000
Ireland	300,000
Germany	270,000
Scotland	150,000
Netherlands	100,000
Wales	10,000
France	15,000
Jews	2000
Sweden	2000
Other Europeans	200,000
Total	3,906,000

Meyerink, K., Szucs, L., 1984. The Source: A Guidebook to American Genealogy, Ancestry, Provo, UT.

Thornton (2000) and Gibson and Jung (2002) were the sources for African population in that year. The white population for this period was divided by the many European national origins in the same proportion as they had in 1790. Jews and other Europeans were divided among other Europeans that are not in Table 6.1 in the same proportion as immigrants entering the United States between 1820 and 1824 of each particular nationality.

Evolution of the indigenous population was estimated as a constant growth rate between the years whose data are presented by Campbell and Jung (2002). The same method was used to estimate African population for each year from the data appearing in Thornton (2000) and Gibson and Jung (2002). The nonblack or indigenous population each year was estimated following the rule embodied in Eq. (6.2), which can be defined as:

$$P_{it} = (1 + p_t)P_{it-1} + M_{it-1} \qquad (6.2')$$

This rule is that population each year is equal to new immigrants last year plus the stock of population within the previous year multiplied by one plus the total natural population growth rate of the US population. The sum of all other national origins was made each year as equal to total US population from Maddison (2011) minus African and indigenous populations, which were all estimated for the whole period and were the basis to estimate the natural growth rate of all other origins together.

As there is no detailed data on emigration by national origin from the United States, the total amount of this sums to a subtraction of the natural growth rate, which implies that emigration, like death, was proportional to the total population of each nationality. This is an assumption that is not fully correct, but certainly was not sufficient to distort the results significantly.

Another important assumption was made for indigenous population per capita GDP. As this population was treated by the US government and white population similarly to Africans, this per capita GDP was simply made equal to the average for Africa, as was done for all Afro-Americans independently of their country of origin.

Given these estimations of population in all the years, Eqs. (6.1) and (6.3) and data by Maddison (2011) with Bolt and van Zanden's (2013) corrections are combined to generate a predicted per capita GDP in the United States between 1820 and 1900. This time series is presented with actual data in Fig. 6.2. It can be seen that until 1878 the two series are very close. After that year their distance widened a little, but their proportion still falls in a small range between 0.90 and 1.22. Only after 1878 does the US actual per capita GDP start to outgrow the one that would be predicted by the composition of its population and arbitrage in the labor market, with all the other hypotheses of the previous section also holding.

Brazilian surrogated per capita GDP is more complicated to estimate, as there is no detailed data on immigration by nationality for the whole period under analysis. Therefore, the option was to estimate only in 1820 and 1900.

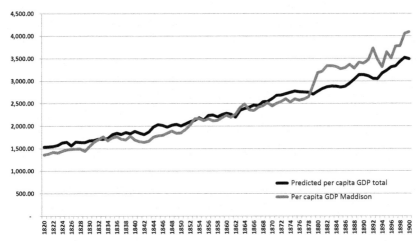

FIGURE 6.2   Actual and surrogated US per capita GDP, 1820 and 1900. *Bolt, J., van Zanden, J.L., 2013. The First Update of the Maddison Project: Re-Estimating Growth Before 1820, Maddison Project Working Paper 4 and author estimations as described in the text.*

Total population in these years was divided in three groups: European descendants or immigrants, African or indigenous population, and mixed population. Per capita GDP for each of these groups was defined as that of a particular country or group of countries. Europeans were supposed to be all Portuguese or Portuguese descendants. For 1820 this is a very good approximation, but it is less accurate for 1900, as there was much migration of Germans, Italians, and Japanese-born people at the end of the 19th century. The per capita GDPs of other groups were fixed to be equal to that prevailing in Africa, as both natives and slaves brought from Africa had very precarious standards of living in Brazil in the 19th century, and multiracial individuals were marginalized in Brazilian society until the 20th century.[15]

Data for population of each group was obtained from Maddison (2001) and is originally taken from IBGE compilations of historical data (IBGE, 1990). Data for per capita GDP is from Bolt and van Zanden (2013) for both Portugal and Africa, and is originally from Goldsmith (1986) and Leff (1982). This data combined gives the figures presented in Table 6.2 and Fig. 6.3. As the year 1900 saw a particular fall in per capita GDP, the average between 1895 and 1906 was used in Table 6.2.

Data for both the United States and Brazil shows that the forecast values from the expected embodied human capital of immigrants, which has been called the surrogated per capita GDP, are very close to the actual figures. Nonetheless, while the United States per capita GDP departed positively from

---

15. Ribeiro (1995, Chapter 2) gives an analysis of the difficulties faced by the mixed population in integrating in Brazilian society.

TABLE 6.2 Brazilian Population by Origin and Per Capita GDP, Actual and Surrogated

| | Brazilian Population by Race | | | | | | |
| | (1000 people) | | | | | | |
Race	1500	1600	1700	1800	1820	1870	1900
Indigenous	1000	700	950	556	500	400	350
Black and mixed		70	200	1924	2500	5700	9346
European		30	100	1155	1500	3700	7622
Total	1000	800	1250	3635	4500	9800	17,319
	Per capita GDP of relevant origin in 1990 US$ international PPP						
Per capita GDP of relevant origin	1500	1600	1700	1800	1820	1870	1900
Indigenous	400	400	400	400	430	430	430
Black and mixed	400	400	400	400	430	430	430
European (Portugal)	606	1164	975	1024	923	975	1302
Total							
Brazilian per capita GDP (Maddison)	400	443	485	683	683	713	720,9
Surrogated	400	429	446	598	594	636	814

Note: The actual figure for Brazilian per capita GDP is the average for 1895 and 1906, as the figure for 1900 is an outlier in the original series by Bolt and van Zanden (2013). Data for populations of black, mixed, and Europeans for 1800 is simple estimates based on the data for 1820.
Maddison, A., 2001. The World Economy: A Millenial Perspective, OECD, Paris; Bolt, J., van Zanden, J.L., 2013. The First Update of the Maddison Project: Re-Estimating Growth Before 1820, Maddison Project Working Paper 4.

its surrogated values in the last two decades of the 19th century, Brazilian actual values fell short of the predicted figures. Certainly this was one source of divergence of these two economies in the 19th century, but differences in the evolution of the surrogated series across the whole period also played a relevant role. This is the subject of the next sections.

6.5 SIMPLE EXERCISE COMPARING AMERICAN AND BRAZILIAN PER CAPITA GDP

The Brazilian population is composed mainly of three ethnic groups: native Indians, Africans, and Europeans. Until the 19th century Portuguese were the main Europeans who migrated to Brazil. However, there was a major change

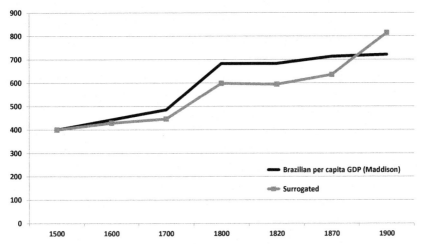

FIGURE 6.3   Actual and surrogated Brazilian per capita GDP, 1500 and 1900. *Bolt, J., van Zanden, J.L., 2013. The First Update of the Maddison Project: Re-Estimating Growth Before 1820, Maddison Project Working Paper 4 and author estimations as described in the text.*

in migration profile from the colonial period to the last decades of the 19th century. While before the 1830s most immigrants moved to Brazil to prosper as business people or potential managers, the second half of the 19th century saw an important inflow of Portuguese immigrants who sought to escape hardships imposed by an agrarian crisis in that country.

Only at the very end of the 19th century did other Europeans and Japanese emigrants start arriving in Brazil. Although they often also came to escape hardships in their countries of origin, they were better-qualified workers and changed the Brazilian economy, as they did in the United States over most of the 19th century. Nevertheless, their impact in Brazilian society over the 19th century was still quite small, given the proportion of immigrants to local population in that period. In the 20th century, however, they had a larger impact, especially in south Brazil.

In 1872, a Census year in Brazil, there were 3.7 million European descendants living in the country, and 80% of them were of Portuguese origin. In addition there were 1.9 million African descendants and 4.1 million ethnically mixed people, including natives and their mixtures.[16] These numbers imply that 38% of the Brazilian population was formed by European descendants. Maddison (2011) estimated that in 1900 the share of European born or their descendants reached 44% of the Brazilian population. According to Census data, 7.3% of the population that year was foreign born, most of them from Europe.

---

16. Data is from IBGE, 1872 Census.

The United States, in turn, had 88.1% of its population as European descendants in 1900, according to data by Maddison (2011). Our own estimations using the method described in the last section are that this number was 84%. They were spread among many nationalities, but were mainly from United Kingdom, Ireland, and Germany. England, Scotland, and Wales together accounted for 44% of the population origin, while Irish accounted for 14.1% and Germans for 14.9%.

Two important relationships arise from these figures. First, the proportion of European descendants was much higher—actually double—in the United States than in Brazil. This in itself could generate a great difference in per capita GDP in 1900, as pointed by some recent studies on the role of European descendants in development.[17]

In addition to this difference in the share of European descendants in population composition, most European descendants in Brazil were of Portuguese origin, while North Americans in 1900 had English and Germans as their major forebears. The United Kingdom per capita GDP was 3.5 times that of Portugal in 1900, according to data by Maddison and Bolt and van Zanden. Germany had a per capita GDP 2.3 times that of Portugal. These differences in the development of the original population who migrated to these two countries could have some role in their relative development.

Table 6.3 gives a summary of the statistics presented in Figs. 6.2 and 6.3. The data is for the Brazilian and US actual and surrogated per capita GDP in 1820 and 1900. This data indicates that estimations for both Brazil and the United States are good approximations for the actual figures, as seen before. In all years presented, estimated values for both countries are under a 17% deviation of the actual number. This data also shows that the United States has grown faster than would be predicted by simple human capital accumulation through imports, while Brazil has grown slower than predicted through this same type of accumulation.

6.5.1 Migration and Per Capita GDP

When people migrate, they carry with them many embodied productive attributes. Most of these are nowadays considered human capital. This involves basic education, which determines logical and analytical abilities, discipline, working behavior, and abilities to plan, to control a sequence of activities, to cooperate, and to manage oneself and other people. In addition, people carry specific skills, such as how to undertake certain tasks and generate particular outputs. Beyond these embodied productive attributes, they can also carry with them valuable goods and even financial assets that could eventually be used as capital. Thus migration of people implies also a migration of human and physical capitals.

---

17. See, for example, Easterly and Levine (2012) and Putterman and Weil (2010).

TABLE 6.3 Actual and Surrogated Per Capita GDP in Brazil and the United States in 1820 and 1900 (1990 US$ International)

		Brazil	United States	Proportion United States/Brazil
1820	Actual (a)	683	1361	1.99
	Surrogated (b)	594	1318	2.22
	Proportion (a)/(b)	1.15	1.03	
1870	Actual (a)	713	2445	3.43
	Surrogated (b)	636	2639	4.15
	Proportion (a)/(b)	1.12	0.93	
1900	Actual (a)	721	4091	5.67
	Surrogated (b)	814	3530	4.34
	Proportion (a)/(b)	0.89	1.16	

Bolt, J., van Zanden, J.L., 2013. The First Update of the Maddison Project: Re-Estimating Growth Before 1820, Maddison Project Working Paper 4 for actual data and author's estimation for surrogated based on data from IBGE, 1990. Estatísticas Históricas do Brasil, IBGE, Rio de Janeiro; Bolt, J., van Zanden, J.L., 2013. The First Update of the Maddison Project: Re-Estimating Growth Before 1820, Maddison Project Working Paper 4; Dillingham, W., 1911. Statistical Review of Immigration 1820–1910, Government Printing Office, Washington; Maddison, A., 2011. Historical Statistics of the World Economy: 1-2008 AD, Maddison Project.

The higher the per capita income of a country, the higher tends to be the human capital of its population. Therefore, the higher the per capita income of a particular country, the higher tends to be the human capital that emigrates with outflows of its population, *ceteris paribus*. It is common that when the average human capital of a country increases, all social strata have their own human capital elevated, although at different increasing rates. This is why there is a positive correlation between human capital embodied in emigration and the human capital and income of a particular country, especially regarding nonformal education human capital, which represented a larger share of the total in the 19th century, when schools were not so important in human capital building as they are nowadays.

Of course, it is possible to have a bias in the attributes of the emigrating population. For example, it is possible that although the population of a country has on average 10 years of schooling, the set of those who emigrated in a particular period had only seven years of schooling. This bias, however, does not eliminate the expectation that the higher the per capita income of a country, the higher the human capital embodied in its emigrants.

The bias in the migrating population, however, can be severe. For example, it is known that Portuguese migrating to Brazil after the 1830s were mainly peasants from the Minho region. Crises in the peasant economy of that region worked as a major motivation for such emigration. If these immigrants had average abilities that were only able to generate per capita income that was 80% of the Portuguese average and all immigrants in this period came from this region,[18] the predicted per capita GDP in Brazil in 1900 from the source population would be US$699.14, instead of the US$814 appearing in Table 6.3. This new figure is even closer to the actual figure in Table 6.3, varying by only 3.1%.

Bias in the embodied human capital of immigrants could also reduce the US gap between actual and projected per capita GDP figures appearing in Table 6.3. If instead of the weighted average, as described earlier, the projection relies on the hypothesis that all European descendants living in the United States in 1900 had the English average productive abilities, instead of those of their original countries, the estimated local annual per capita GDP would be US$4587.11, which is 12% above the actual figure. This would happen under two circumstances: (1) if they and their descendants could easily build productive abilities similar to those of English descendants after their arrival in the United States; or (2) if there was already an upward bias in the average abilities of migrants of other nationalities, when compared to the population of their country of origin, as they were going to compete in an economy with relative prices similar to England.

It is reasonable to think that the true stories for both Brazil and the United States are actually in between the two assumptions presented. Brazilian Portuguese migration was not all from Minho, and also the migration of Italians, Germans, and Japanese at the end of the 19th century should be included. Thus the actual per capita GDP is above that predicted with all the European population coming from Minho. This could make the surrogated per capita GDP even closer to the one actually found. In the case of the United States, not all immigrants would expect and be able to replicate English productivity in the New World, as they did not do so in previous years. Thus the true value would be somewhere between US$3530.29 of Table 6.3 and the figure obtained with English standard for all Europeans, which was US$4587.11. This correct value could be even closer to the actual figure (US$4090.79) than these extremes. A simple nonweighted average of these two extremes would depart only 1.4% from the actual figure.

6.5.2 Potential Role of Embodied Human Capital in Development Differences in 1900

All this discussion and data indicate that embodied human capital in migration could have played a relevant role in the growth inequalities between Brazil and

---

18. This proportion of Minho's per capita GDP to the Portuguese average is higher than that reached in the existing statistics for the last 50 years. Therefore it is a conservative assumption.

the United States. Taking into account that migration to Australia, New Zealand, and Canada was also predominantly of Europeans, as in the United States, and was strong in the 19th century, this same logic would apply to these countries. The migrating population also carried more embodied human capital, and this could have led to faster growth in this century.

To have an idea of the role of this hypothesis, it is possible to use a simple metric established from the difference between per capita GDP in Brazil and the United States in 1900.

$$Y_{US} - Y_{BR} = \left(\overline{Y}_{US} + D_{US}\right) - \left(\overline{Y}_{BR} + D_{BR}\right) \tag{6.4}$$

where Y_{US} and Y_{BR} are the 1900 per capita GDP in the United States and Brazil, respectively. $\overline{Y}_{US}$ and $\overline{Y}_{BR}$ are the expected per capita GDP, given the average human capital in immigrating populations and their descendants, in the United States and Brazil, respectively. D_{US} and D_{BR} are deviations from these expected per capita GDPs in the United States and Brazil, respectively. Eq. (6.4) was built on the assumption that $Y_i = \overline{Y}_i + D_i$ for $i = BR$ or $i = US$. D_i is tautologically defined by this relationship, so it is necessarily correct.

Deviations D_{US} and D_{BR} have many potential determinants. They could represent the bias in the embodied human capital of immigrating populations, as discussed earlier, or the ability of immigrants to replicate their human capital in their herds, which could be different from a one-to-one relationship in any direction. The level of efficiency of the local financial market and cross-border flows of capital could also affect how quickly migrants reach the optimal capital—labor—natural resources relationships in new enterprises that were necessary to reach their expected income after immigration. Thus there are many potential sources of such D_i's.

Eventual deviations from a rational expectation equilibrium, in which a large group of immigrants do not reach their expected income and do not have resources to proceed to an immediate reversal of migration, could also explain D_i's in some particular years. Nevertheless, such deviations would be short term, small in size, or both, and are thus of minor interest here.

Eq. (6.4) can be rearranged to generate:

$$\frac{\overline{Y}_{US} - \overline{Y}_{BR}}{Y_{US} - Y_{BR}} + \frac{D_{US} - D_{BR}}{Y_{US} - Y_{BR}} = 1 \tag{6.4'}$$

Eq. (6.4') indicates that it is possible to split the total difference in actual per capita GDP between the United States and Brazil into two components. One captures the differences in expected per capita GDP given the profile of immigration, the hypothesis that there is full intergenerational transmission of human capital, and all other assumptions discussed in Section 6.3. The second component is the difference between the two deviations from the predicted per capita GDP in the two countries, as defined earlier. The division by $Y_{US}-Y_{BR}$ makes Eq. (6.4') generate the proportion of each of these two components in the total inequality found in 1900. Given that Brazilian deviation in 1900 is actually negative, it is possible to split the difference in the second term of the left side of Eq. (6.4') between the one arising from US deviations and another emerging from Brazilian deviations. The three components together still would add to 100%. This is the procedure taken to generate the statistics appearing in Table 6.4.

Two cases are presented in Table 6.4. In one there was no bias in the migration and citizens moving had the average human capital of those remaining in the source country. The second decomposition considers that all immigrants to the United States in the 19th century had the same average human capital as that of England, and those Europeans migrating to Brazil came from Minho and consequently had average human capital that was 80% of the Portuguese average. All these statistics indicate that the major part of the differences between Brazilian and US per capita GDPs is explained by the differences in human capital embodied in the immigrants that headed to each of these countries. The share of this difference goes from 80.6% in the unbiased case to 115.4% within the two biased cases. The correct number easily stands between these two assumptions, and could be much closer to the 100% level.

6.5.3 Role of Embodied Human Capital in the Rise of Disparity Over the 19th Century

The decomposition of per capita GDP underlying the decomposition defined in Eq. (6.4) was an additive one. The analysis of the role of immigration-embodied human capital in the widening of the per capita GDP gap between Brazil and the United States in the 19th century would be simpler if the original decomposition of this variable was multiplicative. So per capita GDP for country i at year t, y_{it}, is now defined as:

$$y_{it} = v_{it}\bar{y}_{it} \tag{6.5}$$

where $\bar{y}_{it}$ is the surrogated per capita GDP for country i at year t and v_{it} is the deviation parameter, also at period t for country i, whose values is such that $v > 0$. From this definition, it is possible to generate a proportion between Brazilian and US per capita GDP in any year t:

$$\frac{y_{ust}}{y_{brt}} = \frac{v_{ust}\bar{y}_{USt}}{v_{brt}\bar{y}_{BRt}} \tag{6.6}$$

This proportion between per capita GDP for the two countries increased from 1820 to 1900, as discussed in Chapter 2. This rise in proportion is the variable whose decomposition is better analyzed. A proportion between the proportions represented in Eq. (6.6) at 1900 and 1820 was created and called π. A natural logarithm of this statistics would yield:

$$\begin{aligned} \ln\pi = & \left(\ln\bar{y}_{us1900} - \ln\bar{y}_{us1820}\right) - \left(\ln\bar{y}_{br1900} - \ln\bar{y}_{br1820}\right) \\ & + \left(\ln v_{us1900} - \ln v_{us1820}\right) - \left(\ln v_{br1900} - \ln v_{br1820}\right) \end{aligned} \tag{6.7}$$

TABLE 6.4 Sources of Inequalities in Per Capita GDP Between the United States and Brazil in 1900

Variable	Absolute Value	Calculation Formula	Percentage With Respect to Actual Difference (%)	Absolute Value	Calculation Formula	Percentage With Respect to Actual Difference (%)
Actual difference of per capita GDP between the United States and Brazil	3370	(4090.79 −720.90)	100.0	3370	(4090.79 −720.90)	100.0
Predicted difference of per capita GDP between the United States and Brazil, given embodied human capital of immigrants	2717	(3530.34 −813.74)	80.6	3888	(4587.11 −699.14)	115.4
Deviation of predicted difference of per capita GDP between the United States and Brazil generated by US deviation from its predicted value	560	(4090.79 −3530.34)	16.6	−496	(4090.79 −4587.11)	−14.7
Deviation of predicted difference of per capita GDP between the United States and Brazil generated by Brazilian deviation from its predicted value	93	(813.74 −720.90)	2.8	−22	(720.90 −699.14)	−0.6

Author estimations based on data by Maddison, A., 2011. Historical Statistics of the World Economy: 1-2008 AD, Maddison Project; IBGE, 1990. Estatísticas Históricas do Brasil, IBGE, Rio de Janeiro; Dillingham, W., 1911. Statistical Review of Immigration 1820–1910, Government Printing Office, Washington.

TABLE 6.5 Share of Total Proportional Variation of the Proportion of Per Capita GDP in the Two Countries

Component	Unbiased Immigration Assumption (%)	Biased immigration assumption (%)
Predicted	64.1	95.7
Unpredicted	35.9	4.3

Author's calculation using data by IBGE, 1990. Estatísticas Históricas do Brasil, IBGE, Rio de Janeiro, Dillingham, W., 1911. Statistical Review of Immigration 1820–1910, Government Printing Office, Washington; Maddison, A., 2011. Historical Statistics of the World Economy: 1-2008 AD, Maddison Project; Bolt, J., van Zanden, J.L., 2013. The First Update of the Maddison Project: Re-Estimating Growth Before 1820, Maddison Project Working Paper 4.

The right side of the equation can be decomposed into two components: (1) change of immigration-predicted components, which are the first and second terms within brackets, respectively; and (2) change of other determinants of per capita GDP in both countries. Table 6.5 shows these two components for the period between 1820 and 1900 as a share of the natural logarithm of π.

Data in Table 6.5 indicates that the role of the immigration human capital building predicted component in the variation of the total proportion between US and Brazilian per capita GDPs would be somewhere between 64.1% and 95.7%, depending on the assumption of skill bias in immigration for the two countries. Thus this role could be quite high. Imported embodied human capital was the major determinant causing Brazil to lag behind the United States in the 19th century. If it is similar for other countries such as Canada, New Zealand, and Australia, the particular role of these countries in the mass migration of the 19th century would be a major determinant of the widening of Brazilian relative backwardness in that century.

It should be noted that there was also a great widening of the gap between Brazilian per capita GDP on one side and the benchmark countries in the European periphery on the other, as shown in Chapter 2. As these countries were actually exporting their populations, immigration cannot be considered as the source of this jump ahead by these countries. Their particular circumstances are further discussed in later chapters.

6.6 CONCLUSIONS AND ADDITIONAL COMMENTS

This chapter highlights an important feature of Brazilian relative backwardness in the 19th century. It is stressed that the way the country featured in the European mass migration of that century played an important role in shaping the relative development reached by Brazil and the other ex-European colonies, such as Canada, Australia, New Zealand, and the United States. Some simple simulations comparing the role of European migration in the relative development of Brazil and the United States indicate that, under conservative assumptions, this migration could respond for something between 80.6% and 115.4% of total disparities emerging in 1900 between these two countries.

Some further empirical estimation also indicates that the growth of the proportion of US per capita GDP to Brazilian GDP had the imported human capital accounting for something between 64.1% and 95.7% of the total. This means that this variable is the major determinant of the increase in Brazilian relative backwardness in the 19th century when compared to the United States.

These basic conclusions leave us with two broad hypotheses to understand Brazilian relative backwardness, especially as it developed in the 19th century. The first is that the composition of immigration in that century was a major determinant of such backwardness. The second is that, despite the apparent role of immigration composition, it was not a relevant cause of the disparities emerging. Under this second hypothesis, the features of immigration distribution could be a consequence of these other factors, rather than the determinant of inequalities themselves. The next chapters further explore these alternative hypotheses.

Chapter 7

Genesis of Brazilian Human Capital: From Colony to the 19th Century

7.1 INTRODUCTION

The last chapter shows that immigration had a major role in determining the backwardness of Brazil relative to the United States, and probably also to Australia, Canada, and New Zealand. These countries benefited from a sizable inflow of skilled Europeans, who migrated in search of new opportunities in the New World. While Brazil and other Latin American countries also benefited from such migration, they did so on a smaller scale.

The 19th century was the period in which most of the current disparity between Brazil and the European periphery was built. Chapter 2 shows that the gap between per capita GDP (gross domestic product) in Brazil and these European countries widened sharply in this century. As they were all sources of migrants rather than their target, international population flow cannot explain the relative performance of these countries directly. Furthermore, although immigration played a substantial role in US relative performance when compared to Brazil, it did not answer for all the widening in the per capita GDP gap, as acknowledged in the previous chapter. Therefore a sizable part of the story still needs to be understood, especially regarding the European countries.

Before focusing on this still-unidentified source of Brazilian relative backwardness, this chapter aims to give an idea of Brazilian social structure at the beginning of the 19th century and how it emerged from the Portuguese colonization strategy. This is used in the next chapter to explain the way it evolved in the 19th century and, consequently, to understand why Brazil lagged behind with respect to the so-called European periphery.

More precisely, the formation of the Brazilian population is reviewed, with special focus on its consequence for local human capital building. This factor of production is not seen as a one-dimensional concept, but rather one with many particular features, which are further discussed in Section 7.2. Section 7.3 elaborates on the human capital status of the major groups involved in the initial setup of Brazilian society, while Section 7.4 deals with the evolution of their human capital up to the beginning of the 19th century. Section 7.5 uses a hypothetical exercise of the structure of Brazilian society, taking as reference the British social structure in 1800–1803 from Milanovic et al. (2007). Its goal is to show that it was possible to have perfect capital mobility and arbitrage in commodities markets and still have the level of per capita GDP inequality between Brazil and England found in the period. The necessarily high share of specific social strata that arises from this exercise is used to explain the relative evolution of per capita GDP in European countries and Brazil throughout the 19th century. Section 7.5.1 presents the consequences of this exercise for the per capita income of the three ethnic groups forming Brazil. This discussion is important to understand some of the leverage of the figures presented. Section 7.6 summarizes the major conclusions of the chapter.

7.2 SOME COMMENTS ON THE NATURE OF HUMAN CAPITAL

Although human capital is often taken as acquired cognitive skills, this is not the most appropriate idea. Human capital corresponds to any stock of knowledge or characteristics a worker has (either innate or acquired) that contributes to his/her potential productivity, measured in output per time of work spent.[1] This definition stresses that not only years of schooling, school quality, and previous training are important determinants of individual human capital but also other noncognitive individual attributes,[2] such as creativity, initiative, personal abilities in relationships with colleagues, self-esteem, and attitudes toward work like discipline, persistence, and commitment. Thus the concept includes all individual traits that affect the productive ability of individuals.

It is possible to divide the human capital of an individual into four broad components.

---

1. Concept adapted from Acemoglu and Autor (2013, p. 3).
2. See, for example, Heckman et al. (2006).

1. *Personal innate traits*, such as height, beauty, and even intelligence. A recent study also placed some of the principles of common sense as an innate trait, arguing that the human mind is equipped with innate intuitive theories or modules for the major ways of making sense of the world.[3] These human features affect the productive abilities of individuals, and as such can be considered as human capital.

2. *Acquired cognitive abilities*, which are productively relevant information and capacity to replicate and adjust processes, both acquired through experience, training, or schooling. These are the human abilities that are mostly related to human capital by economists. Certainly they are crucial components determining human productive capacity, but they are not the only component of human capital.

3. *Socially inherited abilities*, acquired through culture and social relations, which determine behavior in specific circumstances. These are important components of common sense, as they are learned not only from personal experience, as stressed by some authors,[4] but also transmitted among persons and generations. These ideas, norms, taboos, and behavioral parameters are important determinants of human productive abilities. In the past, when formal education was less important in skills development, these socially acquired abilities played a major role in the determination of individual total human capital.

4. *Attitude or personality factors*, as named by modern psychology. Heckman and Kautz (2012) present the big five personality factors, shown in Table 7.1 with more information on their description in the *American Psychology Association Dictionary* and correlated trait adjectives.

Estimations by Heckman et al. (2006) conclude that these noncognitive abilities, which include personal innate traits, socially inherited abilities, and attitude or personality factors, have a relevant role in labor income determination in the United States, either directly or through educational achievements, similar to that of acquired cognitive abilities.[5] They rely on data from the US National Longitudinal Survey of Youth (1979) for males age 30 to reach such conclusions. Other studies have shown that such attributes are relatively more important in wage determination for labor market positions demanding less complex tasks than education itself (Schmidt and Hunter, 2004).[6]

Two of these components, socially inherited abilities and attitude or personality factors, are both strongly influenced by social and historical

---

3. Pinker (1997).
4. See, for example, Redekop (2009).
5. Heckman et al. (2011) presented evidence on the strong effect of the educational attainment channel mechanism.
6. Almlund et al. (2011) show a survey on the role of personality traits in labor market and other economic outcomes.

TABLE 7.1 Big Five Personality Factors and Some of Their Facets

Big Five Personality Factors	American Psychology Association Dictionary Description	Facets (and Correlated Trait Adjectives)
Conscientiousness	Tendency to be organized, responsible, and hardworking	Competence (efficient), order (organized), dutifulness (not careless), achievement striving (ambitious), self-disciplined (not lazy), and deliberation (not impulsive)
Openness to experience	Tendency to be open to new esthetic, cultural, or intellectual experiences	Fantasy (imaginative), esthetic (artistic), feelings (excitable), actions (wide interests), ideas (curious), and values (unconventional)
Extraversion	Orientation of one's interests and energies toward the outer world of people and things rather than the inner world of subjective experience; characterized by positive affect and sociability	Warmth (friendly), gregariousness (sociable), assertiveness (self-confident), activity (energetic), excitement seeking (adventurous), and positive emotions (enthusiastic)
Agreeableness	Tendency to act in a cooperative, unselfish manner	Trust (forgiving), straightforwardness (not demanding), altruism (warm), compliance (not stubborn), modesty (not show-off), and tender-mindedness (sympathetic)
Neuroticism/ emotional stability	Emotional stability is predictability and consistency in emotional reactions, with absence of rapid mood changes; neuroticism is a chronic level of emotional instability and proneness to psychological distress	Anxiety (worrying), hostility (irritable), depression (not contented), self-consciousness (shy), impulsiveness (moody), vulnerability to stress (not self-confident)

Extracted from Heckman, J., Kautz, T., 2012. Hard Evidence on Soft Skills, NBER Working Paper, # 18121, NBER, Cambridge, Mass, who adapted from a version by John, O.P., Srivastava, S., 1999. The big five trait taxonomy: History, measurement and theoretical perspectives. In: Pervin, L.A., John, O.P. (Eds.), Handbook of Personality: Theory and Research, The Guilford Press, New York, pp. 102–138 (Chapter 4).

determinants.[7] Therefore they evolve over time in any particular society depending on its social dynamics, including relationships among social classes and groups and the way local culture and social norms change. Certainly the smallest social cells, such as families, have the most influence on these attributes, but their nature and structures are strongly influenced by social relationships within more complex social groups.

Personal innate traits, in turn, are mainly genetically determined and as such tend to be stable over time in any society. Their distribution may vary among societies and social groups, however, as normally there are more genetic similarities in people living in the same space and with similar cultures. Intracultural marriage is more frequent than intercultural marriage. Intracity or intratribe marriages are also more common than intercity or intertribe marriages. This generates more genetic convergence in contiguous spaces and similar cultures.

Acquired cognitive abilities are strongly determined by economic factors as rational incentives motivated by individual welfare perspectives. The model in Chapter 5 stresses that family income is a major determinant. As often there are increasing returns to scale in the potential productive efforts to generate these abilities, political economy outputs can also play a major role in their determination, in addition to individual incentives.[8] Obviously, the development level of a society has a positive impact on the resources allocated in the mechanisms of cognitive ability enhancement, but social determinants, such as social priorities and political power distribution among social segments or classes, also play a major role. These basic relationships are the underlying ideas behind the forthcoming analysis of Brazilian human capital building up to and throughout the 19th century.

7.3 AFRICANS, NATIVE AMERICANS, AND EUROPEANS IN THE BRAZILIAN SETUP

The current Brazilian population has its roots mainly in Africans, Native Americans, and Europeans, especially from the Iberian Peninsula, and particularly from Portugal. When Portuguese colonizers arrived in Brazil and brought Africans to the country, the three major racial sources of current Brazilians had very distinct development levels. This diversity was crucial in shaping the social relations and interactions built in the Portuguese colony and the development path taken since the 16th century.

When the Portuguese arrived in Brazil, the local native population was living in conditions resembling those from the prehistoric Mesolithic era to the

---

7. See Section 8 of Almlund et al. (2011) for a survey.
8. See, for example, Alexopoulos and Cavalcanti (2010).

beginning of the Neolithic era in European history.[9] They lived mainly from hunting, fishing, and gathering, although a very incipient agriculture existed and a few animals were domesticated as livestock. Although local tribes used fire, they did not work with metals, but mostly with bonds and woods as a basis for their instruments. They already had knowledge of ceramics for domestic utensils. Their productive technologies were thus similar to those normally classified as part of the Mesolithic era.

Regarding foundations of social life which also affect economic productivity, they did not have writing skills and lived in temporary villages, moving when resources started to become scarce, so they were seminomads. They had no state organization with tax collection and separation of justice and defense organization from other regular activities, although fights against other tribes were frequent. They did not have monetary units, and the few exchanges were made through barter. Intertribe exchanges were rare, although there is some evidence that they existed. These features also resemble European Mesolithic settlements between 13,000 and 6000 BCE, depending on the country and European tribes selected for comparison. This means that when the Portuguese arrived in Brazil, European societies were technologically ahead of the local native population by about 10,000 years.

Division of labor within tribes was made through rudimentary specializations, mainly based on sex and age. The lack of metalwork and more sophisticated agricultural technologies are evidence that they worked using very restricted processes as regards their complexity, so they were not easily trained in processes that demanded more discipline and cooperation. This limited their employment on plantations, as they generated very low productivity in these activities, even under slavery.

Thus the first entrepreneurial sugarcane plantations in Brazil had to rely on African slaves to be efficient. Natives soon died when subjected to such work, because they did not have the emotional stability to handle complex activities under the authority of someone else; and with no previous intense contact with Europeans, they were easily infected by diseases brought by the colonizers. Together, these two facts resulted in short lives for the natives when they were made slaves. They would also frequently try to escape, as they had low notions of submission and hierarchy skills, and this raised their operational costs. Altogether, with the high costs to capture them, as there was no large-scale slavery and trade practice among Brazilian natives, these characteristics led to the import of African slaves as a more competitive source of labor.

Africans were brought to Brazil as slaves from the beginning of the Brazilian colonization. According to data from the Transatlantic Slave Trade

---

9. Darcy Ribeiro (1995, Chapter 1) mentions the Upper Paleolithic, but dated the period in European history as about 10,000 years before the Portuguese invasion of Brazil, which was in 1500. Under such classification, the final relative backwardness ends up very similar to that predicted by the classification in the Mesolithic era.

Database,[10] in the second half of the 16th century Brazilian sugarcane production started booming and the import of slave also increased. It only officially ceased in 1850, when Brazil suppressed the slave trade, and really ended after 1866, when smuggling started to collapse. More than 5 million Africans were sent to Brazil between 1500 and 1866. This represented 47.7% of slaves disembarked from Africa through transatlantic trade, which includes all American countries as destinations.

The slave trade in Africa started long before Brazilian imports. There is evidence of trade in 1400 which involved three other routes besides the transatlantic trade: the trans-Sahara, Red Sea, and Indian Ocean routes. The first sent slaves from the south of the Saharan desert to Northern Africa; the second route exported slaves from inland Red Sea areas to the Middle East and India, while the third route sent slaves from Eastern Africa to the Middle East, India, and plantation islands in the Indian Ocean.[11] Altogether these other three routes traded around 6 million slaves, about half the number traded through the transatlantic route.

In the period of transatlantic slave trade, Africa was much more developed than the Americas were before the Europeans arrived. Africans already had frequent contacts with other civilizations, such as Egyptians, other Moors, and even Europeans. They thus had contact with new technologies and productive processes that were known to Europeans. They already engaged in long-distance trade for many goods, including agricultural commodities and even manufactured goods such as textiles, in which western sub-Saharan Africans had some productive experiences.

In addition to ceramics and basic metalwork, they knew about gunpowder and guns, and these were some of their objects of demand in the slave trade.[12] They were also acquainted with blacksmithing technologies that were not even available in Europe and had some sophistication in architecture: many temples were built in Africa, not only in Northern Africa, but also in east, west, and central sub-Saharan Africa.[13] The two latter regions were the most important sources of slaves sent to Brazil.

Africans had more knowledge of mathematics than Brazilian natives. They worked with numbers and numeral systems, and had quantitative precision when comparing relative amounts. They also had experience with monetary units and price systems, as there were many states or kingdoms that collected taxes even before the Portuguese arrival in the Americas. They had basic

---

10. Available at www.slavevoyages.org.
11. For more details see Nunn (2007).
12. There is a reference in the literature to a gun—slave cycle, a vicious cycle in which Africans demanded guns to protect themselves against slavery and paid for these guns with captured slaves. See Lovejoy (2000).
13. See, for example, Lovejoy (2011).

arithmetic and geometric notions, which were much more developed than those found among South American natives at the same time.

African social spatial organization was also much more sophisticated than that found among American natives in the same period. There were already reasonably populated cities, like Lagos, and communities whose specialized production was sufficiently high to justify long-distance trade with European and Middle Eastern countries and other African communities. Furthermore, there is evidence that there were already plantations in Africa for some commodities, such as cotton, rice, and millet. There was not only higher population density than in the Americas, but also higher division of labor and all the necessary management skills and notions of hierarchy associated with it.

Some African states and kingdoms had existed since the first 10 centuries of the Christian era. These states and kingdoms had some sophistication in tax collection systems, justice, and management of some public services. Thus not only was a higher degree of division of labor already common in Africa, but also more sophisticated political organizations than those found in Brazil when the Portuguese arrived there. Naturally, the higher labor skills in Africa generated the necessary productivity to allow such phenomena.

An obvious byproduct of the higher division of labor and sophistication of political organization, when placed together with the more extensive abstract knowledge in mathematics and geometry, is that there were higher levels of *socially inherited abilities* and *acquired cognitive abilities* among Africans than Brazilian natives. Many African personality traits were also better adjusted to labor under supervision and productivity demands. African's *conscientiousness, openness to experience, extraversion,* and *emotional stability* were certainly higher than those of native Brazilians in a slave system, as slavery was known to them centuries before it was first introduced to Brazil. Thus it is reasonable to think that Africans had much more human capital than Brazilian natives in the colonial period.

Before concluding this section, it is worth mentioning that in the Brazilian colonial period most countries had a very wide spectrum of income and human capital. It was possible, for example, in an African country to have people with a standard of living little above that of Brazilian natives, while others were living at standards close to European middle classes of the period. This also happened in European countries at the time. Some people lived under very precarious conditions, while others were lived like kings or nobles in castles, with high levels of comfort. It is reasonable to assume that per capita income distributions in Europe, Africa, and Brazil in 1500 were such as those appearing in Fig. 7.1. $\overline{Y}_A$, $\overline{Y}_N$, and $\overline{Y}_E$ stand for average per capita income of Africans, Brazilian natives, and Europeans, respectively. The lines are for the income density functions by population ordered by income levels (Y).

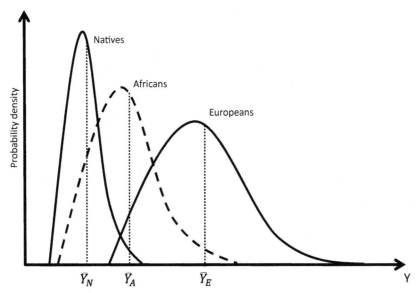

FIGURE 7.1 Predicted distribution of proportion of people by income level (Y). Note: $\overline{Y}_A$, $\overline{Y}_N$, and $\overline{Y}_E$ stand for average per capita income of Africans, Brazilian natives, and Europeans, respectively. The lines are for the proportional distribution of population by income levels (Y). The populations they refer to are identified above the lines. *Author's elaboration.*

Fig. 7.1 relies on some reasonable assumptions. First, as native Brazilians lived in tribes with consumption defined collectively, the distribution of individual (inputted) incomes had very low standard deviation. There was some dispersion in standards of living, arising mainly from intertribe differences, which justifies this distribution. Such differences arose from technologies, knowledge, and labor organization, but also from environmental conditions. Some tribes were settled in regions where nature was more generous. Such differences explained the standard deviation in the income density function appearing in Fig. 7.1.

Secondly, Africans had higher average per capita income $\left(\overline{Y}_N\right)$ than Brazilian natives $\left(\overline{Y}_N\right)$, but they were on average poorer than Europeans $\left(\overline{Y}_E\right)$. The dispersion of their incomes was higher than that among Brazilian natives. Their better productive technologies and human capital were not evenly spread among nations and kingdoms, or even among tribes within the same nation when there was tribal organization. Thus there were tribes with standards of living similar to those of Brazilians natives, while some social groups, normally living in cities, were much more advanced. They were 10,000 years ahead in knowledge and human capital than the most backward tribes, and had standards of living similar to the European middle class of the same period.

Thirdly, Europeans had inherited all the intellectual development of the ancient societies and had worked to advance this. There were already well-established universities, such as Oxford, Cambridge, Bologna, Coimbra, Salamanca, etc. Science was much more advanced and widespread in Europe, and many sizable cities already existed.[14] Thus human capital, knowledge, and technologies were much more advanced on this continent. Nevertheless, there were villages and isolated communities where the standard of living was very low. It is possible that some Europeans were living in harsher conditions than the wealthy Brazilian natives (not necessarily true) and many Africans (more probable). Thus average per capita income was higher in Europe than it was in Africa or Brazil, but the standard deviation of the income density function was also higher in this continent.

It is possible to say that dispersion of income was higher in wealthy societies, as some people still lived under very precarious standards while others enjoyed wealthy conditions. This happened because the existing technology and social organization allowed some people to accumulate wealth privately. This could be used to generate income beyond that extracted from their labor. Furthermore, this last source of income also relied on a more disperse stock of human capital among individuals. Knowledge, technologies, and human productive abilities were higher and more efficient in Europe than in Africa, and in Africa than in Brazil. However, they were more unevenly distributed among individuals, as there were few formal public policies to ensure more equal opportunity of access. Communication systems restricted their flow among individuals, and much more among communities and countries.

Density functions for human capital distribution were similar to those for income, especially if all sources of human capital are taken into account and are all transformed to the same unit to generate a one-to-one relationship with individual potential productive power. Perhaps some narrowing in the distribution would exist, as the richest people extracted a considerable share of their income from the previously accumulated stock of wealth. This second set of density functions indicates that there was more average human capital among Europeans than Africans, and among Africans than among Brazilian natives. The standard deviations of these density functions also followed this same order.

When Europeans, mainly Portuguese, came to Brazil and brought African slaves, a new society was created with some particular features. First, although a large share of natives died from simple contact with Europeans, because of the unknown diseases brought by the latter, their number was so large that they still dominated Brazilian per capita labor income in the first years of Portuguese colonization. The very scarce records suggest that Brazilian population

---

14. London in 1530 already had around 50,000 inhabitants. Vienna in 1590 had a similar population. Venice had around 100,000 inhabitants in 1500. Lisbon in 1552 had around 200,000 citizens.

distribution among the three ethnic roots in selected years was as shown in Table 7.2. Natives represented about 35% of the Brazilian population in 1600. In 1700 they still represented around 25% of the population, but by 1800 they had fallen to about 13.3% of the population.

The local density function for human capital, measured as potential productive power arising from individual attributes, is a composition of those for the three ethnic groups that formed Brazilian society in the period. Fig. 7.2 shows these population density functions in their origins and as formed in Brazil in the year 1600, when there were already the three groups with a strong presence in Brazilian society. While native density functions include all those who survived, human capitals for Europeans and Africans are for the populations living in their original continents. Those for Brazilians are for the people living in the country.

The human capital among Brazilians has a higher dispersion than those for the original populations of the three groups, which is reasonable given that these original populations had different means. Nevertheless, some assumptions are important to build this Brazilian hypothetical probability density function adequately for human capital. First, natives have human capital similar to those they have when analyzed separately, as they all lived in Brazil. Secondly, Africans had two biases with respect to the original population living in their native continent. Lower-skilled Africans were captured for slavery in a lower proportions, as they lived in less densely populated regions, which raised the costs of their kidnapping and inland transport and, similarly to native Brazilians, they did not have the emotional stability and discipline to live as slaves and would die, often in the overseas transport. Thus efforts to capture and transport them were less efficient in terms of quantity of people and, consequently, this population group was underrepresented.

The highest-skilled strata of African society were also underrepresented, as they tended to be more protected in their societies, living in cities, with more people surrounding them and often security support, despite records of kidnapping and sale as slaves of people even from African royal families. They also had more access to technologies of protection, such as firearms. Thus there was a bias toward an overrepresentation of people with middle levels of human capital disembarking from Africa. As they had higher average per capita human capital than Brazilian natives, however, when they were put together with the latter in the same population, the Brazilian average per capita human capital increased. Nevertheless, the dispersion of human capital also increased.

Europeans had both higher average and higher dispersion of human capital than native Brazilians and Africans. There is evidence that some renegades were sent from Portugal to Brazil in the initial colonial periods, but the colonizers themselves were people with some wealth and the energy to start new businesses in an unknown place and face the adversities of a new and barely occupied land. Thus it is reasonable to think that there was a positive bias in

TABLE 7.2 Brazilian Population in Selected Years by Ethnic Origin

Year	Total	Population			Share of Total (%)		
		Natives	Africans	Europeans	Natives	Africans	Europeans
1500	2,431,010	2,431,000	0	10	100.0	0.0	0.0
1600	100,000	35,000	35,000	30,000	35.0	35.0	30.0
1700	300,000	74,831			24.9		
1800	3,660,000	488,493	2,160,000	1,011,507	13.3	59.0	27.6
1850	7,256,000	1,248,091	2,151,876	3,856,033	17.2	29.7	53.1
1900	17,438,434	2,912,120	4,808,798	9,717,515	16.7	27.6	55.7
1950	51,944,397	7,863,909	12,985,710	31,094,778	15.1	25.0	59.9
2000	169,799,170	25,358,017	41,873,816	102,567,337	14.9	24.7	60.4
2010	190,755,799	28,475,320	47,021,432	115,259,048	14.9	24.7	60.4

Note: All migrants in the 20th century were considered as Europeans. Africans were taken as migrating to Brazil only with the slave trade. All natives, of course, were descendants of the original population. All ethnic groups were assumed to have grown at the same natural rate since 1850. The share of each ethnic group since that year was equal to the share of population in the year after, redefined by immigration that year. Ethnic composition for 2010 was obtained from a genetic study by Manta et al. (2010).

Built by the author using data from IBGE (1990, Mortara's figures when they were available), and Manta, F., Pereira, R., Vianna, R., Araújo, A., Gitaí, D., da Silva, D., Wolfgramm, E., Pontes, I., Aguiar, J., Moraes, M., Carvalho, E., Gusmão, L., 2013. Revisiting the Genetic Ancestry of Brazilians Using Autosomal AIM-Indels. PLoS One 8 (9), 1–11 for recent composition of the share of ethnic origins. IBGE is also the source for migration since the 19th century.

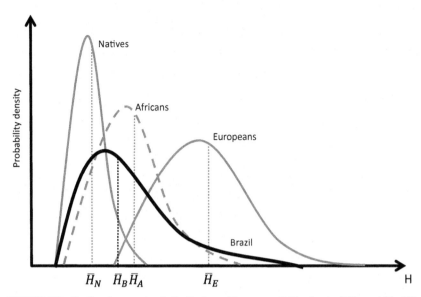

FIGURE 7.2   Predicted proportional distribution of human capital by level of this variable (*H*) among original groups that formed Brazilian society. Note: $\bar{H}_A$, $\bar{H}_N$, $\bar{H}_B$, and $\bar{H}_E$ stand for average human capital of Africans, Brazilian natives, Brazilians, and Europeans, respectively. The lines are for the proportional distribution of population by human capital (*H*). The populations each distribution refers to are identified above the lines. *Author's elaboration.*

their qualification, as they had to trust in their ability to succeed. Consequently, it is reasonable to think that this higher average human capital, in comparison to that of Africans and native Brazilians, existed and that there was also a higher standard deviation because of the inclusion of renegades in the people sent to Brazil. It is worth mentioning that the most skilled professionals at the top of the distribution are unlikely to have migrated, as they had a higher probability of succeeding even in Portugal, so adventures in the colony were relatively less attractive to them. This, however, certainly did not alter much the hypothesis on dispersions presented, although it is represented in the density function drawn in Fig. 7.2.

7.4 EVOLUTION TO THE EARLY 19TH CENTURY

The human capital density functions shown in Fig. 7.2 were established in the first century of Brazilian colonization. The Brazilian density function of human capital evolved over time as a consequence of three determinants: changes in proportions among the three population groups, which had three major sources (differences in mortality rates among these groups, European immigration, and African arrivals); bias in the average human capital of newcomers or of deaths, whatever their origins; and changes in the level of human capital of any of the three populations already living in Brazil as a consequence of education, on-the-job training, family acceleration (deceleration) of human capital building, or other reasons. If there is a close relationship between human capital and per capita GDP, as argued in previous chapters, these determinants were also crucial to determine the evolution of Brazilian per capita GDP.

The Brazilian economy in the 16th century and first three-quarters of the 17th century basically expanded based on sugarcane plantations. In addition to the plantations and mills, many activities were developed in the country to support them. Cattle raising and food production in the interior are the most frequently mentioned,[15] but there was also much petty and wholesale trade, many types of services, and even public sector work in the colony.

The potential biases in population movements were the same as those mentioned before. The local native population was no longer shrinking, but its growth was slow as there were no new incomers, as happened with Africans and Europeans. Slaves continued to be imported from Africa, as they were employed in plantations and other local activities, and Portuguese colonizers were the businessmen and managers in enterprises, so their immigration was mainly from the middle to upper human capital and income strata ranges in Portugal.

In the last decade of the 17th century and most of the 18th century the Brazilian economy moved from its major focus on sugarcane production to add another important export activity, which over the 18th century became at least as important as sugar production: the so-called gold and diamond cycle. There were some discoveries of gold and diamonds in the interior of Brazil, mainly in the current state of Minas Gerais, but some mines were also located in Goiás, Mato Grosso, and even Bahia. Other minerals were eventually found in these regions too, such as silver, but in smaller amounts.

There were radical changes in the composition of the Brazilian population during this period. While the regions that had sugarcane plantations as their major export activity kept the same working logic, the mining activities had a different nature. They were accessible to small-scale enterprises and there were more opportunities to make money in short periods. Furthermore, as they were in the interior of Brazil, they demanded more inland long-distance trade and all the services associated with it. This provided new entrepreneurs with prosperous opportunities.

Demand for trade and services by people engaged in mining activities was more spatially concentrated. As a consequence, a higher share of the

---

15. Furtado (1959, Chapter 10), Prado Jr (1945, Chapter 5) and Simonsen (1957, Chapters 7–8) have extensive analyses of these supporting activities.

population started to live in cities and demanded proportionally more food, energy, and services from the market when compared to rural enterprises, which were relatively more self-sufficient. This created more opportunities for new businesses, which could be more diverse in size and receptive to the introduction of new technologies.

The shape of European immigration changed in this period. People with less capital and more skills started to consider Brazil an attractive option as a place to build a life. This changed the bias of newcomers toward more skilled people with discipline and other attributes of human capital that increased the ability to dedicate effort. The higher demand for control to ensure that taxes were properly collected increased the number of civil servants in the country. This brought a contingent of immigrants with human and physical capitals sizable enough to constitute a middle class in Brazil.

Despite the lack of a relevant change in the human capital of slaves imported from Africa, there was a change in the effective human capital of slaves. While on plantations many productive skills of Africans were underemployed, mining activities demanded more of these skills and enabled slaves to benefit from their employment. Difficulties in controlling the output of labor effort forced employers to create incentives for slaves, which consisted mainly of payment of a share of the results of their labor if performance targets were fulfilled. As a consequence, African technologies were widely used in mines and there was an instantaneous rise in the effective human capital of Africans, as there was effective employment of some of their skills that were not used in previous activities when they had no incentive.

Many slaves bought their emancipation with funds raised through their performance bonus in mining activities. These exslaves were free to employ their skills in market activities. Such freedom raised the efficiency of their work as they started to direct their effort to activities in which they had comparative advantage. Their skills were empowered by their choices, raising their market value. This also raised their effective human capital and its family transmission over generations.

These comments show that in the 100 years after 1690 there was a huge increase in the average human capital availability in Brazil because of the new qualification profile of European immigrants and the new valuation of the skills of Africans. Furthermore, the less-qualified Brazilians, the natives, continued to have a falling share of population. As noted, in 1700 they represented 25% of the Brazilian population, but in 1800 they formed only 13%.

The ability of slaves to earn some income and eventually buy their freedom accelerated the expansion of a lower class of free people in Brazil. They had no physical capital and low levels of human capital, so they lived from petty trade or services in urban areas or as peasants in rural areas. At this time the Brazilian agricultural frontier was still open and they could move to the border of occupation by the big landlords and settle down as small farmers. Once engaged in such enterprises, they did not take possession of large areas because they did not have the necessary funds to buy animals and equipment for large-scale exploitation. This created in Brazil a sizable share of the population with a low standard of living and whose human and physical capitals were also low, although higher than in native tribes.

Many Brazilian natives were incorporated into Brazilian society in colonial times. The disintegration of many tribes due to death of a large share of their population because of the contact with Europeans and the invasion of their lands for farming by the latter left many natives with no organized social group to continue their way of life. These people were incorporated into the cities in the same way as the exslaves and a few poor Portuguese descendants who failed in their entrepreneurial efforts in Brazil. They all had the two options previously mentioned: they could live in cities on petty trade and services or as employees of other urban businesses, or they could migrate to the frontier of productively employed lands and start their own farms as small peasants. The expansion of Brazilian frontiers much beyond Portuguese and Spanish initial agreements was an important consequence of the relevance of this second option.

Thus by the end of the 18th century richer Brazilian social segments were formed by businessmen engaged in farming, mainly of sugarcane, and mining, and those engaged in trade and services. Trade was both long-distance international and local, both wholesale and retail. Very few still lived from mining, as there was a collapse in the availability of precious metals and stones. The middle classes were engaged in farming, trade, and services, either as employers or highly skilled employees. They also worked in government bureaucracy. The low-income classes, the majority of population, worked as slaves, peasants, laborers in husbandry, natives in tribes, hawkers, pedlars, duffers, and artisans, among other occupations.

7.5 SIMULATED STRUCTURE OF BRAZILIAN SOCIETY IN THE EARLY 19TH CENTURY

Table 7.3 shows Milanovic et al.'s (2007) estimates for English and Welsh population distribution among the many working professions between 1800 and 1803. It also shows the estimated average annual income which was transformed from their original data. They gave values in British pounds for the period, but these numbers were multiplied by a constant so the final average value became the estimated per capita GDP (in US$ 1990 international) of Bolt and van Zanden (2013), which was extracted from Broadberry et al. (2011) and represents an updated version of the Maddison (2011) tables.

Table 7.4 has the same structure as Table 7.3, with the same professions shown, but data is an educated guess of population share for each professional category in Brazil in 1800. The absolute number of people in each professional category was built from the assumption that the total is equal to the estimated Brazilian population in 1800. As no assumption was made to estimate the

TABLE 7.3 Distribution of Population in England and Wales in 1800—1803 by Profession and Their Per Capita Contributions to Per Capita GDP

Social Group	Number of People	Percentage of Population (%)	Average Per Capita Income (1990 US$ International)
Paupers	1,040,716	11.5	239.07
Persons imprisoned for debt	10,000	0.11	573.77
Laborers in husbandry	1,530,000	16.9	659.83
Hawkers, pedlars, duffers	4000	0.04	765.02
Laborers in mines, canals	180,000	1.99	851.09
Vagrants	175,218	1.94	956.28
Artisans, mechanics, laborers	2,005,767	22.16	1166.66
Clerks and shopworkers	300,000	3.31	1434.41
Freeholders, lesser	600,000	6.63	1721.30
Farmers	960,000	10.6	1912.55
Innkeepers and publicans	250,000	2.76	1912.55
Lesser clergymen	50,000	0.55	2295.06
Dissenting clergy, itinerants	12,500	0.14	2295.06
Education of youth	120,000	1.33	2390.69
Military officers	65,320	0.72	2658.45
Common soldiers	121,985	1.35	2773.20
Naval officers	35,000	0.39	2849.70
Shopkeepers and tradesmen	372,500	4.11	2868.83
Tailors, milliners, etc.	125,000	1.38	2868.83
Confined lunatics	2500	0.03	2868.83
Freeholders, greater	220,000	2.43	3480.85
Marines and seamen	52,906	0.58	3633.85
Lesser civil offices	52,500	0.58	3825.11
Engineers, surveyors, etc.	25,000	0.28	3825.11
Merchant service	49,393	0.55	3825.11

Continued

TABLE 7.3 Distribution of Population in England and Wales in 1800–1803 by Profession and Their Per Capita Contributions to Per Capita GDP—cont'd

Social Group	Number of People	Percentage of Population (%)	Average Per Capita Income (1990 US$ International)
Keeping houses for lunatics	400	0.004	4781.38
Theatrical pursuits	4000	0.04	4781.38
Liberal arts and sciences	81,500	0.9	4972.64
Law, judges to clerks	55,000	0.61	6693.93
Eminent clergymen	6000	0.07	7965.78
Gents	160,000	1.77	8367.42
Shipowners, freight	25,000	0.28	9562.76
Higher civil offices	14,000	0.15	10,930.24
Lesser merchants, by sea	91,000	1.01	10,930.24
Building and repairing ships	1800	0.02	11,159.75
Warehousemen, wholesale	3000	0.03	12,747.16
Manufacturers	150,000	1.66	12,747.16
Knights	3500	0.04	14,344.15
Esquires	60,000	0.66	14,344.15
Educators in universities	2000	0.02	14,344.15
Baronets	8100	0.09	19,125.53
Eminent merchants, bankers	20,000	0.22	24,863.19
Spiritual peers	390	0.004	25,503.89
Temporal peers	7175	0.08	30,600.85
Mean			**2097.00**

Note: Per capita income was standardized for average income to be equal to per capita GDP in 1800 (1990 US$ international).
Original data from Milanovic, B., Lindert, P., Williamson, J., 2007. Measuring ancient inequality, NBER Working Paper, # 13550, National Bureau of Economic Research, Cambridge, Mass; Bolt, J., van Zanden, J.L., 2013. The First Update of the Maddison Project: Re-Estimating Growth Before 1820, Maddison Project Working Paper 4.

TABLE 7.4 Educated Guess Distribution of Brazilian Population in 1800 by Professions and Their Per Capita Contributions to Per Capita GDP

Social Group	Number of People	Percentage of Population	Per Capita Income Standardized for Per Capita GDP in 1800
Paupers, poor peasants, residents in tribes	465,406	**12.7**	239.07
Persons imprisoned for debt	4026	0.11	344.26
Laborers in husbandry	2,108,160	**57.6**	449.45
Hawkers, pedlars, duffers	5124	0.14	607.24
Laborers in mines, canals	72,307	1.9756	610.10
Vagrants	71,004	1.94	239.07
Artisans, mechanics, laborers	512,400	14	929.98
Clerks and shopworkers	36,673	1.002	1434.41
Freeholders, lesser	128,100	3.5	**1387.08**
Farmers	133,590	3.65	**1338.79**
Innkeepers and publicans	5490	0.15	1912.55
Lesser clergymen	20,130	0.55	2295.06
Dissenting clergy, itinerants	5124	0.14	2295.06
Education of youth	7320	0.2	2390.69
Military officers	7320	0.2	2658.45
Common soldiers	10,980	0.3	**1941.24**
Naval officers	1830	0.05	2849.70
Shopkeepers and tradesmen	43,920	1.2	**2295.06**
Tailors, milliners, etc.	10,980	0.3	2868.83
Confined lunatics	1098	0.03	**2295.06**
Freeholders, greater	3660	0.1	**2784.68**
Marines and seamen	732	0.02	3633.85
Lesser civil offices	732	0.02	3825.11
Engineers, surveyors, etc.	366	0.01	3825.11

Continued

TABLE 7.4 Educated Guess Distribution of Brazilian Population in 1800 by Professions and Their Per Capita Contributions to Per Capita GDP—cont'd

Social Group	Number of People	Percentage of Population	Per Capita Income Standardized for Per Capita GDP in 1800
Merchant service	366	0.01	3825.11
Keeping houses for lunatics	146	0.004	**2390.69**
Theatrical pursuits	15	0.0004	4781.38
Liberal arts and sciences	329	0.009	4972.64
Law, judges to clerks	1098	0.03	6693.93
Eminent clergymen	110	0.003	7965.78
Gents	—	0	8367.42
Shipowners, freight	37	0.001	9562.76
Higher civil offices	37	0.001	10,930.24
Lesser merchants, by sea	183	0.005	10,930.24
Building and repairing ships	256	0.007	11,159.75
Warehousemen, wholesale	366	0.01	12,747.16
Manufacturers	439	0.012	**6373.58**
Knights	—	0	14,344.15
Esquires	—	0	14,344.15
Educators in universities	—	0	14,344.15
Baronets	—	0	19,125.53
Eminent merchants, bankers	146	0.004	**17,404.23**
Spiritual peers	—	0	25,503.89
Temporal peers	—	0	30,600.85
Mean			**634.19**

Elaborated by the author based on data from Milanovic, B., Lindert, P., Williamson, J., 2007. Measuring ancient inequality, NBER Working Paper, # 13550, National Bureau of Economic Research, Cambridge, Mass; Bolt, J., van Zanden, J.L., 2013. The First Update of the Maddison Project: Re-Estimating Growth Before 1820, Maddison Project Working Paper 4; Mortara, G., 1941. Estudos Sobre a Utilização do Censo Demográfico para a Reconstrução das Estatísticas do Movimento da População no Brasil. Revista Brasileira de Estatística, IBGE, 2 (5), 39—89 for Brazilian population.

share of the population that was working, the total by profession is equal to the total population, so not only people actually involved in work are included but also those whose expenses were paid by those active workers. The underlying implicit assumption for this method is that family size and proportion of active population were similar in all professions. Certainly this was not true, but it is still the best possible approximation available.

Other assumptions were made to get Brazilian per capita GDP in 1800. The per capita income of each ethnic group in 1800 was supposed to be the best possible approximation in their country or region of origin, according to figures in 1820. Maddison's figure, as updated by Bolt and van Zanden (2013), of a per capita GDP in Brazil of US$683.49 (US$ 1990 international) was used for 1820. An interactive approach was used to distribute the share of each ethnic group among the professions so the total per capita income in 1820 was as specified (US$683.49) and those for each of the three ethnic groups also reached an expected average income as close as possible to their original levels back home, corrected by a reasonable size of the biases generated by previous arguments. These values, however, were educated guesses, and the share of each ethnic group in each category also had a role to play in the reached equilibrium.

With these income levels for each ethnic group fixed between 1800 and 1820 and the change of the share of each of them in the total population, Brazilian per capita GDP in 1800 is estimated at US$634.19 (1990 international). The combination of income by profession and the share of population in each of them gives this average per capita GDP.

To reach the final figures, some incomes of specific social strata were altered; the reasons for each change are detailed in Table 7.5. In general, most professions whose income was generated directly from the market for services had their incomes reduced in Brazil. This is because Brazil had a lower per capita GDP than England, thus consumers preferred to pay less for lower-quality services. Consequently, lower-skilled services providers could survive in the market, and the average incomes of these professions were lower.

This procedure to alter some incomes in particular circumstances has two underlying rationales. First, as argued in Chapter 3, people with the same human capital tend to have the same income, whatever country they live in, if there is full factor mobility among countries and no transaction costs in the market for goods and services. Although this is not really true, it was argued before that this is a better approximation of reality than that made by models such as Heckscher-Ohlin and the one forwarded by Prebisch (1949), which assume no factor mobility. Secondly, some professional categories in Table 7.3 aggregate many agents and sometimes with very different human capital, so composition in Brazil could be different from that in England and a different average stock of human capital would tend to generate a distinct average income in this category. Table 7.5 shows the categories whose incomes were altered from the English numbers and gives more detailed explanations for the changes made.

TABLE 7.5 Explanations for Changes in Relative Income of Specific Professional Categories

Profession	Reasons for Changing Relative Income When Compared to English Standard
Persons imprisoned for debt	Brazilian imprisoned persons were on average from lower classes than in England, so the standard of living provided in prisons was lower than that found in England.
Laborers in husbandry	Brazilians were less qualified, as many were natives or slaves and exslaves. They all had relatively very low human capital and were unable to generate the same income for landlords or themselves as in England.
Hawkers, pedlars, duffers	Brazilians were less skilled than the English in this category, so on average they had lower productivity and earned a lower income. They had a higher income than the previous category because of the risk involved in their activities and some necessary skills in dealing with clients, but the social origin of these workers and their acquired cognitive abilities were similar to those of the previous category.
Laborers in mines, canals	Brazilians were less qualified for the same reason as stated before, since many professionals came from the same social strata as those in the previous two categories. Nevertheless, as there was proportionately more autonomous labor in Brazil, because of the type of mining activities, the risk partially compensated the lower average individual skills.
Vagrants	Most vagrants in Brazil in those days came from the lowest social strata, so their income was leveled off with this category.
Artisans, mechanics, laborers	This set in Brazil contained mainly artisans. They were peasants with low education but some skills acquired during life, although not much training. They tended to be less skilled than artisans in England, where the practice of apprenticeship was more developed than in Brazil. Thus this category in England earned a premium over peasants because of their additional skills, although their other skills, such as discipline and so on, were not much higher than those of the peasants.
Freeholders, lesser	Among Brazilian lesser freeholders at that time there was an enormous variety of individuals supplying many services. There were more qualified individuals, but also much lesser qualified individuals than were found in England in the same period. Consequently, the average income within this group was lower in Brazil.
Farmers	Brazilian farmers were on average smaller landlords and had lower skills than British farmers, who had a much longer family tradition in working on the land. Therefore, on average, Brazilians had a lower income.

TABLE 7.5 Explanations for Changes in Relative Income of Specific Professional Categories—cont'd

Profession	Reasons for Changing Relative Income When Compared to English Standard
Common soldiers	Common soldiers in Brazil were less qualified as the country was less dangerous than England, with fewer wars and potential attacks by pirates. Therefore, Brazilian soldiers came from different social strata than in England, with a lower share of skilled individuals.
Shopkeepers and tradesmen	Brazil had a wider range of sizes of shops and trade businesses. Smaller units would survive and were headed by less-qualified individuals. This would justify the lower average income of this segment.
Confined lunatics	As Brazilian per capita income was lower, confined lunatics had an average lower standard of living and would cost less to support.
Freeholders, greater	The same arguments for lesser freeholders apply for this case. The variety of services generated a higher range of occupations to be included here. As the population was poor, less-qualified professionals could provide services at lower costs and would survive in the market. This yielded a lower average income for this group.
Keeping houses for lunatics	The high availability of workers with lower skill and subject to lower pay meant the average skills of these workers were lower.
Manufacturers	As Brazilian manufacturing was much less developed than in Britain, the plants were smaller, yielding lower average income for these professionals.
Eminent merchants, bankers	The same argument as for manufacturers applies.

Elaborated by the author.

The Brazilian distribution of people by categories was made by changing the English and Welsh figures using an educated guess. The changes in income were also arbitrary, relying only on educated guesses. Thus the figures in Table 7.4 are completely made up and there is no reason to think they are true. The relevance of this exercise, however, is to transform in numbers the hypothesis of international arbitrage of human capital income and reasonable mobility of physical capital, as well as to give an example of how it could work. This exercise indicates that it is possible to have such hypotheses in a world with higher inequalities in per capita GDP. The solution presented is not unique, as many alternative distributions of the Brazilian population among occupations would yield the same per capita GDP as that in Table 7.4. Nevertheless, the essential conclusions would still be the same.

The poorest 72.4% of the population get only 46.4% of the total income under such hypotheses. Nevertheless, to match the estimated per capita GDP, the proportion of poorer social strata is so high that income distribution ends up as very good. An estimated Gini coefficient with these figures is only 0.057, while it was 0.31 in England. Thus at the beginning of the 19th century Brazil was a country with such a large share of very poor and unqualified people that even the income distribution was very equitable. Although the data in Table 7.4 is simply a guess among many potential alternatives, most of them, when generating the same per capita GDP and taking into account a reasonable arbitrage in the world market for returns to human capital, would generate similar results.

7.5.1 Relative Income of Ethnic Groups

Table 7.6 goes one step beyond the previous guesses and distributes the population of each ethnic group by the occupations presented in Tables 7.3 and 7.4. Of course the solution shown in Table 7.4 is a starting point for Table 7.6. The obvious guesses are that natives and African descendants are more heavily concentrated in the lower classes, which is a straightforward consequence of previous arguments, while European descendants composed all the upper-income social strata. Their human capital availability and political power certainly led to an ethnic distribution among strata similar to that presented in Table 7.6.

A first important conclusion from these exercises is that European descendants also ended up concentrated at the bottom of the income distribution, although they composed all the upper social strata. The low per capita income of the country led to this, even under the hypothesis of perfect factor mobility and arbitrage among markets. Thus a large share of those who freely migrated to Brazil searching for opportunities to improve their income were poor Europeans.

A second important conclusion that can be extracted from a combination of Tables 7.4 and 7.6 is that per capita incomes were very low for natives and African descendants living in Brazil in 1800. Table 7.7 shows these figures for all ethnic groups. Natives lived in tribes, as poor peasants, or in very low social strata in urban agglomerations. Most Africans lived as smallholders, in low social strata in urban agglomerations, or as workers for farmers. In all these cases their incomes were very low given their human and physical capitals.

A consequence of this high concentration of low human capital in the social segments engaged in farming was that the prices of these products on domestic markets were determined by technologies that were relatively very intensive in labor and very low intensive in physical and human capitals. Although to some extent this also happened in regions already engaged in

TABLE 7.6 Guessed Distribution of Population of Each Ethnic Group by Profession

Social Group	Natives	Africans	Europeans
Paupers, poor peasants, residents in tribes	349,055	93,081	23,270
Persons imprisoned	537	3,089	400
Laborers in husbandry	128,225	1,791,936	187,999
Hawkers, pedlars, duffers	0	3,331	1,793
Laborers in mines	0	57,846	14,461
Vagrants	10,676	60,328	0
Artisans, mechanics, laborers	0	149,656	362,744
Clerks and shopworkers	0	733	35,940
Freeholders, lesser	0	0	128,100
Farmers	0	0	133,590
Innkeepers and publicans	0	0	5,490
Lesser clergymen	0	0	20,130
Dissenting clergy, itinerants	0	0	5,124
Education of youth	0	0	7,320
Military officers	0	0	7,320
Common soldiers	0	0	10,980
Naval officers	0	0	1,830
Shopkeepers and tradesmen	0	0	43,920
Tailors, milliners, etc.	0	0	10,980
Confined lunatics	0	0	1,098
Freeholders, greater	0	0	3,660
Marines and seamen	0	0	732
Lesser civil offices	0	0	732
Engineers, surveyors, etc.	0	0	366
Merchant service	0	0	366
Keeping houses for lunatics	0	0	146
Theatrical pursuits	0	0	15
Liberal arts and sciences	0	0	329
Law, judges to clerks	0	0	1,098

Continued

TABLE 7.6 Guessed Distribution of Population of Each Ethnic Group by Profession—cont'd

Social Group	Natives	Africans	Europeans
Eminent clergymen	0	0	110
Gents	0	0	0
Shipowners, freight	0	0	37
Higher civil offices	0	0	37
Lesser merchants, by sea	0	0	183
Building and repairing ships	0	0	256
Warehousemen, wholesale	0	0	366
Manufacturers	0	0	439
Knights	0	0	0
Esquires	0	0	0
Educators in universities	0	0	0
Baronets	0	0	0
Eminent merchants, bankers	0	0	146
Spiritual peers	0	0	0
Temporal peers	0	0	0
Total	488,493	2,160,000	1,011,507

Elaborated by the author relying on conjectures described in the text, using data from Mortara, G., 1941. Estudos Sobre a Utilização do Censo Demográfico para a Reconstrução das Estatísticas do Movimento da População no Brasil. Revista Brasileira de Estatística, IBGE, 2 (5), 39–89; Milanovic, B., Lindert, P., Williamson, J., 2007. Measuring ancient inequality, NBER Working Paper, # 13550, National Bureau of Economic Research, Cambridge, Mass.

TABLE 7.7 Average Per Capita GDP in Each Ethnic Group in 1800 (US$ 1990 International)

	Natives	African Descendants	European Descendants
Per capita GDP (US$ 1990 international)	294.41	472.20	1143.50

Author's elaboration with data from Mortara, G., 1941. Estudos Sobre a Utilização do Censo Demográfico para a Reconstrução das Estatísticas do Movimento da População no Brasil. Revista Brasileira de Estatística, IBGE, 2 (5), 39–89 for Brazilian population; Bolt, J., van Zanden, J.L., 2013. The First Update of the Maddison Project: Re-Estimating Growth Before 1820, Maddison Project Working Paper 4; Milanovic, B., Lindert, P., Williamson, J., 2007. Measuring ancient inequality, NBER Working Paper, # 13550, National Bureau of Economic Research, Cambridge, Mass.

some export output, its relevance was even more important in areas of new occupation which were incorporated in production by these smallholders.

As there was a need to adjust production technologies for livestock and agricultural products to local environmental conditions, these technologies were first adjusted to the relative factor availabilities. Any change in the relative factor employments would demand a fixed cost for adjusting technologies. This introduced uncertainties in the feasibility of potential new technologies which would bring new proportions of factor employment, and created a barrier for entrepreneurs whose intention was to explore rural nonexporting activities using new technologies with the employment of proportionally more human capital.

This in turn created a barrier to the success of new European immigrants as farmers in Brazil. The consequence was that the country ended up not offering as many opportunities for life improvement for these potential newcomers as did the United States, Canada, Australia, and New Zealand in the 19th century. Even the Portuguese did not find many opportunities in rural activities, and ended up migrating mainly to urban areas. This is true even among those coming from rural areas in Minho, who were the majority of Portuguese migrants to Brazil in the 19th century. This apparently small friction may have helped shape the Brazilian role in European mass migration of the 19th century.

7.6 CONCLUSIONS AND ADDITIONAL COMMENTS

The major conclusion of this chapter is that at the beginning of the 19th century Brazil had a society already composed of a population with very low human capital when compared to Europeans. A reasonable share of this population was formed by natives, whose human capital development was 10,000 years behind that found in Europe. African descendants also had much lower human capital than Europeans in the period, although on average it was higher than that of natives. Their human capital was lower in *socially inherited abilities, attitude or personality factors,* and *acquired cognitive abilities,* as society did not have efficient transmission mechanisms, such as schools. Their access to free land and other autonomous working opportunities isolated them from pressure to increase their skills and perpetuated their relative skill backwardness.

The effort to narrow this cultural gap, made mainly by Jesuits and other religious orders, was not sufficiently widespread to engender any relevant result. Most of their descendants still had no education and lived in rural areas with very rudimentary agriculture and livestock at the beginning of the 19th century. Some lived in urban areas, but marginally inserted in society, working in very low-skill services and trade. They did not have enough interactions with more qualified people to learn new skills, such as labor organization, discipline, and so on.

The existence of free land on the borders of occupied territories created a survival alternative for these poor populations with less human capital without creating any relevant social disturbance or social pressure to reduce this gap. This also reduced social interactions and, consequently, the abilities to learn socially transmitted skills. The result was that average income within the country was quite low when compared to European countries.

The chapter also shows that it is possible to have the relatively low Brazilian per capita GDP in 1800 even if there were full arbitrage in the goods market and perfect mobility of factors of production in the economy, as introduced in the model of Chapter 3. Thus it is not necessary to have important market failures to explain Brazilian relative backwardness, as presented in most studies on this subject to date. Only one composition of Brazilian society is presented, but there are many possible alternatives which would generate the relative backwardness found in the data given the ethnical composition of population, the expected human capital of each of these groups, and their share in the social strata.

One more important conclusion is that the existence of this low-skilled population dominating agricultural and livestock production for domestic markets on new lands they occupied, and under the local environmental conditions and using technologies they built from their skills, created a barrier for newcomers who demanded a different factor proportion in their production to generate an attractive income that could justify their migration. Thus an adverse environment for higher-skilled Europeans was built in Brazil by the logic of its previous occupation up to the 19th century. This certainly had an adverse impact on the human capital of the European incomers disembarking in Brazil throughout the 19th century.

Chapter 8

Relative Declining in the 19th Century

Chapter Outline

8.1 INTRODUCTION

By the beginning of the 19th century Brazil had built a society with many poor individuals living in urban and rural areas who had very low human capital. They were mainly descendants of Africans brought to Brazil as slaves and natives, who were incorporated in the society created by the Portuguese colonizers but always left at its margin, with few opportunities to prosper from human capital acquisition through any mechanisms provided by the colonizers.

The structure of Brazilian society built up to the beginning of the 19th century also created a barrier to new immigrants, as the technologies developed in rural exploitation for domestic markets were adjusted to a factor proportion that was less intensive in human capital. This technological trap restricted the potential gains in welfare of European migrants, as they had to overcome its limits to benefit fully from their human capital. This led to a relative loss of potential migrants from Europe with higher human capital than natives and Africans, as they preferred to risk their futures in North America,

139

Australia, New Zealand, and even Argentina, as there were lower barriers to employment opportunities with higher use of their skills in these countries. This restricted the human capital availability within Brazil in the beginning of the 19th century.

This chapter focuses on the way the relative availability of human capital evolved in the 19th century, and how it left Brazil behind European countries that increased their productivity quickly in the 19th century. The next section estimates yearly time series for the stock of human capital in some countries in the 19th century, with data for Brazil, Sweden, Spain, and Great Britain. Section 8.3 compares the relative performance of Brazil and these other countries, which include one from the Northern European Periphery and one from the Southern European Periphery. Section 8.4 comments on historical human capital building in Brazil and some European countries and gives a first evaluation of the origins of discrepancies in the relative human capital enhancement over the century. Section 8.5 links the empirical conclusions to the model in Chapter 5, indicating that they are reasonable under the conclusions reached there, while Section 8.6 summarizes the major conclusions of the chapter.

8.2 LONG-TERM TREND OF BRAZILIAN HUMAN CAPITAL AVAILABILITY IN THE 19TH CENTURY

There is no available data for Brazilian per capita stock of human capital in the 19th century, but using some strong assumptions it is possible to guess its behavior throughout most of that century. This estimation generated time series for this variable so its major long-term trend can be compared to the behavior of similar series in some of the European benchmark countries generated in a similar way.

8.2.1 Estimating Brazilian Per Capita GDP in the 19th Century

Estimation of the long-term trend in per capita stock of human capital starts with an estimation of Brazilian per capita GDP in the 19th century, as there was no available data for this series. The procedure for this first estimation was quite simple. A surrogated per capita GDP, such as those used in Chapter 6, was initially created relying on data from IBGE (1990) for populations from Europe, Africa, and natives. The gaps were filled with simple extrapolations relying on growth rates from extremes of missing periods. Whenever there was more than one population estimation, those made by Mortara (1941) were chosen. When data for a given year was available but generated changes in growth rates considered to be too radical, it was disregarded. Of course, data for 1872 was from the population census of that year.

The 20th-century composition of population from the three major origins was taken from genetic studies in 2010 by Manta et al. (2013). Population growth of each of these genetic groups from 1872 up to 2010 was supposed to be equal to the natural one for the Brazilian population. The growth rate for European descendants was corrected to add immigrants, whose yearly data was obtained from Instituto Brasileiro de Geografia e Estatística (IBGE). Such corrections were also made for growth of European descendants in the 19th century.

Per capita GDPs from Bolt and van Zanden (2013) for Portugal and African countries were used for the 19th and early 20th centuries. Extrapolations through constant growth rates calculated from extremes were used in missing intervals. The per capita GDP of Brazilian natives was assumed to be constant over the whole period at levels obtained in Chapter 7 from English income distribution in 1800 and per capita GDP from Bolt and van Zanden (2013). The generated average income for the lowest social strata was input for Brazilian natives.

GDP growth rates in the interval between 1820 and 1930 were obtained from average growth rates of four available time series: money supply, imports, exports, and government income. All data was in local currency and deflated by a price index created here[1] from an implicit effective exchange rate (UK sterling and local currency) obtained by comparing imports in local currency and sterling. A British GDP deflator from Thomas et al. (2010) was combined with that of Broadberry et al. (2012) to deflate the sterling values before exchanging to Brazilian currency. The justification for this price index is that imports accounted for a large share of consumption in Brazil in the period, so local prices were highly influenced by local prices of imported goods.

After getting the real value in local currency for these four variables, their per capita values were calculated by dividing each by the population figures recomposed from the existing population data. The growth rates of these variables were calculated, and they were adjusted so the average for the period 1820−1900 matched the average growth of the surrogated per capita GDP in the same period. Then an average of the growth rates of these per capita variables was calculated and considered as the yearly growth rate of per capita GDP. The series for this last variable was recomposed for the period 1820−1930. The growth rate for the period 1800−1820 was extracted directly from the surrogated per capita GDP, as there is no macroeconomic time series that is strongly correlated with per capita GDP for this period.

8.2.2 Estimation of Human Capital in Brazil in the 19th Century

A simple aggregated Cobb−Douglas production function, with no natural resources, was the starting point for the estimation of the stock of human capital in the 19th century in Brazil.

$$Y = AK^{\alpha}(HL)^{1-\alpha} \tag{8.1}$$

where Y is total output, and A, K, H, and L are total factor productivity, the stock of physical and human capitals, and the amount of labor employed,

---

1. All this data is from IBGE (1988).

respectively. The Greek letter α is a parameter, so $0 < \alpha < 1$. Under this specification, the stock of natural resources is included as physical capital. This is a standard Cobb–Douglas function used in many development accounting studies.[2]

To date, only Y has been estimated through methods described in the previous subsection. To eliminate L from Eq. (8.1), a simple relationship is introduced:

$$L = \delta P \tag{8.2}$$

where P is population and δ is a parameter so that $0 < \delta < 1$. This parameter defines the proportion of population that is part of the labor force. Substituting this equation back in the production function yields:

$$y = A'k^\alpha H^{1-\alpha} \tag{8.1'}$$

where $A' = A\delta^{1-\alpha}$, $y = (Y/P)$, and $k = (K/P)$. Only y in this equation was already estimated.

The marginal condition of firms for profit maximization ensures that:

$$\frac{\partial Y}{\partial K} = \alpha \frac{Y}{K} = r \tag{8.3}$$

where r is the rate of return to capital. Although there is no data for r, it will be taken to be equal to 0.33 following Gollin (2002), who estimated this parameter for the United States. Although there are alternative estimations for the parameter, which represents the share of capital in total GDP not only for the United States but also for other countries and in many years,[3] it is still common in the literature simply to assume that this is the correct value for this parameter.

There is no data for the rate of return to capital in Brazil in the 19th century, but if there was full arbitrage among factor markets around the world, Piketty's (2014) figures for England could be used. Of course the assumption of full arbitrage has to consider the existence of differences in risk when investing in Brazil and England. Therefore, alternative assumptions on the risk premium are introduced and tested later.

These two assumptions define r and α. As Y is already known, Eq. (8.3) can be used to generate estimated values for K. A second first-order condition for profit maximization yields:

$$(1 - \alpha)Y = wHL \tag{8.4}$$

where w is the wage rate in the economy. As α and Y are already known, either estimated or by assumption, this equation can generate the total flow of income

---

2. See, for example, Caselli (2005), Hall and Jones (1999), Bils and Klenow (2000), Hsieh and Klenow (2010), and Daude and Fernández-Arias (2010).
3. See, for example, Feenstra et al. (2013).

accruing to workers given their human capital. If it is assumed that the market is efficient in human capital investments, the total value of the stock of human capital in any period is equal to the present value of the infinite future income stream that this factor of production generates. The implicit assumption is that a society can reproduce its current human capital forever, only consuming part of its current GDP with actual welfare extracted from such reproduction. Although this is a strong assumption, it is reasonably close to reality, especially at a time when learning by doing from apprenticeship was the major source of human capital building. Under this assumption, the stock of human capital H can be defined as:

$$H' = \frac{(1-\alpha)Y}{1 - \left(\frac{1}{1+r}\right)} \tag{8.5}$$

Dividing H', the total stock of human capital in the economy, by P, the stock of human capital per capita, h is obtained, which is slightly different from H, as this last variable presents the stock of human capital per unit of labor. Therefore:

$$h = \frac{(1-\alpha)y}{1 - \left(\frac{1}{1+r}\right)} \tag{8.5'}$$

As y, r, and α were previously estimated, h can be obtained from this equation. Alternative assumptions made to determine r, the rate of return to capital in Brazil, will generate different time series for h. In the same way, different assumptions on the capital share in total output, α, will alter the values for h. Before discussing these alternative assumptions and the estimated time series, alternative methods for estimation of these same series for Sweden, England, and Spain are introduced in the next subsection.

8.2.3 Estimation of Human Capital in Other European Countries

In addition to the estimations of the human capital stock in Brazil in the 19th century, as described in the previous subsection, three other countries were subject to such estimations: England, which is not in the set of benchmark countries in this book but is the major world superpower of the period, Sweden, and Spain, each of the latter representing one of the regions from which European benchmark countries were drawn—the Northern and the Southern European Peripheries, respectively.

The only difference in the method for England and that used for Brazil is the figures for α were those calculated by Piketty (2014) from 1800 to 1854. From 1855 to 1930 the shares were from Mitchell (1988). The shares between years with available data in Piketty's time series were calculated by inputting a constant yearly growth rate between the two extremes of available data. Then the decennial shares were transformed into yearly data. The data from Mitchell (1988) was already in a yearly frequency. All other steps were exactly the same as pursued in estimation for Brazil. It is worth noting that the rates of return to capital were also transformed into yearly data from decennial data using the same method as described for capital share in total output. Per capita GDPs from 1800 to 1870 were from Broadberry et al. (2012)[4]; after 1870 the figures were from Bolt and van Zanden (2013).

The method for Sweden was slightly different, as there was available data for the physical capital stock. Data for per capita GDP was from Bolt and van Zanden (2013). Capital share α from 1800 to 1849 was fixed at 0.33397, which is the average of the share calculated by Edvinsson (2005), as appearing in Edvinsson (2013), between 1850 and 1865. From 1850 to 1930 data is directly from Edvinsson (2005). The proportion of physical capital stock to GDP from Edvinsson (2005) was combined with Bolt and van Zanden (2013) data for per capita GDP to generate K in US$ 1990 international, and Eq. (8.3) was used to generate the rate of return to capital from data for y, k, and α. Given these series, Eq. (8.5') was used to generate h, the per capita human capital stock. Two alternative series were used in this last step: one relied on the return to capital, as described; and a second relied on Piketty's (2014) English time series for this return to generate an alternative time series for h. This helps comparisons with other countries.

The per capita GDP for Spain was from Bolt and van Zanden (2013). The period 1800−1850 was filled with yearly fluctuations in real wages in Madrid obtained from Allen (2001). The long-term average growth from Bolt and van Zanden (2013) was maintained, but the annual fluctuations were those found in the wage series with yearly growth normalized to generate the growth rate of per capita GDP. The capital return and share, r and α, were from Piketty (2014) for England and set *ad hoc* at 0.33, respectively.

8.3 GENERATED HUMAN CAPITAL SERIES

Two figures were built from the data generated by the methods described. Fig. 8.1 presents the human capital series for the four countries, but all using the return to capital from Piketty (2014) for England. Fig. 8.2 shows these same four calculated series when the return to capital is that estimated for Sweden from the available data for stock of physical capital and capital share for Sweden. This return was used to generate series for Brazil and Spain, as well as Sweden. The return to physical capital in England was its own return obtained from Piketty (2014), even in Fig. 8.2.

---

4. Professor Stephen Broadberry kindly provided access to the whole series discussed in the paper.

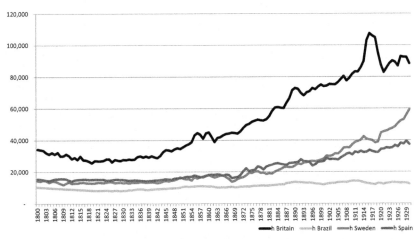

FIGURE 8.1 Per capita human capital stocks for Brazil, England, Sweden, and Spain, 1800–1930, using Piketty (2014) return to capital, 1990 US$ international. *Author's calculation, using data from various sources. See text for details.*

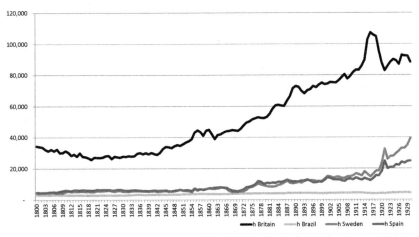

FIGURE 8.2 Per capita human capital stocks for Brazil, England, Sweden, and Spain, 1800–1930, using Swedish data for estimated return to capital for Spain, Brazil, and Sweden, 1990 US$ international. *Author's calculation, using data from various sources. See text for details.*

A higher return to capital in Fig. 8.2 reflects the higher risk involved in investments in these countries other than England. Brazil is the farthest from Britain among these countries, so probably any investment there would be more risky than in Sweden and Spain, and the equilibrium rate of return to capital would be higher than those used in both figures. Thus the stock of human capital calculated for Brazil is relatively overestimated in Figs. 8.1 and 8.2.

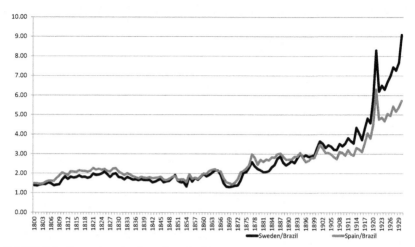

FIGURE 8.3 Proportion of estimated stock of human capital: European countries compared to Brazil, using Swedish data for estimated return to capital. *Author's calculation, using data from Fig. 8.2.*

Figs. 8.1 and 8.2 unveil the same general conclusions. The per capita stocks of human capital in the benchmark countries, Sweden and Spain, were higher than in Brazil throughout the whole 19th century. This difference was relatively stable in the first half of the century and increased thereafter, especially in the last quarter. This trend is reinforced by the proportions presented in Fig. 8.3, whose data relied on Fig. 8.2 as its original source.

England faced a fall in its per capita stock of human capital in the first quarter of the 19th century. This was a consequence of urbanization and subsequent loss of skills that were important in rural work but not relevant in urban activities. However, access to schools started to increase in the first half of the century, eventually leading to a reversal of the trend in human capital, which started to increase. The stock of human capital thus started to depart further from the Brazilian stock.

These three figures indicate that the per capita human capital of the European peripheries departed from that of Brazil in the 19th century, as also identified for the United States in previous chapters using a different method. The data also shows that the Brazilian per capita stock of human capital stagnated in the first half of the 19th century. Its increase in the second half of the century was very mediocre when compared to the performance of this variable in European countries. This could explain why Brazil fell behind in the 19th century, especially in the second half.

8.4 ADDITIONAL COMMENTS ON HUMAN CAPITAL BUILDING IN EUROPE IN THE 19TH CENTURY

A glance at the history of education in many European countries, even those of the periphery, indicates that education became a major concern in these societies in the 19th century, if not earlier. This fact is especially true in the

Northern European Periphery.[5] Schooling in countries such as Sweden, Norway, and Switzerland was widespread very early in the 19th century, and became compulsory in some of these countries during that century.

In 1736 learning to read was made compulsory for all children in Norway, although it only became effective some years later. As early as 1827 the Folkeskole type of primary school was introduced in the country, and attendance for 7 years became mandatory in 1889. In Sweden mandatory reading skills for children were also introduced before the 19th century. Parents were responsible for teaching their children, and priests were required to test the children's abilities in reading. This enforced the development of education in the country. In the middle of the 19th century Sweden already had one of the highest literacy rates in Europe.

Switzerland was among the first European countries to establish free, compulsory primary education in 1830. In the mid-19th century it was already, with Sweden and Norway, among the countries with the highest literacy rates—over 70% of the adult population.[6] Finland had a similar trend to Sweden: family education was demanded from the churches, and Finland also reached high rates of literacy in the early 19th century.

Societies in the Southeast Periphery were not so committed to education as their neighbors in Northern Europe. Portugal and Spain placed less emphasis on such educational policies. The consequence was that they accumulated less human capital and became relatively less developed. Around 1800 the Portuguese literacy rate was less than 20%; in Spain it reached the same level in 1820, and only reached 30% in 1870.[7]

In contrast, the Brazilian population had very low educational levels at the beginning of the 19th century. African and native descendants had almost no access to education. Only those natives engaged in schooling by Jesuits and other Catholic organizations had any access to education, but their share in the total population was very small. Africans who came to Brazil with some education had their skills devalued by the colonial economic activities and there were no incentives for intergenerational transmission of skills, even reading and writing in their native languages. Even the Portuguese who migrated to Brazil were often badly educated, as Portugal, the major source of Europeans migrating to Brazil until the beginning of the 19th century, itself had a very uneducated population.

While there was fast enhancement of access to education in the Northern European Periphery, and less so in the Southeast Periphery, the Brazilian average educational level made almost no progress in the period. The incoming Europeans until the last two decades of the 19th century were mainly Portuguese migrants; after the Portuguese nobility had gone back to Portugal with the king, they were mainly poor and uneducated peasants from Minho,

---

5. See Houston (2011) and UNESCO (2006, Chapter 8).
6. See Graff (1987, Chapter 7, pp. 301–302).
7. Data is from Roser (2014).

which actually reduced the average stock of human capital in Brazil, as shown in Figs. 8.1 and 8.2.

Immigration originating from places other than Portugal became more important in the second half of the 19th century. Germany, Italy, and Spain were the major sources of these other immigrants.[8] Nevertheless, two factors meant this had little impact on the Brazilian average human capital. First, the numbers were small when compared to the existing population in the country: between 1884 and 1913 the share of nonPortuguese immigrants in the average Brazilian population reached only 11.4%. Secondly, most European immigration to Brazil was financed by the Brazilian government and the landlords. These incentives automatically biased the migration to lower-educated and lower-skilled individuals. Those European citizens who had some wealth would rather migrate to the United States, Canada, Australia, and New Zealand, where they already had networks, organized communities, and more confidence that they could improve their lives, as they would not be tied to slaveowning landlords. Furthermore, news coming from the New World told of very different experiences in the different countries. Brazilian experiences were such that some local governments in Germany and Italy deliberately put barriers on emigration to Brazil. This bias in immigrants also reduced the impact of European immigration on the level of Brazilian human capital in the last quarter of the 19th century and first decade of the 20th century.

By 1872 only 23.4% of Brazilian nonslave males were literate and 13.4% of females; 84.8% of the population were free and 15.2% were slaves. These numbers imply that less than 20% of the male population had reading skills, and less than 12% of women. Spain had 30% of its population with reading skills in 1870, a number similar to that in Portugal. Sweden and the United States had an 80% literate population in 1870.[9] These differences are good indicators of the stagnation of human capital building in Brazil when compared to that found in the European periphery and North America.

When the focus moves to higher education, evidence unveils a similar picture but with some different features. The map of existing universities in the 18th and 19th centuries shows many Spanish and some Portuguese universities. The number of universities in Spain is particularly astonishing: in a country with a low literacy rate and low average schooling, it is an apparent contradiction. A similar view arises from analysis of the developments in higher education in Brazil. In 1792 Brazil founded its first engineering school in Rio de Janeiro, the Real Academia de Artilharia, Fortificação e Desenho (Royal Academy for Artillery, Fortifications, and Design), while its first medical school was founded in Bahia in 1808 (Escola de Cirurgia da Bahia). Recife and São Paulo had law schools, both founded in 1827. Thus although

---

8. Japanese immigration only became important in the 20th century.
9. Data is from Roser (2014) for other countries and IBGE (Census data for 1872) for Brazil.

basic education for a large share of the population was not advanced in Brazil and the two Iberian countries, those who had gone through basic education had relatively more access to tertiary education.

This fact unveils the class bias of decisions on education. While Portuguese, Spanish, and Brazilian governments and local institutions were generous in providing access to tertiary education to their elites, they had no special engagement in promoting basic education for the mass population. State control by elites restricted the focus on education to that which would benefit their descendants. Particularly in Brazil, the existing schools were mainly private and expensive for the majority of the local people, even when they had religious backing. The consequence was that only a small share of the population had access to basic and tertiary education, although access to the latter for those who had access to the former was proportionally more generous.

This difference in social policies and institutions regarding education, when European peripheries and Brazil are compared, explains the widening of per capita GDP disparities in the 19th century and also the differences in performance between the two sets of European peripheries focused upon by this book.

8.5 MODEL INTERPRETATION OF THE WIDENING EDUCATIONAL GAP IN THE 19TH CENTURY

Eq. (5.5$'$) from Chapter 5 presents a rate of intergenerational evolution of human capital, which is defined as:

$$\frac{H_O}{H_P} = \left(\frac{vwL_0\delta}{1+r}\right)^{\frac{\delta}{1-\delta}}$$ (8.6)

where H_O and H_P are the human capital of the offspring and the parent, respectively; w and v are wages and 1.0 plus the expected rate of growth of wages, respectively; L_0 is the total labor supply of the offspring; r is the rate of return of capital; and δ is the elasticity of the human capital with respect to the amount of resources dedicated to this investment, which can be public or privately supplied by families.

It is argued in Chapter 5 that this intergenerational growth rate of the stock of human capital tended to be similar among nations if there was no public investment in human capital accumulation determined politically. This is true if δ, w, v, L_0, and r are the same. Although it is one of the major hypotheses of this book that w, v, and r are close enough among countries that the assumption that they are the same is a better approximation to reality, it is argued in Chapter 5 that this is not the case. Another determinant of r is introduced, which is the risk premium associated with each economy. Furthermore, it is argued that $r_b > r_i$, where b stands for Brazil while i stands for any European periphery country.

If $r_b > r_i$, Brazilian human capital accumulation in the 19th and early 20th centuries would be lower than in the European peripheries, as is concluded in this chapter. Furthermore, if Brazil was a less urbanized country, it is also reasonable to assume that $\delta_b < \delta_i$, as education is subject to increasing return to scale. Hence this second relationship also implies that the growth rate of human capital was lower in Brazil than in the European periphery. Reasonable deviations from the full arbitrage hypothesis tend to strength the conclusion that there was lower human capital growth in Brazil throughout the 19th and early 20th centuries.

These conclusions arising from probable deviations of the hypothesis of full arbitrage in the international markets for factors of production under the risk-neutrality simplifying assumption strengthen the conclusion of the preceding section, which stresses the role of public effort through policies to increase human capital accumulation. The determinants of these stronger engagements in the social effort to promote human capital accumulation are the subject of further analysis in the forthcoming chapters.

8.6 CONCLUSIONS

This chapter makes an educated guess at the evolution of the stock of human capital in Brazil, Sweden, Spain, and Great Britain in the 19th and early 20th centuries. It is seen that the scarce data available and simple assumptions on the way markets work point to an expected completely different evolution of the stock of human capital in these countries. While stocks in Sweden and Spain started to depart from that in Brazil, they also narrowed the gap with Great Britain, especially in the second half of the 19th century. The Brazilian stock, however, continued to depart from that in Great Britain, and consequently lagged behind the European periphery.

It is worth noting from Chapter 7 that Brazil's initial labor force in the 19th century did not have the minimum skill to perform with dexterity jobs that were considered unskilled in Europe. They did not have the organization in work, notion of sequence, and hierarchy that would enable them to perform these simple tasks. They were mainly descendants of the native population and Africans. This restricted the relative average productivity within the country when compared to European peripheries.

It is worth stressing that the evolution of the educational systems sketched in the previous sections indicates that some countries had the growth of skills spread more widely over the population (Northern Periphery), while others had more concentration in a smaller share of the population (Southern Periphery). Brazil, similar to the countries in the Southern Periphery, had its educational system concentrating skills on the richer social strata. An important difference in the evolution of human capital in Brazil from that in the Southern Periphery, however, was that the share of population with some access to these facilities for improvement of skills was much more restricted in Brazil.

Chapter 9

Stabilization of Relative Backwardness

Chapter Outline

9.1 INTRODUCTION

The major logic of the main hypothesis to explain the proximate causes of Brazilian relative backwardness has been built in the previous chapters of this book. It starts with the underlying hypothesis that the world economy works as close to an integrated system, with perfect mobility of factors of production, goods, and information, which implies that access to technology is not a constraint to development of any particular country. Of course these hypotheses are not correct in literal terms, as there are transaction costs and restrictions to mobility of many factors of production and information. The implicit assumption introduced here is that such deviations from the initial hypotheses are not so important as to change significantly the relative performance of per capita output among countries. These deviations may be important in explaining relative economic performance for a few decades, but under the hypothesis of this book they are not relevant to the very long-term achievements of countries.

A second pillar of the hypothesis is that the relative per capita output among countries in a world economy with perfect mobility of factors of production, goods, and information is determined from an exogenous spatial distribution of human capital and natural resources, especially the former. Given these, there are adjustments in the local supplies of physical capital so the spatial distribution of total production among countries is finally determined. Such accommodation of this other factor of production and the consequent spatial distribution of output can generate stable inequalities in per capita GDP among countries.

Another important theoretical conclusion underlying the hypothesis forwarded here is that, once initially determined, the spatial distribution of human capital tends to be reproduced over the years, if only market forces work. Chapter 5 relies on the rational behavior of families with different stocks of human capital to generate such a result. If the existing disparities are reproduced over generations, this will also replicate inequalities among countries over generations if there are no public policies to change this dynamic equilibrium.

Using such theoretical arguments, the analysis of the historical formation of Brazil's current population indicates that it had as background a proportionally less-educated population than those of the benchmark countries, both the new colonies, such as the Western Offshoots, and the European countries lying on the periphery of that continent. The relevance of imported Africans, the role of natives in the social composition of the Brazilian population, and the composition of European immigrants explained this original setup. This could already explain the gap built up to the 19th century, and even its widening over that same century.

The current hypothesis departs radically from that forwarded by Latin American structuralists, which sites Brazilian relative backwardness on technological restrictions. They saw such restrictions as the source of international specializations in the world market which impeded the development of some nations. In their view, primary commodity specialization left Brazil out of most technological development of the 19th century and condemned its population to an average low per capita GDP.

The hypothesis of this book turns this idea upside down, suggesting that the low human capital of the local population and consequent low average ability to generate income built this low per capita GDP. As relative availability of factors of production gave it comparative advantage in producing primary commodities, Brazil specialized in such goods in the world market. The failure to attract or generate endogenously a more qualified workforce was the true source of Brazilian relative backwardness and the primary commodity specialization was one of its consequences, not the other way around.

Nevertheless, an important question still remains: why were there no public policies to rescue Brazil from this relative backwardness in the 20th century, after the world migrations were halted? Other countries, such as South Korea and Taiwan, managed to come from behind and narrow their differences in per capita GDP with the advanced economies. The answer to this question is presented in the next chapter. Before that, this chapter analyzes further the data on Brazilian relative performance, restricting the focus to a smaller set of benchmark countries, but with yearly data since 1800. This closer look at their long-term performance sheds some light on the development of the Brazilian economy and consequently offers support to the answer to the previous question.

Section 9.2 presents data on Brazilian long-term relative performance compared to a small set of benchmark countries. Section 9.3 proposes the major explanation for the end of the divergence found over the 19th century, which ceased in the early 20th century for most countries included in the sample. Section 9.4 gives comments which help to build a bridge between the theoretical arguments of the previous section and historical facts, while Section 9.5 focus on the role of immigration over the late 19th and early 20th centuries as a source of this change in the long-term trend established in the 19th century. Section 9.6 summarizes the major conclusions and discusses the state of our understanding of Brazilian relative backwardness, building a bridge to the discussions in forthcoming chapters.

9.2 LONG-TERM DYNAMICS OF BACKWARDNESS

A new presentation of the proportion of Brazilian per capita GDP to those of a sample of countries, but relying on yearly data since 1800 when there is data for the sample country, can help understand the dynamics of Brazilian relative backwardness. Brazilian per capita GDP for 1800−1930 is as generated in the previous chapter. Only in 1930 it is merged with Bolt and van Zanden's (2013) series. Figs. 9.1−9.5 show the proportions of Brazilian per capita GDP to those of the United States, Sweden, Australia, Spain, and the United Kingdom (UK). With the exception of the United Kingdom, all the other countries were chosen to represent the regions from which the benchmark countries were drawn. Yearly data availability was the criterion to choose the representative country in each group. As no European Southern Periphery country had data for per

FIGURE 9.1 Proportion between Brazilian and US per capita GDP, 1800−2013. *Bolt, J., van Zanden, J.L., 2013. The First Update of the Maddison Project: Re-Estimating Growth Before 1820. Maddison Project Working Paper 4; IBGE (see Chapter 7); The Conference Board, Total Economy Database, http://www.conference-board.org/data/economydatabase/, January, 2014.*

FIGURE 9.2   Proportion between Brazilian and Swedish per capita GDP, 1800–2013. *Bolt, J., van Zanden, J.L., 2013. The First Update of the Maddison Project: Re-Estimating Growth Before 1820. Maddison Project Working Paper 4; IBGE (see Chapter 7); The Conference Board, Total Economy Database, http://www.conference-board.org/data/economydatabase/, January, 2014.*

FIGURE 9.3   Proportion between Brazilian and Australian per capita GDP, 1820–2013. *Bolt, J., van Zanden, J.L., 2013. The First Update of the Maddison Project: Re-Estimating Growth Before 1820. Maddison Project Working Paper 4; IBGE (see Chapter 7); The Conference Board, Total Economy Database, http://www.conference-board.org/data/economydatabase/, January, 2014.*

capita GDP from 1800, Spain was chosen, as it is the country with the longest series available.

These five figures show that throughout the 19th century Brazilian relative backwardness increased. Only in the first half of the 20th century was this trend ceased for all countries but Australia, whose proportion had stopped

FIGURE 9.4 Proportion between Brazilian and Spanish per capita GDP, 1840−2013. *Bolt, J., van Zanden, J.L., 2013. The First Update of the Maddison Project: Re-Estimating Growth Before 1820. Maddison Project Working Paper 4; IBGE (see Chapter 7); The Conference Board, Total Economy Database, http://www.conference-board.org/data/economydatabase/, January, 2014.*

FIGURE 9.5 Proportion between Brazilian and UK per capita GDP, 1800−1913. *Bolt, J., van Zanden, J.L., 2013. The First Update of the Maddison Project: Re-Estimating Growth Before 1820. Maddison Project Working Paper 4; Broadberry, S., Campbell, B., Klein, A., Overton, M., van Leeuwen, B., 2012. British Economic Growth, 1270−1870: An Output Based Approach, Studies in Economics, # 1203, Department of Economics, University of Kent; IBGE (see Chapter 7); The Conference Board, Total Economy Database, http://www.conference-board.org/data/economydatabase/, January, 2014.*

falling in the last quarter of the 19th century. Table 9.1 shows the years in which the long-term downward trends in the proportion between per capita GDP of each benchmark country and Brazil were halted. These years vary from country to country and their identification is subjective, relying only on

TABLE 9.1 Approximated Year of End of Divergence

Country	Approximated Year of End of Divergence
United States	1926
Sweden	1929
Australia	1883
Spain	1929
United Kingdom	1917

Author's elaboration.

the visual behavior of the series. No statistically rigorous method to define the years was used. Sweden and Spain had longer divergences, while the United Kingdom had the shortest, after Australia.

In the 20th century the United Kingdom and Spain faced reversals of the increasing proportion between their per capita GDPs and the Brazilian one that was found in the 19th century. There was stabilization of this trend in the 20th century for the United States, Sweden, and Australia, after the fall inherited from the previous century was halted. There were fluctuations thereafter. Nevertheless, even for the United Kingdom and Spain the reversals ended some years later and there was stability afterward. It is worth mentioning that the trend reversal for the United Kingdom made the proportion reach levels seen only in the early 19th century. As the United Kingdom was already a leading economy in the early 19th century, it had slower growth in the 20th century, as this country did not benefit from the catching-up bonus to enhance its performance.

9.3 EXPLAINING THE STABILIZATION OF RELATIVE BACKWARDNESS

The preceding chapters explain how the human capital stock evolved in Brazil and the other benchmark countries in the 19th century, and why there was a relative decline in the Brazilian stock of this factor of production. Certainly the argument also works for the period in the early 20th century in which divergence was still happening. The year in which the proportion of Brazilian per capita GDP ceased to fall varied among benchmark countries, depending on particular features of their development. The arguments in previous chapters, however, are not enough to explain why this negative trend in Brazilian relative per capita GDP eventually ceased. This question is faced here.

A continuous representation of Eq. (5.5′) in Chapter 5 was made in Fig. 9.1 of that chapter. This figure drew the evolution of the natural logarithm of the stock of human capital over the years for a family in a continuous time.

For convenience, the original equation of Chapter 5 is reproduced here as Eq. (9.1).

$$H_O = \left(\frac{vwL_O\delta}{1+r}\right)^{\frac{\delta}{1-\delta}} H_P \qquad (9.1)$$

where H_P and H_O are the stocks of human capital from the parents and the offspring, respectively. It is worth noting that human capital is measured as the productive ability to generate units of the basic wage rate over a given period, so it is not necessarily a linear function of the time spent on human capital accumulation. L_O is the amount of labor spent by the offspring, which can be set equal to 1; w is the basic wage rate, $v = (1 + g_w)$; g_w is the expected growth rate of w over generations; and r is the interest rate. δ is the elasticity of the human capital of the offspring with respect to the resources invested in human capital building. From these definitions, it is reasonable to assume for the moment that w, v, L_O, r, and δ are the same for all families in a given economy. This equation represents the stock of human capital of the offspring given that of the parent, when there is an interior solution for utility maximization. Conditions for an interior solution demand that $E \geq 0$, where E is the amount of resources invested by the family in the human capital building of the offspring.

Define a set of families as I, and assume that the number of families included in this set is sufficiently large. Also assume that all the variables and parameters on the right side of Eq. (9.1) are equal for all families within this set, and that they are also constant over the periods. Furthermore, assume that the reproduction moments of the families are spread evenly over the periods, so that in each moment there is the same number of families reproducing. Under such assumptions, the growth rate of the average human capital stock of this set i for an interior solution can be represented as:

$$\frac{H_{it} - H_{it-1}}{H_{it-1}} = \left[\frac{vwL_O\delta}{1+r}\right]^{\frac{\delta}{1-\delta}} - 1 \qquad (9.2)$$

When expenditures on human capital building by the government are high enough to force E to a corner solution, so that $E = 0$, the model of Chapter 5 and the three assumptions of the previous paragraph imply that the growth rate of the average human capital stock in set i becomes:

$$\frac{H_{it} - H_{it-1}}{H_{it-1}} = \frac{\pi^\delta}{H_{t-1}^\delta} - 1 \qquad (9.3)$$

Suppose that there are n sets of individuals in this economy, each corresponding to a social group. Furthermore, each individual belongs to one and only one social group. Under such assumptions, the growth rate of the average stock of human capital for the whole economy is:

$$\frac{H_t - H_{t-1}}{H_{t-1}} = \sum_{i=1}^{n} \phi_i \frac{H_{it} - H_{it-1}}{H_{it-1}} \qquad (9.4)$$

where H_t is the average stock of human capital for the whole economy, so that:

$$H_t = \sum_{i=1}^{n} \eta_i H_{it} \qquad (9.5)$$

η_i is the share of individuals in the total population who belong to set i, and ϕ_i is the share of human capital of set i in the total for the whole population, so it is defined as:

$$\phi_i = \eta_i \frac{H_{it-1}}{H_{t-1}} \qquad (9.6)$$

It is worth noting that the growth rate for the average stock of human capital when $E = 0$ only holds if:

$$\frac{\pi^{\delta}}{H_{t-1}^{\delta}} \geq \left(\frac{vwL_0\delta}{1+r}\right)^{\frac{\delta}{1-\delta}} \qquad (9.7)$$

Thus the growth rate expressed in Eq. (9.3) is necessarily equal to or higher than that expressed in Eq. (9.2). This means that if government investments in education for a social group are such that they reduce to zero family expenditures on education in this social group, the growth rate of the human capital in this social group is higher than or equal to that of those social groups in which such private expenditures are still positive, if all the parameters and variables in the inequality expressed in Eq. (9.7) are the same for all social groups.

Therefore, when the government sets up an investment in education equal to π_1, so that:

$$\pi_1 > \left(\frac{vwL_0\delta}{1+r}\right)^{\frac{1}{1-\delta}} H_{it-1} \qquad (9.8)$$

for $0 < i \leq v$, but

$$\pi_1 < \left(\frac{vwL_0\delta}{1+r}\right)^{\frac{1}{1-\delta}} H_{it-1} \qquad (9.9)$$

for $i > v$, then the human capital of the v poorest social groups will grow faster than that of the other social groups. Their growth is defined by Eq. (9.3), while other groups have their growth rates defined by Eq. (9.2). This means that the level of per capita stock of human capital of these lower-income social groups will be converging with the per capita stock of human capital of the others. If π_1 is kept fixed over time, eventually the human capital stock of all groups will reach the point at which:

$$\pi_1 = \left(\frac{vwL_0\delta}{1+r}\right)^{\frac{1}{1-\delta}} H_{it-1} \qquad (9.10)$$

Therefore $E = 0$ will prevail, but as a limit of an interior solution, not a corner solution, and the growth rate of the stock of human capital will be determined by Eq. (9.2) thereafter. As this rate is equal to that of all the richest groups, which has $E > 0$, convergence will cease. Each social group that was in the lowest income group will switch its growth rate of the stock of human capital when it reaches this level. So this economy will eventually end up with many social groups with $E = 0$, but as an interior solution, and the others with $E > 0$. All will have the same growth rate of their stock of human capital. After all the social groups with $E = 0$ as a corner solution reach this new level in which $E = 0$, but as an interior solution, the economy will evolve with stability in the relative stocks of human capital among families.

Assume now that the world economy is divided into two countries, A and B, but v, w, L_O, δ, and r are the same in both countries and for all social groups. Initially these two countries are in equilibrium, with $\pi_A = \pi_B = 0$, where π_A and π_B are public expenditures on education in countries A and B, respectively. Under such conditions, the growth rate of the stock of human capital is the same in both countries, and both are determined by Eq. (9.2). If per capita GDP growth rate keeps a constant and equal proportion to the growth rate of per capita stock of human capital in these two countries,[1] they will be also growing at the same rate. Consequently, the proportion between their per capita GDP will be constant.

Suppose that suddenly the government in country A starts to finance education so that $\pi_A = \pi_1 > 0$, while there is still no such government expenditure in country B and $\pi_B = 0$. All social groups in country B would continue to have their stock of human capital moving through a growth rate determined by Eq. (9.2), as before. However, those social groups in country A for which the inequality represented in Eq. (9.8) holds would have an increase in the growth rate of their stock of human capital: it would jump from that defined in Eq. (9.2) to that defined in Eq. (9.3). As a consequence, Eq. (9.4) implies that the growth rate of the total stock of human capital in country A will be faster than that of country B. If the previously assumed relationship between the growth rates of the stock of human capital and per capita GDP holds, country A would grow faster than country B and the proportion between their per capita GDP (Y_B/Y_A) would fall. This fall would cease when the increase in H_{it-1} for all social groups in country A is enough to ensure that the inequality in Eq. (9.8) no longer holds for any of them. Per capita GDP for the two countries would again grow at the same rate thereafter.

The rise of public investments in education in the benchmark countries in the 19th and early 20th centuries and the modest or almost nonexistent educational policies in Brazil in the same period were the causes of the fall in

---

1. The Lucas—Uzawa model as presented by Barro and Sala-i-Martin (2003, Chapter 5, Section 5.2.2) has this characteristic. See also Lucas (1988).

the Brazilian relative per capita stock of human capital and GDP in this period. As these policies matured in these developed countries, with a low increase in π_A thereafter, while Brazil started to make some timid progress in such policies, with a noticeable π_B, the fall in the per capita GDP relationship was eventually halted, with some temporary reversal in some cases, as seen in the previous section.

9.4 ADDITIONAL COMMENTS

Reality certainly was not as radical as described in the previous section, as the discussions relied on an economic model and its consequences to derive the major conclusions. It assumes, firstly, the same social groups, even in different countries. Actually, social groups will most probably have different parameters and variables, whether or not they are in the same country. Nevertheless, the necessary implicit assumption to explain the relative trends among per capita GDPs unveiled in Section 9.2 is that variations among these parameters and variables are not enough to jeopardize the conclusions reached using the assumption that they are the same in all countries and social groups.

Furthermore, governments of the benchmark countries did not promote a single jump in their expenditures on education, as was postulated. They actually made many changes in these investments, and the argument suggested a single leap as a simplification. What is essential for the argument is that the upward changes in these investments were higher than those in Brazil in the period, and affected the human capital accumulation of a higher share of total human capital in these countries than in Brazil.

Also, the expenses of governments on education were not the same for all families, as there are differences among regions, countries, and even levels of education for most of these countries. In the same way, the only relevant fact is that such investments were higher than those by the Brazilian government, and were able to increase the growth rate of the average stock of human capital in their societies for a larger proportion of their total stock of human capital.

The Brazilian government also did not have a uniform and static position on investment in education. The many spheres of government had different responsibilities and engagements in public education. Most, however, engaged in efforts that were far below the involvement found in the benchmark countries. Nevertheless, some differences in effective efforts in public education by authorities generated important regional disparities within the country.[2]

Even the religious orders, which often engaged in education in Brazil, did not promote local public education at levels that resembled those found in the benchmark countries. Most of their efforts focused on private education, which

---

2. See Barros (2011, 2013) for discussions on Brazilian regional disparities and their causes.

was mainly directed towards local elites who were economically self-sufficient. Many of their schools were founded in the 19th century. The costs of these private schools were shared by the students' families, so they were inaccessible to the poor populations with limited resources to bear such costs. There were very few public schools, which limited substantially the access to cheap or free education for the majority of the population.

It is easy to understand why there was no public financing of education in Brazil in the 19th century. From the data in Chapter 7 for England and Wales social classes and their per capita income in 1800, one can see that if government taxed the population at a rate of 5% of their total income to finance schools, and the cost of education per instructor was 1.5 times the per capita income of those people involved in education of youth, it would be possible to have school classes with an average of 34.19 students per instructor, so all income generated through taxes would be spent.[3] In Brazil, this same number of students per instructor would be 113.1, under the educated guesses made for the Brazilian population distribution over the social strata of England and Wales and the hypothesis of arbitrage in the labor market for most professional categories.

If Brazil had the same average number of students per instructor as in England and Wales (34.19), the income tax rate to finance that would be 16.5%, under the hypothesis that Brazilian per capita income in 1800 was as estimated in the last two chapters. If the social classes from clerks and shopworkers to the richest strata spent only 6.14% of their income, they could generate the resources necessary to have a school quality similar to the average one in England and Wales, but only for their own children. Thus a preferred strategy for these social strata would be no public financing of education and they would privately bear this cost for their children in schools with similar average quality as that found in England and Wales. If the necessary costs of tax collection from a large poor population are added to this exercise, the case is even stronger to support the private financing of education by local elites when income is as concentrated as it was in Brazil. Thus if the richest social strata in a country control the government, they would choose this privately financed educational strategy.

The rest of the population in 1800 (social segments whose income was lower than that of clerks and shopworkers), which was 88.5% of the total under the educated guesses forwarded in Chapter 7, would not be able to finance education for their offspring through these commercial schools. As their income was low, they could not invest in teachers with the same skills as those found in British schools. Thus the main strategy was domestic education. Parents spent part of their time educating their children. As they had limited skills, the children would tend to reach this same limit. Books and other

---

3. Each family was supposed to have one parent and one heir.

teaching aids were scarce and expensive. Thus heirs tended to reproduce the skills of their parents, with only very low increases. Productivity of these social strata therefore tended to grow very slowly in Brazil over the 19th and early 20th centuries.

This evolution over the 19th century generated a society in Brazil in which the richest social strata followed European standards in productivity growth arising from education, while the poorest social strata were left outside this trend and relegated to follow the standards of the most backward societies in Africa, Asia, and other parts of Latin America. As they had low skills and little resources for education, their heirs made little progress in their productive abilities. Thus despite the ability of some richer social groups to keep up with the new European standards of education, the majority of the population were unable to do so.

In other words, the extensions of the model from Chapter 5, which were discussed in the last section, grasp the major logic of the true reason for the fall in the relative per capita GDP and stock of human capital. Nonetheless, they are not fully correct, as they simplify some relevant aspects of reality. For example, Brazilian elites increased their educational efforts to avoid falling behind their counterparts in Europe. In the simplifications of the model, their rationale could be seen as a reaction to an increase in v, the expected growth rate of their income, as new possibilities for future income were opened, and so more resources could be allocated to education. The majority of the population, however, did not go through such a change in v and continued to dedicate a low amount of resources to education. The essence of the arguments derived directly from the model remains, even under this and the previously discussed deviations of its assumptions from reality.

9.5 ROLE OF IMMIGRATION TO HALT THE RELATIVE DECLINE

Brazil was the target of considerable international migration in the second half of the 19th century, extending through the first half of the 20th century. Fig. 9.6 shows the yearly share of this immigration in the total change in local population. Between 1887 and 1898 this share was always over 20%; between 1905 and 1914 it was under 10% only in 1907. In addition to Portuguese, there were relevant inflows of Italians, Spanish, Japanese, and Germans. Table 9.2 shows some statistics on these migrations by major sources and in different periods.

Fig. 9.7 shows an estimated share of the descendants and immigrants who entered Brazil after 1852. The growth rate of the number of immigrants and their descendants was supposed to be equal to the natural rate for the whole population, so this should be considered as an approximation rather than the exact data. Data shows that since the end of the 1950s the share of immigrants and their descendants in the Brazilian population has stabilized around 23.4%.

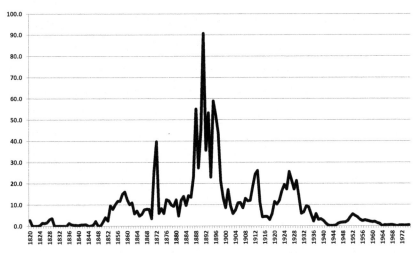

FIGURE 9.6   Share (%) of immigrants in total growth of Brazilian population, 1820—1975. *Calculated from data by IBGE. See discussions for calculation of Brazilian population in Chapter 8.*

TABLE 9.2 Share (%) of Each National Origin in Total Immigration to Brazil for Selected Periods

	Period			
	1884—1900	1901—30	1931—60	1884—1960
Germany	1.8	5.2	4.7	4.0
Spain	11.9	16.2	11.6	13.9
Italy	59.7	19.5	12.8	31.1
Japan	0.0	4.4	12.8	4.7
Portugal	18.6	35.8	38.1	30.7
Russia	2.7	2.8	0.3	2.3
Others	5.2	16.1	19.6	13.3
Total	100.0	100.0	100.0	100.0

IBGE.

The Brazilian per capita GDP and stock of human capital were quite low over the whole period under focus (1800—2013) when compared to European countries and Japan. Most immigration to Brazil was from Europe and Japan within the period for which there is data available on national origin

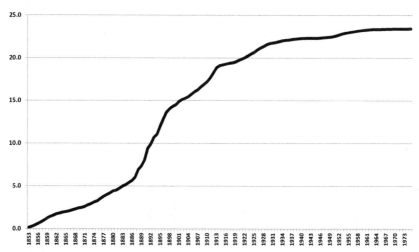

FIGURE 9.7   Share (%) of immigrants and their descendants in Brazilian total population, 1853–1975. *Estimated from data by IBGE.*

Note: Includes Portuguese, Germans, Italians, Spanishes, Japanese, and Russians.

FIGURE 9.8   Share of major sources in Brazilian total immigration, 1884–1960. Note: Includes Portuguese, Germans, Italians, Spanish, Japanese, and Russians. *Calculated from IBGE data.*

(1884–1960), with the exception of 1943, when these countries together account for less than 50% of total immigrants. Fig. 9.8 shows these figures for the whole period (1884–1960). The average per capita human capital stock of immigrants tended to be above the Brazilian average. Consequently, immigration helped to increase the Brazilian per capita stock of human capital, especially in the 20th century and more strongly after 1920.

It is worth mentioning that a large share of incomers to Brazil came through government programs to attract immigrants. As their part in the deal, they had to spend some years in rural areas supplying labor for coffee plantations or expanding colonization of parts of Brazil which were not properly exploited.[4] Thus some of their productive skills were often under-employed in the first years after arrival, as many had more urban skills or were more acquainted with rural technological skills that were not much used in Brazil. This postponed by some years the full impact of their skills on Brazilian per capita GDP. Nevertheless, after the First World War such skills started to have a significant impact on productivity in Brazil. This was an important cause of the end of the relative decay of the Brazilian per capita GDP, which was halted mainly in the first quarter of the 20th century, as seen in Table 9.1.

Furthermore, foreigners migrated to Brazil to improve their lives in relation to what they expected in their home countries. Thus a simple rational expectation assumption would imply that per capita income of the social groups included in Fig. 9.7 should grow proportionally more than that of their country of origin, if there was no change in the income distribution of the home country and their social origins were evenly distributed among the many social strata. Certainly, none of these conditions really holds, but if at least one of them is close enough to reality, this rationale could also explain some of the relative acceleration of the growth in the Brazilian per capita stock of human capital in the first half of the 20th century.

9.6 CONCLUSIONS AND ADDITIONAL COMMENTS

This chapter advances one more step in understanding Brazilian relative backwardness. Particularly, it proposes some hypotheses which could explain why Brazil had a persistent fall in its relative per capita GDP over the 19th and early 20th centuries when compared to a set of benchmark countries. This fall was eventually halted, mostly in the early 20th century, with some stabilization and even some recovery thereafter, depending on the country of comparison.

There were two major sources of these relative dynamics. Firstly, the beginning of the engagement of the public sector in investment in education in the benchmark countries was such that there was accelerated accumulation of human capital in these countries to an extent that was not matched in Brazil, where the public sector had little involvement in education in the 19th century. When it started to engage in this activity, the effort was so modest that it had little effect on the rate of accumulation of local human capital. The second major source of these dynamics, halting the relative decline, was the immi-gration of Europeans and Japanese, which not only increased the local human

---

4. These were mainly in the south of the country.

capital but also pushed up its rate of accumulation. These two changes, together with the maturation of public policies on education in the benchmark countries, led to a halt of this increase in Brazilian relative backwardness in the second and third decades of the 20th century.

It is worth noting once more that the hypothesis to explain the behavior of the evolution of Brazilian relative per capita GDP relies on the idea that the world economy is more closely represented by the assumption that markets are fully open and there are free flows of commodities and factors of production across country borders. Although there are transaction costs, which can arise from natural barriers such as the need to overcome distances or socially imposed barriers like taxes, trade tariffs and quotas, they are not enough to make the assumption of no free flow of commodities and markets a better characterization of reality.

Furthermore, the hypothesis forwarded here does not challenge the modern endogenous growth models found in textbooks.[5] However, it assumes that these models work at a world level. Therefore technical progress and human and physical capital accumulations, as they are generated from individual incentives to accumulate knowledge and these factors of production, are seen as the major determinants of long-term dynamics in the overall world economy.

These endogenous growth models normally assume that local spatial differences are not relevant to determine economic dynamics within a country, as the existence of many goods is important to explain local dynamics and these models normally assume that there is only one good in the economy. The hypothesis of this book relies on this same assumption. Nevertheless, countries frontiers, when they appear, are not seen as relevant enough to demand the introduction of a different treatment of state and county frontiers. In the same way that state borders in the United States are not seen as relevant to understand US growth dynamics in most analyses of its growth, country borders are not seen as relevant to understand world growth dynamics from the standpoint of this book.

Migration of factors of production and trade of goods and services among countries are seen here as relevant mechanisms to generate a reasonable arbitrage among country markets. Nonetheless, the nature of markets is such that there is one factor of production with a very sluggish adjustment process through migration, which is human capital stock. Physical capital moves across country borders to adjust its optimal spatial employment to the local availability of this factor of production.

Before concluding, it is worth stressing that political decisions on education policies were highlighted in this chapter as a major determinant of the accumulation of human capital not only in Brazil but also in other countries.

---

5. Acemoglu (2009), Aghion and Howitt (1998), and Barro and Sala-i-Martin (2003) are examples.

The behavior of families, which has very important consequences for economic development, was seen as responding directly to public policies on education. However, no comment was made on how these policies are determined, despite their crucial role in the upsurge of Brazilian relative backwardness. The next chapters deal with this problem in the search for the fundamental causes of Brazilian relative backwardness.

Chapter 10

Alternative Explanations for Brazilian Relative Backwardness

Chapter Outline

10.1 INTRODUCTION

We have seen that human capital differences arising from colonization and world migration routes of the 19th century shaped populations in Brazil and other ex-European colonies. Some, such as Australia, New Zealand, Canada, and the United States, were the target of more educated people migrating from Europe; consequently their populations engaged in more sophisticated production processes, relying on more efficient methods. This shaped their production structures and led these countries to a higher per capita gross domestic product (GDP) in the late 20th century.

Brazil, like other Latin American countries such as Argentina, Chile, and Uruguay, managed to attract important inflows of Europeans but not enough to build societies with the high human capital level of the previously mentioned colonies. Consequently, its production structure was more adapted to recruit a less-qualified labor force, which was less efficient productively but also would accept lower returns to its labor, as its members had lower embodied human capital.

Two questions arise from these basic historical facts. First, why did Brazil not attract as many educated Europeans as the United States, Canada, Australia, and New Zealand, so it could create a society with proportionally more human capital per inhabitant? Secondly, why did local organization of production not allocate more resources to human capital building so the country could develop faster and catch up with European developed countries over the 20th century?

The religious would give a very simple answer to these questions: it was God's will. The "new religious" also have a very simple answer: institutions explain these differences. Neither of these answers is minimally convincing, so an alternative hypothesis has to be forwarded. Before that, however, this chapter discusses existing hypotheses explaining Brazilian relative backwardness.

The next section presents a simple general framework that could be the starting point of most of the hypotheses raised in the literature. Exposition of these hypotheses becomes easier with this common starting point. Section 10.3 sketches the major Latin American structuralist hypothesis, forwarded by Furtado (1959). Section 10.4 discusses the dependency theory hypothesis, which has Cardoso and Faletto (1970) as its main proponents. Section 10.5 forwards the new institutionalist approach, with a discussion of a particular institutionalist hypothesis introduced by Faoro in 1958 before the recent institutionalist developments. Section 10.6 summarizes the major conclusions and presents some additional comments.

10.2 GENERAL FRAMEWORK TO UNDERSTAND ALTERNATIVE VIEWS EXPLAINING BRAZILIAN RELATIVE BACKWARDNESS

To understand growth and development, the literature on development normally works with a production function such as:

$$Y_i = A_i K_i^{\alpha} H_i^{\delta} N_i^{\beta} L_i^{1-\alpha-\beta-\delta} \tag{10.1}$$

where Y_i is GDP in country i, while A_i is a productivity parameter. K_i, H_i, N_i, and L_i stand for physical capital, human capital, natural resources, and labor, respectively, all employed in country i. The Greek letters are parameters that are specific for each country, although it is not uncommon in international comparisons to assume they are constant over all countries. These parameters are not negative and are normally all taken as smaller than 1. Additionally, $(\alpha + \beta + \delta) < 1$.

Of course a Cobb–Douglas-type production function was used here as a simplification, but it is not necessarily the starting point for most development theories, at least explicitly. Natural resources are also included as a factor of production, as in Chapter 4, but are often disregarded in development analysis under the assumption that they do not bid and do not accumulate. Chapter 4 argues that this is a simplistic assumption, as new infrastructure investments, technologies, and consumer preferences can change substantially the availability of potentially exploitable natural resources.

From this production function, the level of development of a country tends to be seen as proportional to the GDP per unit of labor. Therefore, a country is more developed the higher is:

$$\frac{Y_i}{L_i} = A_i \left(\frac{K_i}{L_i}\right)^{\alpha} \left(\frac{H_i}{L_i}\right)^{\delta} \left(\frac{N_i}{L_i}\right)^{\beta} \tag{10.2}$$

The output per unit of labor can be transformed into per capita GDP, the most commonly used statistics, if the labor force is taken as $L = \phi P$, where P is population and ϕ is labor participation rate. Substitution of this equation in Eq. (10.2) yields:

$$\frac{Y_i}{P_i} = A_i' \left(\frac{K_i}{P_i}\right)^{\alpha} \left(\frac{H_i}{P_i}\right)^{\delta} \left(\frac{N_i}{P_i}\right)^{\beta} \tag{10.2'}$$

where $A' = A\phi^{1-\alpha-\delta-\beta}$. It is worth noting that ϕ depends on population growth rate, mortality rate, and cultural factors, and can also vary with institutional arrangements in a society. As with all other Greek letters in this model, this can vary over time.

If small letters represent capital letters in per capita terms, so, for example, $y = (Y/P)$, this equation could be expressed as:

$$y_i = A_i' k_i^{\alpha} h_i^{\delta} n_i^{\beta} \tag{10.2''}$$

It is worth mentioning that other ingredients of development not explicitly included in the production function, such as culture, can be incorporated in the production function within the productivity parameter A. The stock of infrastructure is better incorporated as part of the stock of physical capital. All dimensions of development outside per capita GDP, such as level of freedom of a population, which was stressed by Sen (1999), are not included in this simple representation. Under the current view there is a unique correspondence between development level and per capita GDP, which is not necessarily correct.[1]

Using this simple framework, it is possible to understand alternative development models that are relevant to the current discussion on Brazilian development and the causes of its relative backwardness.

10.3 LATIN AMERICAN STRUCTURALIST HYPOTHESIS

The Latin American structuralist hypothesis was first proposed by Prebisch (1949) as a general hypothesis to explain why Latin American countries lagged behind European and North American economies. An in-depth study of Brazilian development using this proposal was made by Furtado (1959), and it has been the major hypothesis explaining Brazilian relative development since then, although many local well-trained local economists nowadays disagree with it.

The major hypothesis is that Latin American countries specialized in the world market in the production of primary commodities, while they imported mainly industrial goods. This had odd consequences for these countries. Firstly, there was a deterioration of the net barter terms of trade for primary commodities, and this led to a constant need to increase their production and export to get a given amount of industrial goods in exchange, regardless of any correspondent change in relative productivity that could motivate such change in relative prices. This made Latin American countries relatively poorer over time.

Differences in market structures among the two set of goods, with industrial goods working under monopolistic competition while primary commodities worked under perfect competition, justified such behavior. Stronger labor unions in developed countries forced relatively higher gains in wages when productivity increased, but market structure allowed these cost increases to be incorporated in prices. Differences in demand elasticities between these two types of goods could also generate this tendency to deterioration of the net barter terms of trade.[2]

These arguments were combined with others, such as that local elites in underdeveloped countries would copy the consumption profile of elites in rich nations. The consequence was that the former ended up with proportionally less savings to accumulate physical capital; it also reduced the relative growth rate of these countries and forced them to lag behind.[3]

---

1. Under such assumptions, Qatar and the United Arab Emirates are more developed than the United States, Norway, and Iceland, according to 2013 data from the Conference Board Total Economy database (extracted in October 2014). In the same way, Kuwait is more developed than the United Kingdom, Denmark, and France.
2. These arguments are from Prebisch (1949).
3. Notice that this argument assumes there is no international free flow of capital.

Furtado (1959) applied this theory to the particular case of Brazil. He stressed that in all primary commodity exporting cycles—sugar, precious minerals (gold and diamonds, mainly), coffee, and rubber—there was always expansion with initial high profitability and high growth rates, but eventually a fall in world market prices led to crisis in the economy that was working around this major commodity export.[4] According to him, only the coffee cycle generated demand that could justify industrialization, and this was the background to the Brazilian catch-up.

Given this particular circumstance in which demand was so high that it could justify some industrialization, policies further promoting local industry would be the passport to overcome Brazilian relative backwardness. This transition, however, would generate many imbalances in the economy that had to be properly dealt by public policies, otherwise the catch-up would be delayed.

It is argued in Chapter 4 that the aggregated production function expressed in Eq. (10.2″) emerges from the grouping of individual production functions in the many firms in the economy. Furthermore, it is argued in Chapter 3 that the sectoral structure of any local economy is determined by its availability of human capital, which is exogenously determined by its accumulation rules, as discussed in Chapter 5. Structuralists assumed that the availability of labor was exogenously given in each country and differences in average per capita human capital were determined by the demand of physical capital. It is important to note that structuralists did not greatly take into account the role of human capital, as all developments related to the role of this factor of production did not exist when they proposed their major ideas, and its role only was stressed by economic theory in the last few decades.

Normally Furtado and other structuralists assumed that:

$$h_i = f(k_i) \tag{10.3}$$

where $f(.)$ represents a function of the argument, k_i in this case. This function is such that $f'(k) > 0$, or in words, h grows automatically when k grows. In Furtado's view, whenever firms start to need better-qualified workers, they invest on training and press governments to provide better education and training opportunities.

Structuralists also took the natural resources availability as given, but its abundance would lead to a higher propensity to specialize in primary commodities' export, so they viewed with suspicion abundant availability of this factor of production. Normally, in their view, availability of natural resources would lead to aggregated production functions with high β proportionally to α. But an economy would develop faster if it had proportionately higher α.

---

4. In the case of gold and diamonds, the fall actually was in production due to exhaustion of reserves.

To understand this argument, take the natural logarithm of Eq. (10.2″) and its derivative with respect to time:

$$\frac{\dot{y}}{y} = \frac{\dot{A}}{A} + \alpha\frac{\dot{k}}{k} + \delta\frac{\dot{h}}{h} + \beta\frac{\dot{n}}{n} \tag{10.4}$$

where the dot over a variable indicates that it is its derivative with respect to time. If a linear form for Eq. (10.3) is taken as correct, Eq. (10.4) could be rewritten as:

$$\frac{\dot{y}}{y} = \frac{\dot{A}}{A} + (\alpha + \delta)\frac{\dot{k}}{k} + \beta\frac{\dot{n}}{n} \tag{10.4'}$$

As they did not assume a constant return to scale, $(\alpha + \beta + \delta) < 1$ would not necessarily be true. Nonetheless, they still took this sum as given. Consequently, the higher β is, the lower tends to be α, as δ was not relevant in their arguments. As the stock of natural resources was given, the last term on the right side of Eq. (10.4′) would be nil. Thus for a given growth rate of total factor productivity (TFP) of A, the higher α is, the higher the output growth rate. Furthermore, they postulated that:

$$\frac{\dot{A}}{A} = g(\alpha) \tag{10.5}$$

where $g'(\alpha)>0$. This assumption strengthened even further the relationship between α and the per capita GDP growth rate.

Another important assumption was that industry had higher α than other sectors, thus promotion of industry would increase its share in total output and consequently would raise the average α for the whole economy. This is why fostering domestic industry was seen as the major development policy.

The fact that Brazil had abundant natural resources in the colonial era created incentives to establish primary commodities' enterprises in its territory. They directed most of their output to exports to Europe at the time. Under Furtado's hypothesis, this specialization limited productivity and capital accumulation, so k was low.

Altogether, this theory implies that Brazil was poor because it had relatively lower k and α than developed countries. It is worth mentioning that an analysis of Brazil's history is necessary to explain why k remained low over time. Primary commodity specialization and deterioration of the net barter terms of trade were the major causes of such low values for k and α. The low domestic saving rates are also sometimes given as an argument, because of standards of local elite consumption in copying the profile of their counterparts in developed countries.

An important feature of this model is that market forces alone would generate the relative backwardness of underdeveloped countries, instead of promoting any tendency to convergence of development levels. At the time this conclusion had a very important impact on mainstream ideas prevailing in American and European universities, as the idea of eventual convergence was dominant. This made the Argentinian economist Raul Prebisch a prestigious scholar around the world in the second half of the 20th century.

The analysis of Brazilian economic history by Furtado (1959) introduced one more feature of this model to explain the historical evolution of the Brazilian economy. His view was that not only industrial economies worked in cycles, but primary exporting countries also faced business cycles. These were very important to understand the industrialization of these countries and why there were inner forces in the dynamics of their economies that would lead to overcoming the primary exporting specialization and the fragilities it generates for economic performance.

Furtado argued that when there was an expansion of an economic cycle based on the growth of exports of primary commodities, normally it was such that prices and profitability of activities were high in the exporting countries. Nevertheless, markets for these commodities would eventually reach a saturation point in the demand from industrial economies. After this, demand growth would slow down and prices normally would fall.

Underdeveloped economies would have increased their per capita income over the period of expansion of their exports, so their consumption of industrial goods would increase during this period because of their prices and income elasticities of demand. When prices and/or volumes of exports started to fall, import capacity for industrial goods faced foreign currency shortage and/or real price increases in underdeveloped countries. As most of the economies exporting primary commodities had few exported goods, this crisis in their exports led to local currency devaluations and imported industrial goods would become relatively more expensive. This would foster local competition for these goods on the domestic markets.

In each of these crises, local industry added new goods to its portfolio, increasing its diversification and scale of production. Eventually, domestic industry had grown so much that investments in its production capacity would start to lead local businesses cycles. Then the model would start to be overcome by its own internal evolution. After this, primary exports would allow the import of intermediaries and capital goods, although they would no longer be the major determinant of business cycles. Only when the country had its own intermediary and capital goods industry would it reach the economic maturity of the industrial economies.

Public policies could be used to accelerate this process of economic maturation. Exchange rates could be affected by such policies, so they would boost local industry and its local integration, even promoting the development of the capital goods industry. Import tariffs or any other kind of restrictions to imports could also protect domestic industry and enhance its competitiveness, so it would grow and anticipate the maturity of the domestic economy.

All these policies would increase α (in the language of the previous section) and the equilibrium growth rate of per capita GDP, as a consequence of Eqs. (10.4′) and (10.5). Brazilian governments did not manage to adopt such policies efficiently, so the country did not overcome its relative backwardness.

10.4 DEPENDENCY THEORY

The trust in markets' ability to generate reasonable outcomes was low when Latin American structuralists forwarded their model, presenting a theory arguing that market forces would lead to underdevelopment in some countries. A corollary of this approach was that markets did not work properly and governments should intervene in the economy to correct the market outcome to a more adequate dynamic equilibrium. Governments were seen as able to speed up the catch-up if they adopted adequate policies to promote industrialization.

Studies on the history of Latin American economies have shown that government interventions always happened, but often did not affect the equilibrium in the "right" direction; rather, they increased further primary commodities' specialization and more underdevelopment. Therefore, some researchers in the region started to ask a simple question: why do public policies not promote industry and reduce this primary commodity specialization if governments can work in this direction?

Studies from sociology forwarded what was called dependency theory. According to this view, local governments or elites contribute to the continuity of specialization in primary commodities because they benefit from such specialization, even if their attitudes retard development of their countries.[5] Part of the local elite made alliances with foreign companies engaged in industry or international trade, to strength economic relationships through policies that would restrict local industrialization and economic development.

These theories, however, had the same underlying economic model as Latin American structuralism. Such political or social relationships would strength primary commodities' exports and lower saving rates and capital accumulation domestically. Multinational companies contribute to local industrialization, but also drain local savings and end up reducing local potential growth. Thus the economic transmission channels from market dynamics to underdevelopment were similar to those forwarded by structuralists. These theories added explanations for the slow growth and the persistence of underdevelopment.

The contribution of dependency theory was to identify the incentives of local elites and/or governments to foster this model, even when it showed signs

---

5. The most important contribution on this theory was introduced by Cardoso and Falleto (1970), although Frank (1967) also made an important contribution. Both studies focused on Latin America but also narrowed their analysis to the Brazilian case.

of crisis. Particularly important in this hypothesis for the ideas forwarded in this book is the recognition that agents place their own interest ahead of the social interest. Their own interest is often shared with other agents from their same social classes. Under this hypothesis, there was a conflict of interest between segments of the local elites, who controlled the state, and the best path for development catch-up.

Figs. 10.1 and 10.2 show the internal logic of both theories. Arrows represent causal relationships, and differences between them become easily understood in these figures. The same causal relationships going from historical circumstance to stagnation, slow growth, and underdevelopment running through economic specialization is found in both Figs. 10.1 and 10.2. Nonetheless, there is a second causal chain in the dependency theory, which goes from social classes emerging from the original economic structure to public policies, and from these to stagnation, slow growth, and underdevelopment.

Under this theory, Brazilian relative backwardness arose from an initial colonial relationship that set up initial primary commodity exploitation of Brazilian lands and created a society adjusted for such production. This

FIGURE 10.1   Internal logic of structuralist model.

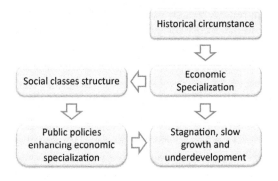

FIGURE 10.2   Internal logic of dependency model.

economic environment generated social classes that interacted among themselves and with sectors in other countries, so policies strengthening the determinants of underdevelopment would prevail and contribute to their reproduction thereafter.

10.5 NEW INSTITUTIONALISTS

The recent literature on growth and development has restated that there is no relevant absolute convergence of per capita GDP among nations. Proportional differences in development levels could exist forever, or at least for very long periods, if differences in some features of these countries are not narrowed.[6] Although this could be seen as a support to some Latin American structuralists'[7] or dependency theorists' conclusions, new theories stressing other determinants of growth and development claimed the empirical support forwarded by these conclusions.[8]

The role of human capital accumulation was seen as the major source of no convergence among development levels of nations.[9] This hypothesis had both theoretical and empirical support, and the problem became to explain why human capital accumulated faster in some countries than in others in some periods, and there was no market mechanism narrowing these differences thereafter. Under this view, physical capital accumulation became secondary, as would be the case if there were reasonable free flow of capital among nations, as postulated in Chapter 3.

More recent research has stressed the role of TFP as a major source of differences in per capita GDP among nations, as mentioned in Chapter 4.[10] This hypothesis, together with the role of human capital differences, is seen as important support to the role of differences in institutions in growth and relative development. Alongside theoretical and empirical research by Acemoglu and his associates,[11] this strengthens the hypothesis that the nature of institutions is the major source of differences in per capita GDP among nations.

Although this theory has not been recently applied with its new concepts to explain Brazilian relative backwardness, Faoro (2001)[12] forwarded a hypothesis using a similar theory for the particular case of Brazil. His approach, however, drew on Max Weber's theories on bureaucracy and its role in

---

6. See for example Rodrik (2011).
7. Not all of them share the hypothesis of Furtado that there is an internal dynamics that eventually will lead to its overcoming.
8. Spolaori and Wacziarg (2013) give a survey of these more recent theories.
9. This was initially stressed by Lucas (1988) from a theoretical standpoint. For a recent empirical study see Barro (2012).
10. See Caselli (2005) and Hsieh and Klenow (2010) for important surveys.
11. See, for example, Acemoglu et al. (2001, 2002, 2005) and Acemoglu and Robinson (2012).
12. The first edition of his book was published in 1958.

development. Although it is a hypothesis that institutions are the cause of Brazilian relative backwardness, its review is postponed until after a general argument on how institutions could have determined Brazilian relative backwardness, as postulated by Acemoglu et al. (2005), is discussed.

The most commonly used definition of institutions comes from North (1990, p. 3): "Institutions are the rules of the game in a society or, more formally, are the humanly devised constraints that shape human interaction." Although very generic, normally institutions include the laws, formal and informal rules, and public policies that affect the shape of economic agents' interactions. In the words of Acemoglu and Johnson (2005, p. 950), institutions are "the social, economic, legal, and political organization of a society." It is often stressed that the structure of property rights and their protection and the strength of market mechanisms are the major institutions that matter. These can be seen as "property rights institutions" and "contracting institutions," respectively.[13]

Before proceeding to the arguments of the new institutionalists, it is worth obtaining the marginal conditions for equilibrium in domestic markets for the factors of production in an economy where the production function is expressed as in Eq. (10.1). They are:

$$\alpha \frac{Y}{K} = r \tag{10.6}$$

$$\delta \frac{Y}{H} = \rho \tag{10.7}$$

$$\beta \frac{Y}{N} = \tau \tag{10.8}$$

$$(1 - \alpha - \delta - \beta)\frac{Y}{L} = w \tag{10.9}$$

where r, ρ, and τ stand for the rate of returns to physical and human capitals and natural resources, respectively, while w stands for the wage rate. The other parameters and variables are as defined earlier.

These four equations can be used to get equations for K, H, N, and L as a function of their return rates, output, and parameters. But instead of Eq. (10.9), the fact that $L = \phi P$ is used to substitute for L and the variables are all redefined in per capita terms. Then all the expressions for the amounts of factors of production can be substituted back in Eq. (10.1). This yields:

$$y = A'^{\frac{1}{1-\alpha-\beta-\delta}}\left(\frac{\alpha}{r}\right)^{\frac{\alpha}{1-\alpha-\beta-\delta}}\left(\frac{\delta}{\rho}\right)^{\frac{\delta}{1-\alpha-\beta-\delta}}\left(\frac{\beta}{\tau}\right)^{\frac{\beta}{1-\alpha-\beta-\delta}} \tag{10.10}$$

---

13. Concepts are from Acemoglu and Johnson (2005).

For two economies, i and b, it is possible to get the proportion of their per capita GDP, y, when Eq. (10.10) is used, as:

$$\frac{y_i}{y_b} = \frac{A_i'^{\frac{1}{1-\alpha_i-\beta_i-\delta_i}} \left(\frac{\alpha_i}{r_i}\right)^{\frac{\alpha_i}{1-\alpha_i-\beta_i-\delta_i}} \left(\frac{\delta_i}{\rho_i}\right)^{\frac{\delta_i}{1-\alpha_i-\beta_i-\delta_i}} \left(\frac{\beta_i}{\tau_i}\right)^{\frac{\beta_i}{1-\alpha_i-\beta_i-\delta_i}}}{A_b'^{\frac{1}{1-\alpha_b-\beta_b-\delta_b}} \left(\frac{\alpha_b}{r_b}\right)^{\frac{\alpha_b}{1-\alpha_b-\beta_b-\delta_b}} \left(\frac{\delta_b}{\rho_b}\right)^{\frac{\delta_b}{1-\alpha_b-\beta_b-\delta_b}} \left(\frac{\beta_b}{\tau_b}\right)^{\frac{\beta_b}{1-\alpha_b-\beta_b-\delta_b}}}$$ (10.11)

Define the surrogated per capita GDP of country i as:

$$y_i^* = A_i'^{\frac{1}{1-\alpha_b-\beta_b-\delta_b}} \left(\frac{\alpha_b}{r_i}\right)^{\frac{\alpha_b}{1-\alpha_b-\beta_b-\delta_b}} \left(\frac{\delta_b}{\rho_i}\right)^{\frac{\delta_b}{1-\alpha_b-\beta_b-\delta_b}} \left(\frac{\beta_b}{\tau_i}\right)^{\frac{\beta_b}{1-\alpha_b-\beta_b-\delta_b}}$$ (10.12)

where it represents the output that would be observed in country i if all parameters in its production function were as those in country b, but the prices for factor of production and TFP were those actually prevailing within its economy.

Therefore, the proportion in Eq. (10.11) can be expressed as:

$$\frac{y_i}{y_b} = \frac{y_i}{y_i^*} \cdot \frac{y_i^*}{Y_b} = V_1 \cdot V_2 \cdot V_3 \cdot V_4$$ (10.13)

where,

$$V_1 = \left(\frac{A_i'}{A_b'}\right)^{\frac{1}{1-\alpha_b-\beta_b-\delta_b}}$$ (10.14)

$$V_2 = \left(\frac{r_b}{r_i}\right)^{\frac{\alpha_b}{1-\alpha_b-\beta_b-\delta_b}} \left(\frac{\rho_b}{\rho_i}\right)^{\frac{\delta_b}{1-\alpha_b-\beta_b-\delta_b}} \left(\frac{\tau_b}{\tau_i}\right)^{\frac{\beta_b}{1-\alpha_b-\beta_b-\delta_b}}$$ (10.15)

$$V_3 = \frac{\left(\alpha_i^{\alpha_i} \beta_i^{\beta_i} \delta_i^{\delta_i}\right)^{\frac{1}{1-\alpha_i-\beta_i-\delta_i}}}{\left(\alpha_b^{\alpha_b} \beta_b^{\beta_i} \delta_b^{\delta_i}\right)^{\frac{1}{1-\alpha_b-\beta_b-\delta_b}}}$$ (10.16)

$$V_4 = \frac{\left(r_i^{\alpha_b} \rho_i^{\delta_b} \tau_i^{\beta_b} A_i'\right)^{\frac{1}{1-\alpha_b-\beta_b-\delta_b}}}{\left(r_i^{\alpha_i} \rho_i^{\delta_i} \tau_i^{\beta_i} A_i'\right)^{\frac{1}{1-\alpha_i-\beta_i-\delta_i}}}$$ (10.17)

V_1 is a term representing the relative TFP in the two countries, V_2 represents the relative equilibrium in the factor prices in these countries, V_3 represents strictly structural differences between the two economies, and V_4 represents the structural differences but conditional on the levels of factor prices and TFP in country i.

The new institutionalist school stresses that differences in per capita GDP arise mainly from V_1, differences in TFP, and V_2, differences in equilibrium returns to factors of production. Nevertheless, some new institutionalist approaches point to some role for V_3 and V_4, structural differences in the economies.[14] Each of these arguments is now discussed.

10.5.1 Differences in Total Factor Productivity

Differences in TFP arise when $A_i' \neq A_b'$. There are many possible sources for variations in A_i' across countries, but the list includes the most commonly mentioned.

1. Differences in incentives for research and development and technological innovation incorporated by local firms. Tax systems and *protection for intellectual property rights* are among the potential causes for such differences.
2. Differences in infrastructure availability, which are a consequence of government role and rules to determine infrastructure investment, *protection for property rights*, and *working of financial markets*, among other possible sources.
3. Differences in *contract enforcement*. Countries with higher and more efficient contract enforcement institutional frameworks allow firms to engage in more efficient economic relationships, which they would avoid if there were no such protections.

These are the sources of what I term the *TFP transmission channel from institutions to development or growth.*

10.5.2 Differences in Equilibrium Return to Capital

Despite the belief that there is international arbitrage in capital markets, some institutionalist approaches argue that the asset returns risk perception by international agents differs among countries. Thus markets reach an equilibrium in which those countries whose risk perceptions are higher would end up with higher rates of return to physical capital. Comparing countries i and b, the higher the relative risk perception in country b, the higher will be the proportion between r_b and r_i. According to Eqs. (10.13)–(10.17), this implies that country b would be relatively less developed. This relatively higher risk perception by international agents would arise from local institutional fragilities, such as lower protection for private property rights and poorer institutional arrangements for contract enforcements.

These are the major sources of what I term the *risk perception transmission channel from institutions to development or growth.*

One important result would be that equilibrium would emerge in which poorer countries have relatively lower stock of physical capital per capita.

---

14. See Rodrik (2011) for an example.

Thus the explanation of Brazilian relative backwardness when compared to the so-called industrialized economies could be observationally equivalent to the structuralist or dependency theory explanations of this particular item, if this relatively higher risk hypothesis is the only consequence of institutional differences.

10.5.3 Differences in Equilibrium Return to Human Capital

It can be seen in Eqs. (10.13) and (10.15) that the higher the domestic return to human capital, ρ_b, when compared to this same return in country i, ρ_i, the lower will be the relative per capita GDP in country b. Unlike the international flow of physical capital, most institutionalists, albeit implicitly, assume there is no international arbitrage in human capital markets. International migration restrictions would justify such approach, although rigorously they are also disregarding the factor price equalization theorem when they assume that $\rho_b \neq \rho_i$. It is noted in Chapter 3 that this theorem only holds under particular assumptions, which are not necessarily true. This probably is the source of the abandonment of the hypothesis.

If there is no international arbitrage through human capital flow across borders and no factor price equalization, the return to human capital is determined by domestic accumulation of this factor of production when compared to the relative accumulation of other factors, physical capital being the major one. Thus institutional arrangements that limit the relative accumulation of human capital are an alternative source of differences in per capita GDP, according this view.

Inadequate educational public policy, as there are positive returns to scale in this factor's accumulation, is normally the most stressed source of limits on human capital building within a country. Some cultural determinants could also play a relevant role, such as family and religious evaluation of female access to education. Institutions that do not create appropriate incentives to human capital accumulation are also often cited as an important source of low accumulation of this factor of production, as are restrictive opportunities to enhance future income from personal skills and restrictions to private property.[15] These institutional arrangements determining relative human capital accumulations are the *human capital transmission channel from institutions to development or growth*.

10.5.4 Differences in Equilibrium Return to Natural Resources

Natural resources are not prompted to arbitrage in international markets through migration, as they remain within the territory of countries. Relative prices of commodities traded in the world market could force their returns to

---

15. See for example Acemoglu and Robinson (2012, Chapter 3), comparing the two Koreas.

equalization through the logic of the factor price equalization theorem. Nevertheless, as mentioned, this theorem only works under special conditions. This fact probably justifies why rules on exploitation of natural resources are often included among institutional sources of relative backwardness.

Some economists argue that differences in the return of such exploitations can also justify relative backwardness. Restrictions in such investments raise the domestic return τ_b in relation to τ_i in alternative countries. It is also possible that low protection for property rights could force market equilibrium to generate high τ_b to justify natural resource exploitation. This would increase the relative per capita GDP in country i when compared to country b. Thus the institutional framework generating restrictions to exploitation of natural resources or the demand for a premium on their domestic exploitation is *the natural resource transmission channel from institutions to development or growth*.

10.5.5 Disparities Emerging From Productive Structural Differences

The parameters involved in V_1 and V_2, whose role of their differences on development are stressed in Eqs. (10.16) and (10.17), can generate inequalities in per capita GDP among countries. Most institutionalist approaches disregard this source of per capita income disparities, although some have stressed it.[16] International trade and fiscal policies, as well as rent-seeking lobbies, could bias the sectoral distribution of domestic productive resource allocation. This would affect the parameters of the aggregated production functions, which are represented by α, β, and δ for the two countries b and i in the equations presented earlier. Some of these biases could reduce the relative equilibrium of per capita GDP of a particular country in the comparison expressed in Eq. (10.13).

The policy framework affecting these parameters can be considered as the *structural determinant transmission channel from institutions to development or growth*.

10.5.6 Disparities Emerging From Social Determination of the Labor Participation Rate

Although economic incentives help determine the labor participation rate in the population, ϕ, embodied in A' in Eqs. (10.13) and (10.14), there are cultural and other social determinants of ϕ. Child labor rules, female labor market engagement, and retiring ages are some of the determinants of ϕ, which are governed by institutional rules and social values. Labor market institutions, such as those shaping unemployment benefits and dismissal costs, are also important to determine ϕ. Normally most of the cultural determinants and

16. See, for example, Rodrik (2011).

social values are embodied in labor market institutions, so it is a good approximation to argue that labor market institutions determine ϕ.

The proportion between ϕ_i and ϕ_b is a relevant determinant of the proportion between per capita GDP within two countries. The higher this proportion, the higher will be y_i/y_b. Thus labor market institutions also help in explaining the relative per capita backwardness of a country. This source of differences in per capita GDP can be termed the *labor participation rate transmission channel from institutions to development or growth.*

10.5.7 Dynamics and Static Comparisons

Most concepts in the new institutionalist approach were built from economic growth theory rather than from development, so the ideas have roots in dynamic models. All the exposition hitherto has relied upon a static system of equations, including Eqs. (10.13)−(10.17). This was a simplifying device to make exposition easier. At any moment an economy always has a steady-state dynamic path to which it is converging and a dynamic transitional path, which includes all the states between today and the moment this economy will reach its steady-state path. Of course, before the economy actually reaches its steady-state path, shocks will move this dynamic path to other positions and the economy normally never reaches its steady-state path.

Fig. 10.3 shows an example of an economy whose current state places it at point a, where the natural logarithm of its per capita GDP is $\ln y_0$. This economy will follow its dynamic transitional path I up to the point where it reaches the steady-state path I. If there is a shock to this economy which

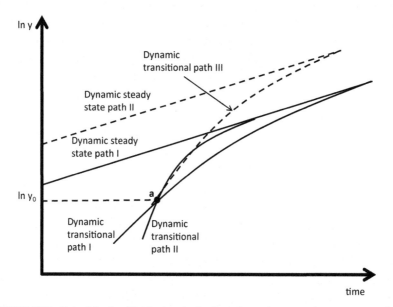

FIGURE 10.3   Potential role of institutions in the dynamic steady-state and convergence paths.

moves its steady-state path to the dynamic steady-state path II, it would also move its evolution to the dynamic transitional path III. It is possible that the shock does not affect its dynamic steady-state path but only its dynamic transitional path, which could change from the dynamic transitional path I to dynamic transitional path II. In this case it will grow faster and also reach the dynamic steady-state path I earlier.

Most institutionalists argue that better institutions move up the steady-state path of an economy, so it starts growing faster when institutions improve. Nevertheless, it is possible that the immediate short-term impact is that growth slows down, although it rises again over time. This possibility, not shown in Fig. 10.3, would have more complicated transitional dynamics than those shown in Fig. 10.3. It is not uncommon to face arguments that the transitional dynamics also speed up when there are institutional improvements, which would move the equilibrium of the dynamic transitional path from I to III and the dynamic steady-state path from I to II.

10.5.8 Determinants of Institutions

The role of institutions in shaping economic growth and development in this approach is so important that it becomes crucial to explain how institutions appear and evolve temporally. Acemoglu et al. (2005) dedicate part of their presentation of this theory to answering these questions. They identify historical origins for institutions in any country. For ex-European colonies, their nature and individual incentives in the colonial period were the major determinants of the quality of their original institutions.

These authors also present a theory on the way an initial institutional arrangement evolves over the years. The essence of their argument is shown in Fig. 10.4. In their view, political institutions and the distribution of resources determine the political power in a society, both *de jure* (as defined by laws) and de facto (as actually prevailing). The exercise of political power determines current economic institutions in this society and future political institutions (represented as $t + 1$ in Fig. 10.4). Current economic institutions determine current economic performance and the future distribution of resources.

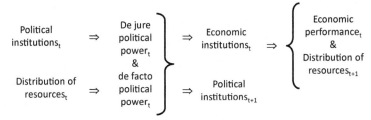

FIGURE 10.4 Determination of political and economic institutions. *Acemoglu, D., Johnson, S., & Robinson, J. (2005). Institutions as a fundamental cause of long-run growth. In P. Aghion, & S. N. Durlauf (Eds.), Handbook of economic growth: Vol. 1A, (pp. 385–472). Amsterdam and Boston: Elsevier, North-Holland.*

As current political power is the determinant of economic and political institutions in the future, an institutional framework tends to be reproduced over the years. Only shocks that move de facto political power would change this vicious circle.

Technological shocks could also change the distribution of resources in the future, given a set of economic institutions, and then change future de facto political power. This would introduce potential changes in political institutions that would alter future economic institutions, and again the distribution of resources. This society, then, would be under a process of institutional change, which could either increase or decrease future growth and relative performance.

10.5.9 Faoro's Institutional Hypothesis Explaining Brazilian Backwardness

Using Max Weber's framework, Faoro (2001)[17] relied on Brazil's Portuguese colonial background to explain the initial set-up of Brazilian institutions. According to Weber, the circumstances of Portuguese history, with the state emerging from wars to expel the Saracens and keep the Spanish out of Portugal, gave much power and property to the kings, who then built a patrimonial state.[18] The extent of their possessions was such that they created a reasonable bureaucracy of control and set up important channels of direct contact with the majority of the population, such as legal and military structures and tax collection mechanisms. Thus, according to Faoro, there was not a typical feudal structure in Portugal, as in North and Central European countries. The king was more powerful over the whole society, and did not transfer rights of justice, military power, and tax collection to the lords.

The control of the economy through the patrimonial logic was extended to merchant and industrial activities, which needed the king's authorization to flourish; consequently, those engaged in such activities always had obligations to the monarch. In this situation the bureaucracy surrounding the king became very powerful, as its members were the instruments of power of the king. Furthermore, the extent of patrimonial relationships was such that the bureaucracy placed between the king and the population grew in size and became a social class itself, with common interests in state control and privileged access to its handouts. It also gained an internal logic of reproduction through personal relations, as its expansion depended on trust, and the monarch did not have access to so many people who deserved his direct trust.

These power relationships of the patrimonial state, built initially around the king, were extended to Brazil as a Portuguese colony. They evolved over

---

17. The first edition of this book (1958) contained the essence of the hypothesis.
18. See Weber (1968, Vol. 2, Chapter 12). This is a translation of the German fourth edition from 1956.

Portuguese and Brazilian histories, but never lost their essence. In the Brazilian case, even after independence (1822) and the republic proclamation (1889), when the power of the Brazilian emperor ceased, this power structure was not challenged. Such relationships continued to exist under the logic that Weber (1968, Chapter 2) called the patrimonial state, with no direct dependency on the king, but with the head of state at the center of a bureaucracy that reproduced itself over time. The same kind of relationship was replicated throughout the power structure, starting from the central government and running to local governments in the counties.

This political structure, plus an accommodation of interests of the local elites, determined the political power, both *de jure* and de facto, which was in the hands of bureaucrats. The political power determined both the economic institutions and the persistence of political institutions in the future. The economic institutions determined the economic performance, according to Acemoglu et al.'s framework, and the persistence of the distribution of resources.

The economic institutions built under this dynamic equilibrium meant a share of local resources was appropriated by the local bureaucracy. Its size, often disproportionately high salaries, and the necessary corruption to overcome obstacles to production made this share considerable. In addition, the bureaucracy forced firms to spend a large share of their scarce resources working to get through the excessive bureaucratic steps necessary to achieve their production and investments. These impacts of the patrimonial state led to a relatively low total factor productivity, or A_b in the model of the previous sections.

Furthermore, the bureaucracy created an adverse selection of firms. The economically most efficient firms were not necessarily those that were productively most efficient, but the most efficient at overcoming the obstacles imposed by the bureaucracy. As a result, the TFP did not rise efficiently over the years and, consequently, at any specific moment A_b would be relatively lower than that existing in countries without this patrimonial state.

The reproduction of the bureaucracy demanded the existence of many laws and rules governing economic activities. The necessary effort to get through all of them reduced investment, as many new investments became unprofitable because of this excess of costly steps to be taken. The consequence was that Brazil lagged behind other countries with less bureaucracy because of shortage in the per capita stocks of human and physical capitals. Therefore, in the language of previous explanations, Brazil lagged behind not only because of a high V_1, arising from local low TFP, but also because of high V_2 due to the high r_b and ρ_b arising from relatively lower stocks of human and physical capitals.

10.6 CONCLUSIONS AND ADDITIONAL COMMENTS

This chapter summarizes the major hypotheses commonly used to explain Brazilian relative backwardness. The structuralist hypothesis forwarded by Furtado (1959) is by far the most important one among local economists in the last half-century. His ideas were rooted in hypotheses that challenged mainstream economic theory, mainly proposed by Prebisch (1949). They incorporate the idea that there is increasing return to scale in industry and no arbitrage in capital markets among countries. He also worked on the assumption that there is no free flow of information among countries, so technology for industrial processes would not flow freely internationally.

In spite of its widespread acceptance in Brazilian academic circles in the 1960s and 1970s, its failure to explain why there was no halt in Brazilian relative backwardness when there was industrial development in the country, as in the last 40 years, challenged this hypothesis, complemented by developments from dependency theory. The latter stressed the role of social and political relationships among local elites and foreign agents to implement policies that strengthened the economic functioning that maintained relative backwardness.

Although dependency theory relied on Furtado's model to explain domestic economic dynamics, it inserted a very important idea in the understanding of Brazilian relative backwardness: the role of social and political relationships in determining the economic dynamic equilibrium, and how these relationships evolved historically to replicate Brazilian underdevelopment over the years. Conflicts among social classes and interest groups were in this view crucial to determining the relative development of a nation. The idea stresses that there is no unique long-term path for any economy: among the many possible options faced by any country at any moment, the chosen one is determined by social conflictual relationships, not only by economic forces.

Recent contributions to understand the wealth of nations presented by the new institutionalists draw on this major contribution of dependency theory to stress the role of noneconomic determinants of the dynamic equilibrium in the relative performance of nations. Nevertheless, the logic of the argument turns the dependency theory hypothesis upside down. While the latter stresses that social classes and group conflicts are the engine of development or underdevelopment and institutions are only instruments to crystallize gains by any party in these conflicts, the former view places the ultimate determinants of class and group conflicts in political and economic institutions. Technical progress, TFP growth, and human capital accumulation are also determined by economic institutions. They work as if institutions were the most stable part on this causal chain, and they only change when there are changes in distribution of resources that could alter the de facto political power equilibrium. This would affect political institutions in later periods.[19]

---

19. It is relevant to stress that some paragraphs in Acemoglu and Robinson (2012) give an impression that they have the same idea as dependency theory. As these contradict other parts and also the hypothesis presented in Acemoglu et al. (2005), I stick to their original explicit discussion of the relationship between institutions and social conflicts.

Dependency theorists rely on Marxian hypotheses that institutions are determined by the social conflicts generated from the role of each social class and group in productive processes. Thus these conflicts and the resulting political power are the determinants of political and economic institutions, not vice versa. Of course future political power and economic outcomes or performance would also be affected by current institutions, but future social conflicts and the productive processes are their major determinants.

The hypothesis to explain Brazilian relative backwardness proposed in the next chapters incorporates the idea that there are social and political determinants of the economic dynamic path taken by an economy, as dependency theory and the new institutionalists argue. It differs from the dependency theory hypothesis because it has a version of mainstream growth theory as its underlying determinant of economic dynamics, like the new institutionalists. But it is closer to the dependency theory argument in the relationship between social and political dynamics and economic and political institutions on one hand and the economic outcome or performance on the other. Institutions are seen as an output of social class conflicts and their final format is not all that relevant for the economic success of a country, although countries with good economic performance tend also to have good institutions.

Chapter 11

The Fundamental Cause of the Emergence of Relative Backwardness

Chapter Outline

11.1 INTRODUCTION

The explanation for Brazilian relative backwardness has been quite simple to this point. It started from the hypothesis that modern growth theory is the basic set-up to understand economic growth. Human capital accumulation and technical progress are the major engines of growth in this theory. The role of the latter, however, has not been stressed only because technological development is a global endeavor: costs of development are high and there are several gains of scale when it spreads spatially, as its output reaches a higher number of consumers. The simplifying assumption that there is full information with no transmission cost rules out any relevance of technical progress in the development of a particular country that is not at the frontier of human knowledge, as was the Brazilian case over the whole period studied.[1]

From world equilibrium with monopolistic competition, when there are many goods and services, there is arbitrary human capital spatial distribution

---

1. Although this radical assumption and its consequence are not correct, they are good approximations for the problem handled here.

which adjusts to local supply and demand, but very slowly, with a higher speed of adjustment of physical capital spatial distribution. Thus from a theoretical and simplistic standpoint, human capital spatial distribution could be considered as exogenous and physical capital would adjust to its local availabilities. This would determine the relative per capita GDP among nations and regions at each moment.

Given these basic theoretical standpoints, a third development focused on the dynamics of human capital spatial availability. A general hypothesis in line with those of perfect flows of factors of production, goods, and services is that there is also the same rate of growth of human capital for families around the world if there is no government intervention. Therefore, initial differences in human capital availability tended to be reproduced over the 19th and 20th centuries. Public investments in education and population movements across country borders changed this initial equilibrium in such a way that Brazil became progressively poorer, relatively, over the 19th century up to some point in the 20th century, when this trend was halted. The exact date for this change in the tendency depended on the country of comparison, as some of its historical particularities also affected this shift.

Public investments in education were consequences of the educational policy frameworks adopted by each country at various times. Understanding Brazilian relative backwardness thus became a question of why Brazilian public efforts to educate its population were so much lower than those in the benchmark countries. This chapter deals with this problem.

In this search, the hypothesis of this book shares with the new institutionalists the idea that there is an important difference between the fundamental and proximate determinants of economic growth and development. Acemoglu et al. (2014) define proximate determinants of growth as those which are part of the process of growth. North and Thomas (1973) state that "they are growth, not its cause." In the language of the previous chapter, they are the channel mechanisms of the causes of growth. Innovation, education, and capital accumulation are transmission channels from institutions or whatever other fundamental causes to growth and development. The accumulation of these factors of production and increases in total factor productivity are not the fundamental causes of economic growth or development. Under this argument, the fundamental causes of growth and development determine the accumulation or growth of these proximate causes, which determine per capita gross domestic product (GDP) growth or development.

Institutionalists argue that institutions are the fundamental or ultimate causes of growth. According to this argument, there are inclusive and extractive institutions. In Acemoglu et al.'s (2014) words:

> *At one extreme, European powers set up extractive institutions to transfer resources from the colony to themselves, and this led to the creation of economic institutions supporting such extraction, particularly forms of labor coercion like slavery, monopolies, legal discrimination and rules which made the property*

rights of the indigenous masses insecure. At the other extreme, Europeans settled and tried to replicate, or in fact improve over, European institutions. This led to inclusive institutions which were much better for economic growth.

Brazilian colonial settlement was guided by all the distortions stressed in this quote regarding extractive institutions. Slavery was the underlying foundation of all the colonial entrepreneurship, so a large share of the population was excluded from all property rights, including their own labor potential. Slaves certainly had no incentives to develop their potential to innovate or enhance their human capital, as they would not benefit from the outcome of such effort. Actually, as has been argued, slaves often wasted human capital: they did not employ all their skills because existing economic incentives did not encourage this.

Even the nonslaves faced monopolies that forbade them to produce locally many manufactured and industrial goods before Brazil became united with Portugal (1808).[2] Furthermore, the working logic of the patrimonial state described in Chapter 10 under Faoro's hypothesis introduced insecurity of property rights and generated risk of legal discrimination in individual fates. This working logic of the institutional framework certainly did not create incentives for the masses to enhance their human capital, as they could be prevented from enjoying the prospective benefits. Thus under the new institutionalist view, Brazilian relative backwardness is easily explained by the institutions that Portuguese colonial policy created in the country. The hypothesis of this book places the major causes of Brazilian relative backwardness on other fundamental sources of growth and development. This chapter further elaborates on these causes and their relationship with the institutionalist hypothesis.

The next section presents a model of determination of the fundamentals causes of economic growth and development, adapted from Acemoglu et al. (2005). Section 3 sets out the major hypothesis of this book on the fundamental determinant of Brazilian relative backwardness in light of this model. Section 4 discusses differences of this major hypothesis to those of dependency theory and the new institutionalist hypothesis, relying on this model as background. Section 5 summarizes the major conclusions of the chapter and discusses some additional ideas that, with the model in Section 2, help understanding the major hypothesis of this book.

11.2 MODEL SET-UP

A simple model extracted from Acemoglu et al. (2005) is presented here,[3] but with small differences that are useful to stress the departure of the major

---

2. See Luz (1978, Chapter 1).
3. See also Acemoglu and Robinson (2015).

hypothesis of this book from that forwarded by those authors. All equations are introduced in a linear format to simplify mathematical manipulation, although there is no indication in Acemoglu et al. (2005) that this should be the case.

$$R_t = \alpha_1 P_t + r_t \tag{11.1}$$

$$F_t = \beta_1 D_t + f_t \tag{11.2}$$

$$E_t = \delta_0 E_{t-1} + \delta_1 R_t + \delta_2 F_t + e_t \tag{11.3}$$

$$P_t = \phi_1 R_{t-1} + \phi_2 F_{t-1} + p_t \tag{11.4}$$

$$Y_t = \overline{Y}_t + \rho_1 E_t \tag{11.5}$$

$$D_t = \eta_1 E_{t-1} + d_t \tag{11.6}$$

where $R_t =$ de jure political power at time t, $F_t =$ de facto political power at time t, $E_t =$ economic institutions at time t, $P_t =$ political institutions at time t, $Y_t =$ natural logarithm of steady-state per capita GDP at time t, $D_t =$ distribution of resources at time t, and $\overline{Y}_t =$ natural logarithm of the world average steady-state per capita GDP at time t.

All capital letters represent multidimensional vectors, with the exceptions of Y_t and $\overline{Y}_t$, which are one-dimensional variables. All small letters are vectors of autonomous shocks to the variable represented by the same capital letter. There are three possible dimensions for these vectors. They are defined by the numbers of social groups (R_t, F_t, D_t, r_t, f_t, d_t), which is represented by n in this model, possible political institutions (P_t and p_t), represented by m, and possible economic institutions (E_t and e_t), which are v. Greek letters are matrices of parameters. From the equations and the dimensions of each variable, which are vectors, it is possible to see that $\alpha_1 = n \times m$; $\beta_1 = n \times n$; $\delta_0 = v \times v$, $\delta_1 = v \times n$; $\delta_2 = v \times n$; $\phi_1 = m \times n$; $\phi_2 = m \times n$; $\rho_1 = 1 \times v$; and $\eta_1 = n \times v$.

It is worth mentioning that the implicit concept of social groups is more restrictive than the social classes in classical and Marxian economics or in Darendorf (1959). Each social group involves all individuals whose economic interests are common and who stand together in disputes on a subset of social priorities at any particular moment. Of course, the higher the set of social priorities included in the identification of groups, the higher will be the number of social groups and the smaller will be each group. As a consequence, there are many more social groups than social classes in a society.

It is also worth introducing a discussion of the meaning, measurement, and dimension of these variables, as some involve qualitative components. A starting point is the identification of the goal of this model, which is to determine the relative development level of a country, measured here as the difference of the natural logarithm of equilibrium per capita GDP within the country, Y_t, and the world average for this variable, $\overline{Y}_t$.

Growth theory normally works with the idea of steady-state paths of per capita GDP and transitional dynamics. So at any moment there are two per capita GDPs, one that represents what it would be if the economy is in a steady state, and the other representing its actual level. If the two do not coincide, which is the most common situation, each economy at each moment has two per capita GDPs. Y_t in the model actually represents the natural logarithm of the steady-state per capita GDP at moment t, rather than its actual level. From now on, Y_t is always referred to as the per capita GDP of a country, although it actually represents the natural logarithm of its steady-state level. In the same way, $\overline{Y}_t$ is often used here as the world per capita GDP, although it is actually the natural logarithm of its steady state.

Under such concepts, it is obvious that if there is no change in the economic institutions of a country from one period to another:

$$Y_t - Y_{t-1} = \left(\overline{Y}_t - \overline{Y}_{t-1}\right) \tag{11.5'}$$

and the steady-state per capita GDP would grow at the same rate as the world average. This growth rate is determined by consumer preferences and parameters of the production functions of knowledge, human capital, and goods, as stated by standard endogenous growth theory. Under the hypothesis of an integrated world economy, these parameters would be for the whole world, not only for a specific country.

Given these definitions, it is possible to think that:

$$Y'_t - Y'_{t-1} = \theta\left(Y_t - Y'_{t-1}\right) + u_t \tag{11.7}$$

where Y'_t is the natural logarithm of actual per capita GDP in period t, Y_t is the natural logarithm of the steady-state per capita GDP, as stated before, u_t is a short-term macroeconomic deviation from the adjustment path $\left(Y_t - Y'_{t-1}\right)$, and θ is a parameter such that $0 < \theta < 1$. Thus the current natural logarithm of per capita GDP Y'_t follows a path determined by Eq. (11.7), while its steady state Y_t follows a path determined by an extended version of Eq. (11.5'), which also can be derived from Eq. (11.5):

$$Y_t - Y_{t-1} = \left(\overline{Y}_t - \overline{Y}_{t-1}\right) + \rho_1(E_t - E_{t-1}) \tag{11.5''}$$

Fig. 11.1 shows an exposition of these concepts, using an example that includes two economies, a and b, and two measures of the natural logarithm of per capita GDP for each country. The first, Y'_a and Y'_b, are the actual natural logarithms of these variables at t_0. The second measures, Y_a and Y_b, are the natural logarithms of the per capita GDPs that would prevail if these economies were already in their steady state at t_0.

Both economies grow at the same equilibrium rate after they reach their steady-state paths, which are identified as the dotted lines in Fig. 11.1, and both are below their steady-state paths in t_0, the current period. This means they are both converging to their equilibrium path, as suggested by Eq. (11.7),

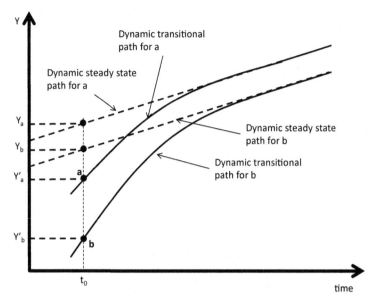

FIGURE 11.1   Dynamic steady states for economies *a* and *b*.

unless u_t is so negative that it offsets momentarily the first term in the right side of Eq. (11.7). It is also obvious that they will not reach their equilibrium paths at the same moment, but this is irrelevant for the forthcoming arguments.

The growth rate of the two economies in their equilibrium paths is determined by the rate of accumulation of human capital and technological progress at a world level, as already argued. The levels of the steady-state paths for economies *a* and *b* normally differ, as represented in Fig. 11.1, because the fundamental or ultimate causes of development are not the same, and they determine the relative steady-state paths of any two economies. In this model, E_t is not the same for the two economies.

Political institutions, which motivate the introduction of the variable P_t in this model, have many features and most are difficult to measure, as they are essentially qualitative. Systems of government—presidentialism or parliamentarism, for example—or political regimes—democracy, authoritarianism, or totalitarianism—are not quantitative variables. The vote system, number and nature of political parties, role and scope of trade unions in society, and shape of (legal) courts are also examples of features of reality that are political institutions of a qualitative nature. Thus many traits of political institutions are not amenable to simple quantitative evaluation.

In the same way, economic institutions have a variety of features. Many have qualitative attributes, such as structure of taxes, with a major focus on consumption, income, production, or trade; nature of bankruptcy laws; rules for access to mineral reserves; rules of protection for property rights; and the level of contract enforcement. Some are easier to quantify within the original context, such as the level of contract enforcement, tax rates for all types of taxes, and legal costs to exploit mineral reserves.

Qualitative features of both economic and political institutions can be adequately split in parts that could be subject at least to a binary quantitative measurement, in which 1 stands for its existence and 0 for its absence. Other features are measurable in the intervals of either the natural or the real numbers. Therefore the assumption that it is always possible to decompose any political or economic institution into several features so they can be fully represented by a set of quantitative variables is introduced here.

To understand the possible measurement of P_t and E_t, it is worth defining the following sets.

Ω = Set of all existing political institutions. Each of its elements is a set of the many possible values for a given political institution or one of its components. If it is a qualitative political institution, such as political regimes, it takes a binary form, with 0 or 1 as its alternatives. Political institutions that are already quantitative variables, such as dispersion of the necessary number of votes to elect a member of the parliament among the many spatial units, are represented by sets of all their possible values. Even if these quantitative features of institutions are defined in any interval in the real numbers, so they are subsets with infinite elements, the number of elements in Ω is finite and equal to m.

Ω' = Set of all subsets of Ω, with a specific value for each of its elements. It is worth mentioning that all subsets of Ω transformed in elements in Ω' have elements composed with one and only one value for each individual element in Ω. Thus each element in Ω' defines a feasible and complete political institutional arrangement that could exist in a country. As some of the elements in Ω have infinite possible values, the set Ω' has infinite elements.

Φ = Set of all possible economic institutions. Similarly to Ω, each of its elements represents an economic institution or one of its components necessary to ensure full representation of the former through quantitative components. Hence all these elements are subsets of numbers, as qualitative economic institutions or their components are transformed into binary variables and the others are included with all their potential values.

Φ' = Set of all subsets of Φ, which has with Φ the same relationship Ω' has with Ω. Thus each element in Φ' defines a feasible and complete economic institutional arrangement that could exist in a country. Furthermore, Φ' has infinite elements, as some of the quantitative economic institutions included in Φ have infinite possible values.

Ψ = Set composed of an interval in the real numbers that includes all potential natural logarithms of steady-state per capita GDP levels of a nation. Therefore, Y_t and $\overline{Y}_t$ are defined in this set.

From these definitions, it is possible to define a mapping from Φ' to Ψ in which each possible economic institutional arrangement contained in the former set has a correspondent equilibrium Y_t included in Ψ. More precisely, for each economic institutional arrangement in Φ' in an economy, given the development level all other countries $\overline{Y}_t$, there is a value of steady-state per capita GDP at any moment represented by Y_t, which is defined in Ψ, associated with that economic institutional arrangement. Some elements in Ψ, which could represent a development level in the steady state, will probably have more than one subset of Φ' mapped to them. Nevertheless, each element of Φ' has one and only one component of Ψ connected. Two subsets of Φ', or economic institutional arrangements, that have the same element in Ψ in this mapping are considered to be equivalents.

This mapping is defined by the vector of coefficients ρ_1 for a given $\overline{Y}_t$. Each element in the vector E_t is multiplied by a coefficient in a column of ρ_1 so that the sums of all these multiplications generate the expected value for Y_t given the existing institutional arrangements.

Most probably, the values of ρ_1 are not constant over the whole mapping defined by Eq. (11.5), as there are many violations to the linear assumptions: nonlinearities in the relationship; discontinuity of the relations represented; dependency of the response to one dimension on the values assumed by other dimensions; dependency of the response to one dimension on past values of this or other dimensions; and dependency of values in ρ_1 on current and past values of $\overline{Y}_t$. All these obvious violations of the linear relationships captured by Eq. (11.5) are disregarded here as a simplifying assumption to keep the focus on the major concern relevant for this book, thus all elements of ρ_1 are taken as constant.

The $n \times 1$ vectors F_t and R_t can show the quantitative strength of a relevant social group in each of its dimensions. Thus if small stakeholders dedicated to a particular crop or mine workers are considered to be a social group, then the higher their political strength, the higher will be the value within the dimension measuring their strength. If de jure (de facto) political power is the dimension measured, this would be a dimension of R_t (F_t). All political groups have the same order in the vectors R_t and F_t.

All five violations of the linear assumptions made in Eq. (11.5) also hold for Eq. (11.3). This demands that the elements of δ_1 are not constant to ensure that the postulated relationships would hold. Nevertheless, the simplifying assumption is made that the implied relationship between the second term in the right hand side of Eq. (11.3) and its left term is linear, and δ_1 is taken as constant. Similar reasoning works for the relationship between E_t and F_t, and the elements of the $v \times n$ matrix represented by δ_2 are taken to be constant, by a simplifying assumption.

The autonomous innovations in Eq. (11.3), represented in the vector e_t, could offset nonlinearities in the relationships discussed in the previous paragraph. There are also all the changes in economic institutions that are not defined by the political power, both de jure and de facto, of the social groups. New ideas, technological developments, the impact of personal leadership, changes in economic institutions in other countries, and historical circumstances could motivate these autonomous innovations. Thus e_t could actually be split in these two components. The compensating component, which captures deviations due to nonlinearities and discontinuities, is disregarded here, however, and the focus is only on these economic institutional innovations.

Eq. (11.4) defines a relationship between the fully measureable vectors R_{t-1} and F_{t-1}, both with all their dimensions measured in real numbers, and the political institutions set P_t, which also contain binary variables in some of its dimensions. All violations of linearity noted for Eqs. (11.3) and (11.5) also appear in Eq. (11.4). Therefore the coefficient matrices ϕ_1 and ϕ_2 are constant only as a simplifying assumption. The vector of innovations p_t would also work as a buffer to force this equation always to hold. Nevertheless, this most realist approach is left out and the simplifying assumption of a linear relationship is introduced again. It should be noted that, unlike E_t, it is not necessary to have a one-dimensional ordering of the political institutional arrangements in P_t, as there is no mapping of this set to any one-dimensional variable.

The autonomous innovations represented by p_t could also be split in two parts. One represents the necessary adjustments for nonlinearities and discontinuities, and a second component is generated by similar determinants as those listed for e_t, namely new ideas, technological developments, the impact of personal leadership, changes in political institutions of other countries, and historical circumstances. However, only the latter source is considered here.

Eq. (11.1) can be easier understood when placed together with Eq. (11.4). De jure political power of each social group is defined from inertia and potential noncorrespondence between de facto and de jure political powers, plus deviations arising from particular circumstances, which are represented in the innovations r_t added to Eq. (11.1). The probable nonlinearities in these relationships are also disregarded in the equation specification as a simplifying assumption. Then r_t represents mainly changes in de jure political power of social groups that arise from sectorally unbalanced technical progress, the impact of personal leadership, and particular circumstances.

Eq. (11.6) defines the distribution of resources in the economy among the many social groups, each represented by one line of the $n \times 1$ vector D_t. The measures of the lines of D_t are in the share of the total resources of the economy, so they are defined as real numbers restricted between 0% and 100%. There are also nonlinearities in this relationship, but they are disregarded as a simplifying assumption. The $n \times 1$ random vector d_t not only adjusts nonconformities in the mapping from binary components of E_{t-1} to real numbers in D_t but also introduces the possibility that particular circumstances change the values of D_t that are predicted by the first term of the right side of that equation. Sectorally unbalanced technical progress, changes in consumer preferences, and developments in other countries reshaping international trade and capital flows are some of the most prominent determinants of these autonomous innovations in the distribution of resources. It is worth mentioning that Marx's hypothesis on the impact of developments on productive forces enters the system through these innovations.[4]

Eq. (11.2) could be seen as representing the simple idea that money (distribution of resources) generates power (de facto political power). Acemoglu et al. (2005) introduced this relationship from a current perspective of Western society, which is basically ruled by this association. Nevertheless, it is not necessarily true throughout world history, and the Weberian views of bureaucracy and examples of its political influence are challenges to this relationship.[5] However, as the model represented by Eqs. (11.1)−(11.6) is built from the relationships defined by Acemoglu et al., Eq. (11.2) was included in this restrictive form.

There is an autonomous component in Eq. (11.2), its error term f_t, that has a special role in forthcoming developments. This autonomous term could arise from inertia from previous distribution of resources, D_{t-1}, but as a simplifying assumption this possibility was left out of the model.[6] Under this assumption, the vector f_t shows all resulting innovations in F_t, the vector composed of de facto political powers of all social groups, which emerge from the social conflicts among these groups. Therefore, all societies always face changes in the relative power of their many social groups as a consequence of social conflicts.

These conflicts are motivated by differences in individual interests of social groups and their permanent search to shape political and economic institutions to satisfy their interests. Their de facto political powers are always changing as a consequence of their exposure to other interests, capturing and losing allies and advancing or retreating in institutional changes. These conflicts are constantly moving society and permanently generating new equilibria, which are immediately challenged by some groups.

11.2.1 Implications of This Model for Steady-State per Capita GDP

If Eq. (11.5) is left to determine Y_t, the other equations can be condensed to yield:

$$R_t = \alpha_1 \phi_1 R_{t-1} + \alpha_1 \phi_2 F_{t-1} + \alpha_1 p_t + r_t \tag{11.8}$$

$$F_t = \beta_1 \eta_1 E_{t-1} + \beta_1 d_t + f_t \tag{11.9}$$

---

4. See Marx (1867, introduction).
5. See Weber (1968, vol. II, Chapter 11).
6. A better representation of the relationships introduced under this hypothesis would include lags of D_t in the specification of Eq. (11.2).

$$E_t = (\delta_0 + \delta_2\beta_1\eta_1)E_{t-1} + \delta_1\alpha_1\phi_1 R_{t-1} + \delta_1\alpha_1\phi_2 F_{t-1} + \delta_1\alpha_1 p_t + \delta_1 r_t$$
$$+ \delta_2\beta_1 d_t + \delta_2 f_t + e_t$$

$$(11.10)$$

These three equations form a system of first-order difference equations in R_t, F_t, and E_t as a function of the autonomous innovations, p_t, r_t, d_t, f_t, and e_t. A recursive solution of this system of equations yields:

$$E_t = A_0 E_0 + A_1 R_0 + A_2 F_0 + \sum_{i=0}^{t} A_{3i} p_{t-i} + A_{4i} r_{t-i} + A_{5i} d_{t-i} + A_{6i} f_{t-i} + A_{7i} e_{t-i}$$

$$(11.11)$$

where the matrices of parameters A_{ji} are nonlinear functions of the many parameters found in Eqs. (11.8)–(11.10), A_0 and A_{7i} are $v \times v$ matrices, and $A_1, A_2, A_{3i}, A_{4i}, A_{5i}$, and A_{6i} are all $v \times n$ matrices. The demand that the values for all elements in E_t are finite imposes restrictions to the possible values of the parameters of the model, but these are of any concern here. Substituting Eq. (11.11) in Eq. (11.5) yields:

$$Y_t = \overline{Y}_t + \rho_1 \left(A_0 E_0 + A_1 R_0 + A_2 F_0 + \sum_{i=0}^{t} A_{3i} p_{t-i} + A_{4i} r_{t-i} + A_{5i} d_{t-i} \right.$$
$$\left. + A_{6i} f_{t-i} + A_{7i} e_{t-i} \right)$$

$$(11.12)$$

Eq. (11.12) stresses that the fundamental causes of the development level of a country depend on initial conditions of its economic institutions and the political power of the many social groups, both de facto and de jure. These variables, however, tend to have small or nil impacts if they are far enough in the past, otherwise Y_t and the many lines of E_t would not all be currently finite numbers. Thus their relevance for determination of current development levels is disregarded.

Hence the terms in Eq. (11.12) involving autonomous innovations are the fundamental determinants of the development level of a country in this model. Boundedness conditions for vector E_t ensures that the further back these autonomous changes were introduced, the lower their impacts on current development level. Given their relevance, these autonomous innovations are summarized in Table 11.1 with their meaning and the major social and economic factors that they introduce to the model.

Many of these innovations introduce apparent conceptually similar factors, but a further analysis shows that in most cases they actually capture the impact of different variables. For example, technological development appears as a source of innovations in e_t, p_t, r_t, and d_t; but while software for trade control

TABLE 11.1 Summary of Autonomous Innovations Determining the Development Level of a Country

Autonomous Innovations	Meaning (Autonomous Innovations in)	What They Capture
r_t	De jure political power	Sectorally unbalanced technical progress, impact of personal leadership, and particular historical circumstances
f_t	De facto political power	Social conflicts among social groups
e_t	Economic institutions	New ideas, technological developments, impact of personal leadership, changes in economic institutions in other countries, and historical circumstances
p_t	Political institutions	New ideas, technological developments, impact of personal leadership, changes in political institutions of other countries, and historical circumstances
d_t	Distribution of resources	Sectorally unbalanced technical progress, changes in consumer preferences, and developments in other countries reshaping international trade and capital flows

Possible captures of nonlinearities and discontinuities in the functions, as well as simple inertia, were left out of this identification of sources of innovations, as they are only noise in the fundamental arguments.
Created by the author.

would enter this system only through e_t, a new machine to reduce energy expenditure in car production would appear in the system only through d_t and perhaps through the lines in r_t representing social groups including car and machine makers. Furthermore, the extent of autonomous increases in de jure political power of these social groups may be completely different from the rise in their share of social income. Thus the same label may represent completely different autonomous innovations.

Despite labeling completely different social and economic phenomena as similar, this spurious aggregation of sources of autonomous innovations in the system helps identify the innovations with some sources of development found in the literature. Table 11.2 organizes data in Table 11.1 by label of shocks, identifying for each the innovations through which they can appear, and relates these sources to previous contributions in the development literature.

TABLE 11.2 Fundamental Sources of Dynamics and Their Representing Innovations in the Model

Fundamental Sources of Dynamics	Innovations in Which They Appear	Authors Stressing the Role of This Source
Social conflicts	f	Marx (1867) and Cardoso and Faletto (1970)
New ideas	e, p	Marx (1867), Schumpeter (1934), new growth theory, Hegel (2001), and Acemoglu et al. (2005)
Technological developments	r, e, p, d	Marx (1867), Schumpeter (1934), and Solow (1956), new growth theory
Impact of personal leadership	r, e, p	Schumpeter (1934) and Acemoglu and Robinson (2012)
Changes in other countries	e, p, d	Cardoso and Faletto (1970) and Frank (1967), Latin American structuralism (Furtado, 1959; Prebisch, 1949)
Consumer preferences	d	Weber (1930), new growth theory
Particular historical circumstances	r, e, p	Arthur (1989) and Acemoglu and Robinson (2012)

Author's own elaboration.

11.3 MAJOR FUNDAMENTAL DETERMINANT OF BRAZILIAN RELATIVE BACKWARDNESS

Eq. (11.12) may be rewritten as:

$$\rho_1 \left[\left(\frac{A_0 E_0 + A_1 R_0 + A_2 F_0}{Y_t - \overline{Y}_t} \right) + \left(\frac{\sum_{i=0}^{t} A_{3i} p_{t-i}}{Y_t - \overline{Y}_t} \right) + \left(\frac{\sum_{i=0}^{t} A_{4i} r_{t-i}}{Y_t - \overline{Y}_t} \right) \right.$$

$$\left. + \left(\frac{\sum_{i=0}^{t} A_{5i} d_{t-i}}{Y_t - \overline{Y}_t} \right) + \left(\frac{\sum_{i=0}^{t} A_{6i} f_{t-i}}{Y_t - \overline{Y}_t} \right) + \left(\frac{\sum_{i=0}^{t} A_{7i} e_{t-i}}{Y_t - \overline{Y}_t} \right) \right] = 1 \quad (11.13)$$

This equation indicates that the deviations of the development level of a country from the world average $\left(Y_t - \overline{Y}_t \right)$ can be decomposed in six terms. While the first one captures the impact of historical initial conditions, which tends to be irrelevant, the other five terms represent the five sources of innovations identified earlier. These innovations capture the effect of seven broad fundamental determinants of development, listed in Table 11.2.

The hypothesis of this book is that the major determinant of Brazilian relative backwardness is the term:

$$0 \leq \rho_1 \left[\left(\frac{\sum_{i=0}^{t} A_{6i} f_{t-i}}{Y_t - \overline{Y}_t} \right) \right] \leq 1 \qquad (11.14)$$

This term introduces the role of social conflicts in Eq. (11.13).

Thus the major hypothesis here is that the working of social conflicts over Brazilian history was such that a large share of the population improved its human capital at very low accumulation rates, determined basically by individual incentives with no relevant contribution of public investments, which was the road taken by European countries and Western Offshoots. Only in the 20th century, after substantial immigration of Europeans and Japanese and the changes such population inflow promoted in Brazilian society through conflicts, was there stabilization of the relative backwardness, with more involvement of government in education locally through the tax system or direct investment. Urbanization in Brazil improved the local productivity of human capital, and stabilization of educational policies in developed countries also reduced the gap.

Later chapters discuss further the transmission mechanisms from social conflicts to the set-up of Brazilian relative backwardness. Before that, however, the next section discusses differences between the hypothesis forwarded here and the important alternative hypotheses presented in Chapter 9 that already extend the debate on Brazilian relative backwardness beyond the simple conclusions obtained from economic theory.

11.4 MAJOR DIFFERENCES FROM ALTERNATIVE HYPOTHESES

A hypothesis placing the major engine of development and potential relative backwardness of a country in social conflict was proposed by Marx (1867) from a general theoretical standpoint. Marx's conceptual focus on revolutions which brought changes in the structure of societies and even modes of production led him to stress the fundamental conflicts of each mode of production as an engine of development. In spite of the undoubted key relevance of these major conflicts, there are others that can play a relevant role for development within the same mode of production. This is why society was divided into social groups here, rather than social classes as in Marx (1867).

11.4.1 Major Differences From Dependency Theory

A Marxian strategy of searching for major sources of Brazilian underdevelopment in social conflicts was used by Cardoso and Faletto (1970). As noted in

Chapter 9, they relied on the underlying structuralist economic model or hypothesis to include social conflicts as major sources of perpetuation of a primary exporting specialization or low investment ability, even when industrialization was close to exhausting the existing model. According to them, political alliances made by some domestic social classes or groups with multinational companies and international wholesale traders reduced local capital accumulation, as they promoted an outflow of the surplus generated domestically. This drain of investment ability arose because of interest and profits paid to foreigners or loss of domestic profits as a consequence of deterioration of the net barter terms of trade.

Some social classes or groups pushed for economic institutional arrangements that promoted the competitiveness and earning abilities of foreign agents in the domestic economy. Among others, these groups included government bureaucrats, often seduced by corruption, local representatives of international traders, suppliers of inputs and support services for multinational companies and international traders, and primary commodities producers. The self-interest of such social groups pushed for institutional arrangements that would generated mechanisms for losses of domestic surplus and investment ability, either through deterioration of the net barter terms of trade or outflow of part of the domestically created surplus through earnings by foreign agents.

A first key difference of the hypothesis presented here from the views of dependency theory is that the latter had Latin American structuralism as its underlying economic model, mainly in its interpretation of the Brazilian case used by Furtado (1959). Here, a version of a mainstream growth model, with multiple goods and services and international integration, where human capital and technological development are the major proximate engines of growth, is the underlying economic model. Thus economic specialization in world markets is not relevant to determine the relative dynamics of a country, as in the structuralist view, but is rather a consequence of development.

If a country changes its relative stable per capita GDP through changes in E_t in Eq. (11.5) of the model in Section 2, and consumer preferences are such that its current specialization in world markets cannot provide the necessary demand for faster growth of this country to reach its new equilibrium level of per capita GDP, new specializations will arise. Examples of the international trade path of countries such as Australia, New Zealand, and Canada attest to this assertion. Thus international trade specialization is neither a barrier to nor a determinant of the relative development of a country according to the view here. This conclusion is also a key difference from the Latin American structuralist hypothesis, which places emphasis on primary commodities specialization on world markets as a major determinant of Brazilian relative development backwardness.

The second key difference of the hypothesis of this book from that of dependency theory is that the major social conflict stressed by the latter was the relationship between foreign enterprises and their local allies on one side and the local businesses which compete with or had antagonistic attitudes to foreign companies on the other. This antagonism drained potentially investable surplus in the Brazilian economy, either through deterioration of the net barter terms of trade or through profits, interest, and dividends remitted abroad.

Here, the major conflict that drives Brazilian development is that involving local elites on one side and the majority of the poor social groups on the other, including mainly peasants and unskilled urban workers, with special emphasis on former slaves. While the elites when determining public policies and institutional arrangements restricted the public effort on human capital building in Brazil, the latter groups would be major beneficiaries of such policies. Political organization, class identities, and other weaknesses restricted the political power of the latter to push such public policies up in state priorities. This reduced the rate of human capital accumulation in Brazil and its current relative development level.

11.4.2 Major Differences From the New Institutionalist Hypothesis

The hypothesis of this book shares with the new institutionalist hypothesis the new growth models as the underlying foundation. Human capital accumulation and technical progress are the major proximate causes of relative development. The only difference here is the emphasis placed on a world economic equilibrium, rather than on many national equilibria with reasonable independence from each other and the world market. However, perhaps many new institutionalists would not react against the postulation of a level of international integration, as made here.

New institutionalists point to innovations in institutional arrangements, both economic and political, as the major determinants of the relative development of a country. Thus the second and sixth terms in the left side of Eq. (11.13), together, would represent the major share of the total relative development indicator, represented by $Y_t - \overline{Y}_t$. Under this hypothesis, most changes in E_t in Eq. (11.5) would arise from the autonomous changes of e_t and p_t.

The hypothesis of this book does not challenge the role of economic and political institutional arrangements in the determination of Brazilian relative backwardness. However, it assumes that they are built mainly as a consequence of the dynamics of social conflicts, which evolve mainly from disputes and permanent clashes among social classes and groups. Thus these should be seen as the major fundamental causes of relative development, rather than the institutional arrangements themselves.

Hence, it was not the role of bureaucracy in the institutional arrangements or import of inefficient Portuguese economic and political institutions that generated Brazilian relative backwardness. It was the relationship among social classes and groups and their permanent disputes and clashes that shaped these institutions gradually and built this poor relative outcome. Definitions arising from such conflicts that affected human capital accumulation, through their potential influence on public policies toward education, were the most relevant determinants of Brazilian relative backwardness.

11.5 CONCLUSIONS

This chapter relies on the distinction between proximate and fundamental causes of economic growth and development to stress the fundamental causes in the Brazilian case, according to the hypothesis forwarded here. These concepts of proximate and fundamental causes of prosperity were drawn from Douglas North and Robert Thomas's (1973) seminal book, which is also used by more recent authors such as Acemoglu et al. (2005, 2014). While proximate causes basically define the mechanics of growth and development, the fundamental causes determine why this mechanism works differently in different countries. The latter determine why the former work better or worse in different circumstances.

The chapter relies on a slightly adjusted model from that presented by Acemoglu et al. (2005). Particularly, the model is enhanced with the introduction of a role for social conflicts as an ultimate cause of growth, together with autonomous changes in economic and political institutional arrangements, as stressed by those authors. This small change, when the model is solved, can turn it upside down, as it allows social conflicts to become the major fundamental driving determinant of growth and development, rather than institutions themselves. The latter, then, can become only a transmission mechanism for the impact of the outcome of social conflicts, as postulated in the hypothesis forwarded here.

It is noted in previous chapters that Brazilian relative backwardness arose because of the low human capital accumulation in the 19th and early 20th centuries when compared to a set of benchmark countries. Human capital accumulation, however, in light of the concepts discussed here, becomes the major proximate cause of Brazilian relative backwardness, while the outcomes of the evolution of social conflicts throughout the history of this country become the fundamental or ultimate causes of its relative lower prosperity when compared to the benchmark countries.

Under this view, institutions are not all that stable, but evolve continually over a country's history. Many small changes in any institutional framework are introduced every week. Although most do not launch any substantial change in the existing institutional structure, cumulatively, in one year or even less, they can generate an overwhelming reform. These small weekly changes are the outcome of the permanent conflicts among social groups which are always pressing for institutional consolidation of their interests.

The emphasis on social groups rather than social classes, as made by Marx (1867), arises from the fact that the focus here is on changes in equilibrium within a given social structure, not changes in structure, if these are seen as stratification among social classes through their political power.

The movements in relative equilibrium per capita GDP, given that prevailing in other countries, could be within the same social structure but with different relative de facto and de jure political powers of social classes, although still respecting the same hierarchy among them. Thus a focus only on social classes could miss most of the social conflicts and the evolutions they cause in economic development.

All the sources of changes in any social system could be classified as internal or external. The latter have roots in phenomena whose causes are exogenous to that society. Changes in other countries in Table 11.2 are examples of this. Natural catastrophes, shocks in world commodity prices, and agricultural disasters in other countries are examples of these external sources of growth and development. For an underdeveloped country such as Brazil, new ideas and technological developments are mostly external shocks for local development. Other sources, such as impacts of personal leadership and consumer preferences, can also be considered to some extent as external to the process of development, as they are often fortuitous. Thus social conflicts are perhaps the most legitimate internal fundamental cause of development among those discussed.

Changes in de facto political power created by social conflicts, although exogenous to the system defined by Eqs. (11.1)–(11.6), are generated permanently by internal developments. Each day there are several battles among the different groups in a society, which are reflected in many social decisions and events. All daily reports in the press or discussions around any social event, such as kidnappings, specific forms of government support after a catastrophe, a fraud in government policies, or changes in taxes or unemployment rates, embody an ideological battle that has many sides, each of which benefits particular sets of social groups. Hence these polemics tend to change socially dominant ideas and move the relative power of the many social groups. These permanent clashes among different ideologies and interests of social groups are the true internal fundamental engine of growth and development. Thus evolution of these conflicts in Brazil caused the relative low development of this country throughout its history.

Chapter 12

Social Conflict as the Source of Brazilian Relative Backwardness

12.1 INTRODUCTION

This book tries to explain Brazilian relative economic backwardness when compared to a set of benchmark countries. All analysis starts from the recent distinction between the proximate and fundamental or ultimate causes of development, as underlined by North and Thomas (1973), Acemoglu et al. (2005, 2014), Spolaore and Wacziarg (2013), and Caselli (2005), for example. While proximate causes highlight the economic mechanics of growth and development, the fundamental causes stress the determinants of this mechanism. Thus the book focuses on both proximate and fundamental causes of Brazilian relative backwardness.

Unlike previous hypotheses to explain Brazilian relative underdevelopment when compared to the benchmark countries, the explanation presented here starts from the hypothesis that modern endogenous growth theory is the basic set-up to understand proximate economic growth and development. Thus the book assumes that no serious deviation from the mainstream growth models is necessary to understand Brazilian development, as made by previous hypotheses such as those of Furtado (1959) and Cardoso and Falletto (1970).

Roots of Brazilian Relative Economic Backwardness.

This simple theoretical perspective already points to human capital accumulation and technical progress as the major engines of growth or proximate determinants of growth and development. Nevertheless, the growth model that supports the view of economic dynamics underlying the hypothesis of this book works at a world level, hence most of the endogenous determinants of technical progress and human capital accumulation operate at a world scale. Local public policies can play some role in both enhancements, however, although these are more relevant in human capital accumulation when local relative performance is the object of analysis.

Thus the role of technical progress has not been stressed, as it works on a world scale. It has a high cost of development, and there are several gains of scale when it spreads spatially and its output reaches a higher number of consumers.[1] Furthermore, the introduced simplifying assumption that there is full information with no transmission cost minimizes the relevance of technical progress for the development of a particular country that is not at the forefront of human knowledge, as was the Brazilian case throughout the whole period studied.

To understand relative development levels among countries or regions, it is necessary to approach the economy from a world equilibrium, but with many goods and services and monopolistic competition. It is seen that this model is only able to determine relative income among countries if there is arbitrary initial human capital spatial distribution. Thus relative per capita gross domestic product (GDP) among nations and regions at any time would evolve from this initial distribution. Physical capital moves across country borders to ensure arbitrage in the markets for factors of production.

Given these basic theoretical ideas, a special focus on the dynamics of human capital spatial availability is necessary. It is also argued that a general hypothesis in line with those of perfect flows of factors of production, goods, and services is that rates of growth of human capital for families around the world, if there is no government intervention, can be very close to each other. Therefore initial differences in human capital availability tend to be reproduced over the centuries. Nevertheless, public investments in education and population movements across country borders could change this equilibrium.

Given these general theoretical standpoints, it is possible to propose a particular hypothesis to explain the proximate causes of Brazilian relative backwardness, as done in previous chapters. However, further theoretical developments, with less consensus than those summarized earlier, are necessary to advance an explanation for the fundamental causes of Brazilian relative backwardness. They are drawn from Marxist social and political theories, but freed from some of their deterministic components. The major theoretical ultimate determinants of growth under this hypothesis are presented in

---

1. See, for example, Rivera-Batiz and Romer (1991a).

Chapter 11. Here, the major social conflicts and how they impacted on human capital development in Brazil are discussed.

The next section introduces the major social conflicts throughout Brazilian history, while Section 12.3 unveils additional details of their consequences for human capital building over specific periods. Section 12.4 summarizes the major conclusions of the chapter. A more detailed discussion of the social conflicts in the most recent period, which started in 1930, is given in the next chapter.

12.2 MAJOR SOCIAL CONFLICTS IN BRAZILIAN HISTORY

The idea of social conflicts relied upon in this book is different from that which fostered a recent huge economic literature.[2] These studies focus on conflicts mostly involving some violence and often associated with ethnic or religious disputes to seize power. Notwithstanding this difference, some of their conclusions are useful for the understanding of the views on conflicts stressed here. Particularly relevant is Esteban and Ray (2011), which stresses that the effort on conflict engagement made by any individual is a positive function of the intragroup altruism or a measure of the extent of within-group monitoring, along with promises and threats. Differences in this measure, α in their model, are relevant to explain distinct levels of engagement in conflicts by members of distinct groups.

The idea here focuses on conflicts that are mainly surreptitious, although sometimes they involve open clashes. Their nature is explained by Marx and Engels (2004, Chapter 1) when they argue that "the history of all hitherto existing society is the history of class struggles," whose concepts were extended to the day-to-day political and ideological battles in the search for hegemony and advancements of their interests by different social groups, as further developed by Gramsci (1971). These conflicts move society continuously, but they are normally not fully disclosed. The battles are predominantly fought in the realm of ideas, such as culture and ideology, and extend their outcomes to the legal system and the organization of the state, or more generally to institutions, under the concepts of modern economic theory. Nevertheless, they shape society and institutions and determine the long-term economic path of a country. Under this theory, institutions are nothing more than the crystallization of the output of these conflicts in social rules and norms.

All social conflicts play some role in these social and economic dynamics, just as any stone dropped on the earth by a child theoretically affects the whole equilibrium among planets in the universe. Nevertheless, some social conflicts are more relevant than others in explaining the long-term economic dynamics

---

2. See, for example, Esteban and Ray (2011), Esteban et al. (2012), Caselli and Coleman (2013), and Bhattacharya et al. (2015).

of a country. Hence it is crucial to identify which are the major conflicts that helped shape Brazilian development, and discuss how they influence the current relative backwardness of this country.

The first conflict, which played a major role in colonial Brazil and the first half of the 19th century, was that between slaves and their masters. Slaves were mainly from Africa, and some were captured from native tribes, while masters were mainly from Europe. This basic social differentiation was transformed into an ethnic cleavage, although its essence was from the relationship among social classes, the two sides in the productive processes. This kind of inversion in the conception of social relations is common in Marx's philosophy, and is why he argued that the appearance did not always fully reflect the essence of the phenomena.[3] This was a typical case in which this happened.

Slaves certainly wanted less work effort and a better standard of living provided by their masters, while the latter's direct interest was in more work effort and less expenses on slaves—the inverse of the former. This opposition of private interests was the origin of the conflicts among these two social classes, which constantly interacted in the many productive processes of the period. From 1500 until at least 1850 this was probably the major conflict underlying Brazilian social and economic evolution, especially as regards human capital accumulation.

A second crucial social conflict that helped shape Brazilian society and history was the standard one in capitalist societies between workers and employers, fought mainly in urban areas but also extending to rural relations. Workers obviously demanded higher wages and lower labor hours and intensity, while their employers sought the opposite. This conflict played a more important role from the 19th century and became stronger thereafter. It has gone through all transformations stressed by Dahrendorf (1959, Chapters 2, 7, and 8) in the 20th century.

Workers in Brazil had the most diverse origins. They were exslaves, acculturated indigenous natives, poor Europeans who migrated to make fortune and did not succeed, and, of course, descendants of all these people, including illegitimate descendants of wealthy Europeans who did not have the support of their rich parents. They had two particularly important features up until the second half of the 19th century. First, they did not have much social identity with the ruling classes, wealthy Europeans and their legitimate descendants, as they had distinct cultures and often also ethnic origin. Secondly, they had a huge diversity among themselves, which reduced their willingness to cooperate in the search for common interests.

---

3. "That in their appearance things often represent themselves in inverted form is pretty well known in every Science..." Marx (1867, p. 537).

A third major social conflict that helped shape Brazilian current development was between small rural stakeholders (peasants) on one side and large farmers on the other. This conflict involved the purchase by landlords of labor and services from peasants, as well as trade in goods and disputes over land and land renting. Relations sometimes became tense and reached open conflict, but mostly among individuals, not among social groups. Only in the second half of the 20th century was there a better organization of landless peasants with political demands for land access. When this conflict became more manifest, it impacted institutions, forging laws on agrarian reform.[4] This social conflict had consequences for Brazilian society, as the dynamic equilibria it generated in ideas, rules, and norms affected the outcomes of other political and ideological conflicts. The roles of patriarchalism[5] and paternalism in Brazilian political organization over its history are examples of this rural conflict playing out.

It is important to emphasize that the two major social groups in this conflict had distinct origins. While the large landlords were mainly European descendants, the majority of the peasants were indigenous natives and slave descendants; very commonly they also had some European ancestry, but normally built from nonfamily-structured relationships. It is worth stressing that these diverse dominant backgrounds of the latter lessened their cultural and ideological identities, at least in their initial set-ups, as happened with workers and slaves.

All these social conflicts arose from opposition among major social classes, as emphasized by Marxian sociology. This, however, does not mean that conflicts among social groups that were subsets of social classes were not important in Brazilian history. On the contrary, many conflicts among segments of the local elites had important effects in the economic dynamics of the country, as they played major roles in shaping institutions.[6] Conflicts among elites spatially settled in particular states or cities and the national political equilibrium were the most common. They even generated open uprisings, such as the Farroupilha Revolution in Rio Grande do Sul, the Constitutionalist Revolution in São Paulo, and the Revolução Praieira in Pernambuco. Other conflicts among social classes were also relevant for the economic evolution. For example, conflicts among international traders and commodity producers, which were common in Brazilian history, impacted on equilibrium exchange rates, import tariffs, and even tax revenues of the public sector.

---

4. Guimarães (1977) gives an analysis of the agrarian question in Brazil, while Alston et al. (1999, Chapter 2) give a history of land reform in Brazil and its political determinants.
5. Freyre (1933) presented the deepest initial analysis of patriarchalism in Brazilian society.
6. Bethell and Carvalho (1989) present many of these conflicts and some of their institutional consequences. Gohn (1995) gives an extensive review of many social conflicts since the 19th century in Brazil.

These economic impacts certainly had consequences for the Brazilian development, at least in the short and medium terms.

12.3 DYNAMICS OF SOCIAL CONFLICTS AND THE RELATIVE BACKWARDNESS LEGACY

All the major conflicts listed in the previous section had two polar social classes as protagonists, a richer one and a poorer. The poor pole of society was composed of slaves, low-skilled workers, and peasants. It also included low-skilled self-employed petty traders and petty services providers, whose income tended to be regulated by those of workers by arbitrage in their markets, as low-skilled laborers could migrate to these self-employed activities if their incomes would rise. Many individuals moved among these positions over their lifetimes. In specific circumstance the particular interests of these poor social groups could diverge, even among those settled in urban areas. Overall, though, the poor social strata tended to have closer identities, especially due to sharing the same neighborhoods, frequent family intermarriages across these social classes, and movements among some of the classes by individuals over their lives.

The rich pole was composed of masters, business stakeholders, including retail and wholesale traders, and large farmers. There were also frequent disputes among these elite groups, which often caused social tensions and even open conflicts, as was the case, for example, in the Revolução Praieira in Pernambuco, in which wholesale and retail traders were the target of revolts by the large landlords. The Constitutionalist Revolution in São Paulo in 1932 also pitted the rural elites against the industrial elites. The state bureaucracy and other skilled professionals associated with this rich pole in Brazilian society, so they tended to align ideologically and politically with these groups, in addition to sharing common social environments. Thus Brazilian society throughout its history was divided into two major poles, which were more or less united and were under higher or lower tension in their conflicts, depending on concrete historical moments and social priorities.

The imbalances in organizational development and social identities within each of the two poles and the income disparities between the rich and poor social strata led to little or no public investment in education. Thus the low-income social strata did not have access to public resources to speed up their human capital accumulation and reduce the relative shortage they faced in this factor of production when compared to the stock belonging to the elites. Hence they replicated their relative poor level of per capita human capital over generations and reduced national average growth of this variable. This ruled out any possibility of fast catch-up of Brazilian per capita GDP with that of European countries and the so-called Western Offshoots.

To understand this impact of social conflicts on the human capital accumulation in Brazil better, it is enlightening to divide Brazilian history into three periods: social formation (1500—1822), backwardness consolidation (1822—1930), and search for national identity, which lasts from 1930 to 2016 and probably will extend to forthcoming years.

12.3.1 Social Formation (1500—1822)

In its first three centuries Brazilian society was formed by a few Europeans (mainly Portuguese), who relied on slaves to build efficient enterprises in the country and integrated to the European economy by exporting sugar, gold, and other primary commodities. When building these enterprises, Europeans imported African slaves and captured local indigenous people to use in their productive systems as slaves. These other two origins of population in this new society or productive system had much lower human capital levels, not only in direct productive skills but also in organizational skills, as discussed in Chapter 7.

When Europeans arrived in Brazil and formed a new society, they originally replicated the institutional structure they had in Portugal. In addition to the enterprise stakeholders, a state bureaucracy and military apparatus were brought from Portugal, whose aim was to safeguard the interests of the Portuguese Crown in this new colony. Some professionals, such as physicians and engineers, were attracted to Brazil, but the majority of the initial European population were businessmen, state bureaucrats, and not unskilled but also not highly skilled professionals, merchants, and traders. Over the 17th and 18th centuries there were also incentives for migrations of Portuguese farmers, especially from the north of Portugal (Minho), to help populate Brazil and defend it against potential invaders. These peasants were poorer than the other social strata, but they were granted access to land and allowed to start enterprises. Although they were less educated than those who came as bureaucrats or businessmen, they were much more skilled than natives and Africans. Thus they came to increase the size of a lower middle class in Brazil.

At the end of the first three centuries of colonization, the majority of the population of the colonial society were non-European slaves (42% of the population in 1798 were black slaves)[7] or other very low-skilled free workers, descendants of Portuguese colonizers, imported Africans, and indigenous people. For example, estimates were that 59% of the Brazilian population in 1800 had African origin. Thus the 17% of free individuals of African origins (59%—42%) were either pure Africans who obtained freedom or African descendants, but not pure in their ethnic origin, whose share was included in African population. They were mostly unskilled workers in the labor market. Table 7.2 in Chapter 7 also indicates that 13% of the population were native descendants, so altogether Africans and natives formed 72% of the

---

7. Data from Marcílio (1984, p. 54).

population's ethnic origin, and were in the majority unskilled workers. Thus at the end of the 18th century Brazilian society was formed by a small elite with some education and a majority of people with very low or no skills.

To keep order in this society, economic and political institutional arrangements were built to ensure the necessary protection of the interests of the European elites and Portuguese royal family. Enterprise stakeholders and state bureaucracy controlled the state and ensured the social order was such that they could get what they came for when they moved to Brazil. As those who adhered to this project voluntarily to get some returns from their efforts were a minority in the total population, the political rules had to ensure that power was in the hands of these few beneficiaries and the economic institutions also replicated this bias toward the benefit of those who engaged voluntarily in the project. Hence the existing and potential social conflicts had one side much more powerful than the other, as it controlled all colonization and built institutional arrangements to protect its minority interests.

The consequence of this initial set-up was that the social structure was rooted in centralization of political power in the hands of these few Europeans. Furthermore, the distance from Europe and consequent high transport costs, together with the low productivity of technologies available at that time and the risk involved in such overseas entrepreneurship, only made viable enterprises whose production costs were very low. That is why slaves brought from Africa were the best option. Consequently, the economic institutional arrangements that were created gave a very low standard of living for unskilled workers, mostly slaves either brought from Africa or mobilized from local natives because of their low standard of living, potential productivity with European production technologies, and ideological potential for submission under firm use of power, even violence when necessary. Thus Brazilian society was created with a high income disparity among social groups.

The enterprise stakeholders were on one side of the social spectrum, trying to maximize profits and spend the least necessary on workers. They had the support of state bureaucrats and providers of other skilled services in this task. Slaves and other unskilled workers were on the other side of the conflict: they wanted to work as little as possible and benefit from the highest standard of living possible. Unskilled workers outside plantations also had major conflicts with their hirers (mainly the Portuguese elite), but faced competition from slaves and other unskilled workers within the plantations, even in domestic service, as alternative suppliers of similar services. As they had low human capital, normally very similar to that of slaves, their labor per hour could not be charged at prices that would allow a much higher standard of living than that of slaves and unskilled workers in plantations. The consequence of this competition was that low-income social groups, even those who were not slaves, were kept by market forces at very low standards of living, similar to those of slaves, at least in what concerns material consumption. This brought another source of social conflicts with slaves, who were seen as challenging some of their economic activities. Thus they ended up adding another conflict in addition to the one they had with the Portuguese elite, who often enough were their hirers.

The cost of slaves was so low that it was cheaper to import them from Africa than to engage in their domestic reproduction. The same can be said of the cost of domestic reproduction of local natives when compared to their capture.[8] Thus the Portuguese and other European colonizers had no interest in investing in human capital enhancement of young generations of slave descendants. This conclusion extended to the education of the heirs of unskilled workers, as their services could eventually be substituted by those of imported slaves.

Other social conflicts also appeared within this period, such as those between wholesale traders on the one side and primary commodities and industrial enterprise stakeholders on the other. These conflicts, however, did not greatly alter the availability of resources for human capital building of the poorest social groups in Brazil. Thus they are of little relevance for the long-term development of the country, although they could affect many of the local economic institutions, such as importing rules and royal concession rules for starting particular industries in Brazil, among others. Furthermore, they were often the origin of open conflicts, such as the so-called *Inconfidência Mineira* (1789).

The existing incentives were such that the poor social strata did not feature in the effort of the local Portuguese elites to foster the human capital of their heirs, as argued before. Furthermore, these elites had to keep costs at the lowest possible level as local production was subject to high risk, with commodity price fluctuations and high costs for transport to Europe. Hence they always pressed for lower costs. Furthermore, their aim was often to return to Europe at some time, so they had no identity with local society and tried to become as rich as possible as quickly as possible. Thus they had little compassion for local unprivileged social groups.

Unskilled workers, both freemen and slaves, did not have the necessary organization to press for better working conditions and public investment in their welfare, including education for their heirs. Africans and local natives had no cultural identity with each other and remained divided over the years, as there was no social environment to foster their integration. Both Africans and local natives also came from many different tribes and even nations within their respective continents, so they had different cultures and did not speak the same home language. Thus even within each of these ethnic groups, there were no social identities which could foster their organization.

---

8. This capture sometimes became more expensive because the Portuguese Crown forbade slavery of Brazilian natives when it had an alliance with slave importers, who paid taxes that could give good returns to the royal family. In these periods and in parts of Brazil where the Portuguese government had the ability to monitor capture, Africans were the preference. This happened, for example, in plantations in northeast Brazil.

Up to 1800, the Brazilian population lived mainly in rural areas and small towns and villages. Cities like Salvador (about 51,000 inhabitants), Rio de Janeiro (47,000 inhabitants), Recife (25,000 inhabitants), and São Paulo (24,000 inhabitants) were very few.[9] Table 12.1 shows the available estimations for the 10 largest Brazilian cities around 1800, when altogether these cities had nearly 211,767 inhabitants. If the average population of all 118 existing towns was 2,000, as in Oeiras in Piauí, the smallest city included in Table 12.1, which is certainly an overstatement, the total population in cities and towns in Brazil had reached 447,767, which represented only 12.23% of the total Brazilian population that year according to Humboldt, presented in IBGE (1990) and used in Table 7.2 of Chapter 7. Thus even after the "gold cycle" (over the 18th century), the Brazilian population lived mainly in rural areas.

The rural population was organized in three major types of productive structures: market-oriented establishments, individual self-consumption farms, and collective tribal production. While the first directed most of their production to urban markets or exports to other regions or countries, the second

TABLE 12.1 Population of Brazilian Cities at the End of the 18th and Beginning of the 19th Centuries

City	State	Year	Population
Belém	Pará	1801	12,500
São Luís	Maranhão	1810	20,500
Recife	Pernambuco	1810	25,000
Salvador	Bahia	1807	51,000
Rio de Janeiro	Rio de Janeiro	1803	46,944
São Paulo	São Paulo	1803	24,311
Porto Alegre	Rio Grande do Sul	1808	6,035
Oeiras	Piauí	1810	2,000
Vila Boa	Goiás	1804	9,477
Vila Bela	Mato Grosso	1782	7,000
Ouro Preto	Minas Gerais	1804	7,000
Total			**211,767**

Alden, D., 1984. Late Colonial Brazil, 1750–1808, In: Bethell, L. (Ed.), The Cambridge History of Latin America Vol. 2: Colonial Latin America. Cambridge University Press, Cambridge, Table 3.

9. Most of the data is from Alden (1984).

type was individually formed by a few families and focused mainly on production for self-consumption by their members. The third type of productive structure was basically formed by native tribes, although some were created by African fugitives, the so-called Quilombos.[10]

The market-oriented establishments, all engaged in primary activities, had their populations mainly divided into slaves, unskilled workers, a few skilled workers, and the stakeholders. Thus the social structure tended to reflect the conflicts previously discussed and its evolution was guided by the evolution of these conflicts. As noted, any public or entrepreneurial policy to accumulate human capital in the majority of the poor population was not a priority for the elites, as it was not a rational investment. Moreover, the poorer classes did not have the necessary organization to push for any investment in this, so the rate of accumulation of human capital embodied in the majority of this population was defined by the rational family rate,[11] as defined in Chapter 5, starting from a very low initial level and at a very low productivity level in their human capital generation.

The second group of rural productive structures, the individual self-consumption farms, formed a substantial share of the Brazilian population at the beginning of the 19th century and kept this position over the whole century and even a reasonable part of the 20th century. They had access to small villages, where they traded part of their output, so their contacts with other economic agents were through the market. Most of their consumption was generated by production on their farms, but part was acquired in the market. Thus the major conflicts they faced were with merchants and sometimes with larger farmers who wanted to expropriate their lands and other productive equipment.

Like tribes, peasants lived very isolated from political decisions, as most of the time they were segregated from other social groups. They had their own incentives for human capital accumulation, as described in Chapter 5, but this was a society with very restricted opportunities to improve standards of living as a result of education (low prospect of increased income accruing from education) and the peasants had low productivity in the human capital production function in their communities. Thus the resulting incentives yielded very low rates of human capital accumulation among this population.

Their demands in their major conflicts did not include education as a priority: their major concerns were assurance of land tenure and good prices for their output. Fair trade rules and protection for land access rights were their

---

10. For further analysis on Quilombos see Moura (1987) and Reis and Gomes (1996).
11. Actually this is not really true, as slaves, if they were free to choose, could prefer to invest more in human capital if they had any hope of being free one day. This could increase their future income. Nevertheless, the time they spent on this effort was bounded by the working hours they were subjected to. Thus the final human capital accumulation was actually below the rational family rate.

major demands in any political activism. Hence these conflicts did not lead to any improvement in human capital accumulation. Over the first four centuries of Brazilian colonization, these conflicts did not lead to any organization of peasants that generated relevant concrete demands for improvements of their human capital.

Tribes, whatever their origins, did not have the political power to demand any state investments in human capital, as they lived independently of the state and did not even recognize its authority. They did not pay taxes and were not engaged in any political decision-making institutions. Any faster improvement in their stock of human capital did not benefit the groups that controlled or had influence on the state, as they had hardly any contact with the tribes. Thus the tribes were left isolated, with a low and almost stagnant per capita stock of human capital. This dynamic of their human capital remained over the 19th and 20th centuries, although there was a slow but persistent fall in the share of these populations in the total.

12.3.2 Backwardness Consolidation (1822–1930)

In Chapter 8 the set-up of a less-educated population is discussed in numbers, with a major focus on the period called here "backwardness consolidation," 1822–1930. The logic of human capital accumulation changed in Europe and the United States in this period, but this did not happen in Brazil to the same extent. Public institutions and churches became more involved in education than before, and concern over this subject was raised in these countries. Although the Catholic Church engaged in education in Brazil, its effort extended only to a very small part of society, as there were limited finances and often parents had to pay the expenses.[12]

In the 1824 Brazilian Constitution, the first after independence, state responsibility for education was introduced.[13] Nevertheless, the 1834 regulation of this part of the constitution transferred the responsibility to provide this service to the states (provinces at the time). Thus priorities in municipal budget allocations were defined by local political elites, and primary education was not among their priorities. Only after the new constitution in 1891 did local government have higher budgets, as the republic decentralized public resources. Nevertheless, only in those states and counties with stronger political demand was there better engagement of the public sector in education.

---

12. The most important religious involvement in education in Brazil was by Jesuit missions through the so-called Companhia de Jesus. Nevertheless, in 1759 they were expelled from Brazil by Marques de Pombal. This reduced the involvement of religious orders in education in Brazil.

13. The 1824 Constitution stated that "A instrução primária é gratuita a todos os cidadãos" (Art. 179, § 32). This means "Primary education is free to all citizens". Extracted from Vieira (2007, p. 294).

The major social conflicts that brought changes to the political and economic institutional frameworks in the period of backwardness consolidation involved mainly social groups of the elites. This was true for groups as varied as sugarcane growers in the northeast, dry meat and grain producers in the south, who objected to taxes and import tariff policies imposed by the central government, and senior army officers, who objected to their salaries. There were very few mobilizations of poor peasants and they were mostly badly organized, as was the case of Arraial de Canudos (1893—97) and the Cangaço in the northeast (1870—1930). Thus the demands of these social organizations of the poor social strata did not include greater access to opportunities to improve their standard of living under alternative social rules crystallized in institutions. Their effective impact was low and they did not work to make important improvements in access to education. Only at the very end of this second period of Brazilian history did these mobilizations have an impact on education, and only in specific regions and states.

This period, however, saw an important change in Brazilian society. Most European immigration to Brazil occurred in this period. It started to pick up from 1850, as discussed in Chapter 9, and the share of these immigrants and their descendants rose to almost 22% of the Brazilian population in 1930 (Fig. 9.7 in Chapter 9). Although the immigrants tended to be less skilled than those who went to the United States and Canada, as there were pecuniary incentives to migrate to Brazil for most of this period, they came to compose a low social strata of workers who were eager to improve their standard of living and have access to education as an important instrument for this. They arrived in Brazil with this ideology built in 19th-century Europe.

It took some time before these immigrants became a relevant social player in Brazil, as their numbers evolved slowly. In 1900 they formed only 14.5% of the Brazilian population. Many lived in rural communities in the south or coffee plantations in São Paulo, still under the initial contracts that financed their immigration, which reduced their freedom to search for better ways to improve their standard of living by their own efforts. Their ability to gather together behind common demands was restricted by this spatial distribution, although their increasing urbanization slowly strengthened their capacities to organize themselves.

Their first social demands were to get basic citizenship recognition in an enslaving society. To this end, they first had to gain freedom to move around and have basic rights respected. Such movement was still very restricted at the end of the 19th century, and the 1891 Constitution brought no relevant assurance of social rights. It ended up as a very liberal constitution, made by local elites under little or no pressure from those interested in affirmation of basic social rights, including access to education.[14] The disputes among local

---

14. See Cury (2001).

elites settled long distances apart were more important at that time, and this led to more decentralized power recognized in that constitution.

As newcomers, the immigrants took some time to gain their basic rights and force the necessary institutional changes in Brazil that could ensure public financing of basic education. Although demands for this started to appear at the end of the 19th century, they spread more broadly in regions with heavy European immigration in the early 20th century. This demand generated results that can be identified at the end of this period in 1930, as can be seen in Table 12.2. The enrollment rate in primary school of children between 5 and 14 years of age increased from 7% to 23% between 1889 and 1933.

The still-incipient association of citizenship with access to publicly financed education in the early 20th century confined this demand and its relevant results to a few counties in Brazil, and it spread unevenly across the country. The data in Table 12.2 was combined with data on the share of foreigners in the total population by state in Brazil in 1920. A simple regression of the growth rate of the enrollment rates between 1889 and 1933 in the natural logarithm of the enrollment rate in 1889 and the share of immigrants (foreigners) in the total population in 1920 was run. Results are shown in Table 12.3. As there were only 21 states at that time, the sample is very small and the results are quite fragile. Nevertheless, it can be seen that there is a measurable, positive, and statistically significant impact of the share of immigrants on the growth of the enrollment rate.

These results indicate that European immigration to Brazil, which was fostered from the second half of the 19th century, initiated an important qualitative change in the definitions of priorities of public policies, as stressed in Chapter 9. This eventually halted the tendency toward widening the gap between Brazilian per capita GDP and that of Europe and the Western Offshoots.

12.3.3 Search for National Identity (1930 to Present)

The third period of Brazilian history is certainly the most complex. Industrialization in Brazil was intense in this period.[15] The role of primary exports in total GDP had fallen since the beginning of the 20th century, so the Brazilian economy was already becoming more diversified. Fig. 12.1 shows that from 1930 to 1986 the share of industry in total GDP rose, mainly at the expense of farming and livestock. Since 1986 services have become the leading sector in Brazilian growth, mainly at the expense of industry.[16]

This diversification of economic activities and rise in the role of industry in total GDP to become more important than farming and livestock in the late

---

15. See for example Baer (2008, Chapters 3 and 4), Bonelli et al. (2013), and Villela (2011).
16. Certainly the rise of outsourcing in industry plays a major role in this growth of services at the expense of industry.

TABLE 12.2 Some Statistics on Schooling in 1889 and 1933 by States

	Enrollment Rate in Primary School, 1889 (% of children in the age group)	Enrollment Rate in Primary School, 1933 (% of children in the age group)	Schools per 1000 Children, 1889	Schools per 1000 Children, 1933	Yearly Growth Rate of Enrollment, 1933/1889 (%)
Ceará	4.2	13.0	1.0	1.8	3.4
Rio Grande do Sul	9.8	33.2	2.0	5.7	3.7
Rito Santo	7.2	25.2	2.9	4.4	3.8
Minas Gerais	5.7	23.4	2.1	2.1	4.2
Rio de Janeiro	14.4	29.1	3.9	3.4	2.1
São Paulo	6.3	31.6	3.1	3.2	4.9
Paraná	10.2	25.2	3.1	3.8	2.7
Santa Catarina	10.0	37.3	2.3	6.4	3.9
Amazonas	10.0	23.2	3.4	8.9	2.5
Mato Grosso	7.9	22.8	2.2	3.3	3.2
Pará	13.5	27.9	3.8	4.2	2.2

Continued

TABLE 12.2 Some Statistics on Schooling in 1889 and 1933 by States—cont'd

	Enrollment Rate in Primary School, 1889 (% of children in the age group)	Enrollment Rate in Primary School, 1933 (% of children in the age group)	Schools per 1000 Children, 1889	Schools per 1000 Children, 1933	Yearly Growth Rate of Enrollment, 1933/1889 (%)
Maranhão	5.7	12.2	1.5	2.3	2.3
Paraíba	2.0	16.0	0.7	2.2	6.3
Piauí	2.9	8.0	1.1	0.9	3.0
Rio Grande do Norte	7.7	20.6	2.3	2.5	2.9
Alagoas	5.4	13.2	1.6	2.2	2.7
Pernambuco	7.5	15.7	2.9	3.0	2.2
Sergipe	4.9	17.4	2.7	3.5	3.8
Bahia	4.4	9.2	1.3	1.7	2.2
Goiás	4.4	12.1	1.6	2.1	3.0
Brazil	7.0	23.3	2.2	3.0	3.6

Musacchio, A., Fritscher, A., Viarengo, M., 2014. Colonial institutions, trade shocks, and the diffusion of elementary education in Brazil, 1889–1930. The Journal of Economic History 74(3), 730–766, Table 2; originally extracted from official sources, such as IBGE.

TABLE 12.3 Regression Results of the Relationship Between the Growth Rate of Enrollment in Primary Education (1933−1889) as a Function of the Share of Immigrants in the Total Population in 1920

Variable	Estimated Coefficient	Standard Errors	t-Statistics	p-Value
Constant	2.409	0.396	6.088	0.0000
Natural logarithm of 5−14 years old enrollment rate in 1889	−0.701	0.199	−3.514	0.0004
Natural logarithm of the share of immigrants on population in 1920	0.112	0.033	3.345	0.0008
$R^2 =$	0.48		$\overline{R}^2 =$	0.43

Note: Estimations were by ordinary least square with correction for heteroskedasticity using the method of Eicker and White.
Estimated with data from IBGE.

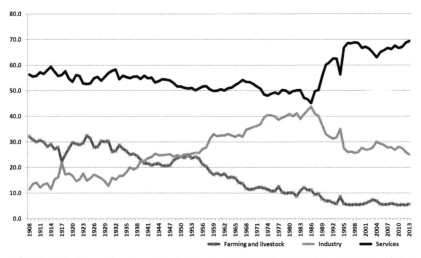

FIGURE 12.1   Share of major sectors in Brazilian GDP, 1908−2013. Note: Data from 1947 to 2013 was forced to add to 100%, which does not happen in the IBGE series. This was done to keep the proportion among the series for sectors. Haddad's series for farming and livestock and industry were made compatible with their counterpart from IBGE, forcing their numbers from 1947 to be equal to those of IBGE. His shares were the index before that. Services shares were obtained as residuals of the shares of the two other sectors before 1946. *IBGE for 1947 to 2013 and Haddad (1978) for 1908 to 1947.*

1930s led to an expansion of the business elites. The newcomers to this elite, mainly in industry and new service sectors, were drawn substantially from middle and low urban classes, composed mainly of immigrants and their descendants.[17] The former moved to Brazil with much better qualifications than the average Brazilian worker and even more than most of the local elite, especially those engaged in rural activities. Furthermore, they also brought eagerness to get rich in their adventure.

The ethnic and cultural identification of these new businessmen with a large segment of the emerging working class, whose demands had more appeal to them as they and their families had often also sought such benefits in the past, were important to generate better outcomes for local workers, including easier access to education. Moreover, the rise of some immigrants to the upper classes increased their social and political influence, so the power of the working immigrants slowly became stronger at county and state levels. Public investment in education was one of the demands that were gradually accommodated, mainly in counties that had a higher proportion of immigrants in south and southeast Brazil.

It is important to stress that there was also intense urbanization between 1930 and 2015. Fig. 12.2 shows Census data from IBGE that indicates the urban share in the total population, rising from around 30% in 1940 to over

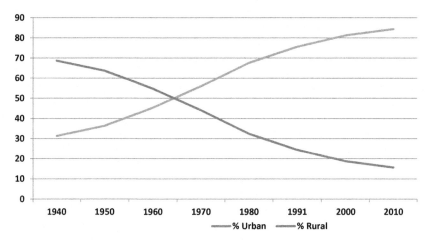

FIGURE 12.2   Share (%) of urban and rural populations in the total, 1940–2010. *IBGE Census data.*

---

17. See Bresser Pereira (1964, 1974, Chapter 3, and 1993). See also Dean (1971) and Cardoso (1964).

84% in 2010. This escalation was steady over the whole period. Thus Brazil became mainly an urban country after 1960. Urbanization led to a more intense exchange of ideas, as emphasized by Glaeser (2011), and consequently strengthened organizations of the poorest social strata demanding better opportunities to improve their quality of life. Education is a natural outcome of this struggle, although access to some social protection, better salaries, and democracy were also important demands in the circumstances, given the historical low standard of living of the poor social strata in Brazil over this whole period.

An important feature of Brazilian urban growth in the early 20th century was the particular increase in the population of two cities, São Paulo and Rio de Janeiro. Table 12.4 shows figures for the major Brazilian cities in the early 20th century. Between 1920 and 1940 the population of both these cities reached over 1 million inhabitants. Estimations are that the population of São Paulo was already almost 1 million in 1930. While Rio de Janeiro was the major political center of the country, where the central government was installed, São Paulo was the center of most urban economic activities connected to coffee production, including trade and financing. Additionally, it was the place where most of the new industries emerged. This growth of these two important centers that were consolidating their leadership in the whole country gave political strength to their urban population. Further organization of the nonelite social classes and the flow of information facilitated by crowding in these cities helped propagation of their demands and promotion of social organization in their favor.

Politically there was the revolution of 1930, which reduced the control of the government by rural elites and brought to power a political alliance including the urban new bourgeoisie, mainly from industry, the state bureaucracy, the urban middle class, workers, and some rural elites that were outside the previously existing pact[18]—which was mainly controlled by coffee growers from São Paulo, livestock farmers from Minas Gerais and Rio Grande do Sul, and sugarcane growers from northeast states and Rio de Janeiro. The new political alliance that emerged, Populism, had to meet some of the demands of all these social groups, as they needed to stay together to retain power. This alliance governed Brazil up to 1964.[19]

All these developments tended to raise public investments in education over the years, especially after the redemocratization of 1946, 16 years after the 1930 revolution, as can be seen in Fig. 12.3. This shows the share of public investments in education in Brazilian GDP between 1933 and 2013: despite long periods of stagnations in this proportion, mainly in periods of

---

18. See Bresser Pereira (2014, Chapters 6 and 8).
19. For further analysis of the new political alliances and developments unleashed by the 1930 revolution, see Skidmore (1967), Fausto (1970), and Ianni (1975).

TABLE 12.4 Evolution of Population in the Largest Brazilian Cities in the Early 20th Century (Number of Inhabitants)

Year	Fortaleza	Recife	Salvador	Belo Horizonte	Rio de Janeiro	São Paulo	Porto Alegre
1872	42,458	116,671	129,109	–	274,972	31,385	43,998
1890	40,902	111,556	174,412	–	522,651	64,934	52,421
1900	48,369	113,106	205,813	13,472	811,443	239,820	73,674
1920	78,536	238,843	283,422	55,563	1,157,873	579,033	179,263
1940	180,185	348,424	290,443	211,377	1,764,141	1,326,261	272,232
1950	270,169	524,682	417,235	352,724	2,377,451	2,198,096	394,151
1960	514,818	797,234	655,735	693,328	3,307,163	3,825,351	641,173
1970	872,702	1,084,459	1,027,142	1,255,415	4,315,746	5,978,977	903,175
1980	1,338,793	1,240,937	1,531,242	1,822,221	5,183,992	8,587,665	1,158,709
1991	1,765,794	1,296,995	2,072,058	2,017,127	5,473,909	9,626,894	1,263,239
2000	2,138,234	1,421,993	2,440,828	2,232,747	5,851,914	10,405,867	1,360,033
2010	2,452,185	1,537,704	2,675,656	2,375,151	6,320,446	11,253,503	1,409,351

Fonte, Recenseamento do Brazil 1872–1920; Rio de Janeiro, Directoria Geral de Estatística, 1872–1930; IBGE, Censo Demográfico 1940/2010. Up to 1991, table extracted from IBGE, *Estatísticas do Século XX*, Rio de Janeiro: IBGE, 2007 in *Anuário Estatístico do Brasil 1994*, vol. 54, 1994.

FIGURE 12.3   Brazilian public investments in education as a proportion of GDP. *INEP from 2000 to 2013 and Maduro (2007) from 1933 to 2000.*

authoritarian governments, there was a long-term increase in the share, which was especially boosted in democratic periods. The most recent rises were such that it reached levels above those found in developed countries in the same periods. It should be noted, however, that this share took a long time to achieve the recent figures, which were only reached after a long process of pressure from the lowest social classes while facing strong resistance from the local elites, especially the most established.

The logic of social conflict underlying the outcome shown in Fig. 12.3 and its consequence for the speed of human capital accumulation in Brazil is discussed in the next chapter.

12.4 CONCLUSION

This chapter unveils the major social conflicts in Brazilian society in three different phases of its long-term development. It is argued that despite the varieties of the existing social groups in each of these periods, there are some major conflicts among social classes that prevail over the many other potential disputes. These class conflicts drove accumulation of human capital over these periods, as they were crucial to determine the shape of most other institutional arrangements, such as those molding the dynamics of the Brazilian economy.

The conflicts and their major logical outcomes were linked to the particularities of each time to explain the evolution of human capital over that particular period. This is related to previous discussions on the social and economic evolutions that are analyzed in previous chapters. A further detailed analysis of the last period, called here "search for national identity," is given in the next chapter, as there is more information available which can help in the analysis. As this was a period in which Brazilian relative backwardness was either partially reversed or stagnated, certainly the increase in human capital was more intense in this period than had been seen previously. What distinguished this period and how the conflicts evolved and impacted on human capital accumulation are introduced in the last part of this chapter, but deserve the deeper analysis pursued in the next chapter.

Chapter 13

Social Conflicts and Human Capital Accumulation in the Period of Search for National Identity

Chapter Outline

13.1 INTRODUCTION

The last chapter presents the major social conflicts underlying Brazilian economic and social history and shows some of their consequences for public investments in education and human capital formation. It is argued that the nature and balances of these conflicts and the interests of the social classes involved led to low human capital accumulation. This was the ultimate cause of Brazilian relative backwardness, which was built throughout its history. Hence the specific social relations and their consequences for the institutional framework that was built and its dynamics, in addition to public policy history, underlie the formation of a less-developed nation.

The last chapter divides Brazilian history into three periods. The first extends from the Portuguese arrival in 1500 to 1822, the year of Brazilian independence from Portugal. The second starts in 1822 and goes up to 1930, when there was a revolution with an important change in the political equilibrium in Brazil. The last period started in 1930 and extends to the present. The class struggles undergone during these periods had particularities, and the equilibrium outcomes were qualitatively different. While there were explicit formal alliances with the Portuguese colonial power in the first period, the second had domestic relations determining the political equilibrium, with the major disputes arising from conflicts among spatially distant local elites. The third period saw new social classes entering social disputes and changing the political equilibrium.

This chapter introduces more details of the class conflicts of the third period and why they did not lead to overcoming Brazil's relative backwardness, although the outcome was enough to halt the widening of per capita income disparities when compared to the benchmark countries. While the two other periods are analyzed in previous chapters, when the concern was with identifying why Brazil lagged behind, this third period, whose major question should be why Brazil did not catch up, has not been analyzed before. Thus the evolution of the class conflicts and their consequences for human capital building are pursued here.

This last period of Brazilian economic history has been the object of many analyses, thus the aim here is not to give an overview of the major social and economic changes over the years, but to focus on the relationship between class conflicts and the evolution of human capital building. The analysis is also useful to differentiate the hypotheses raised in this book from dependency analyses found in the literature on Brazilian social and economic history. Particularly important is the idea endorsed here that classes do not act as a bloc, as if they had a unified command, when they face political and economic disputes.[1] The hypothesis here is that individuals act in their own interest, as rational agents, seeking to maximize their own utility under the restrictions they face, as stated by mainstream economic theory. Only the fact that individuals in the same social class have closer interests justifies the identification of class behavior. Thus despite the existence of class behavior, there are no relevant class strategies in the conflict dynamics and their consequences.

The next section identifies the major class protagonists of this period, while Section 13.3 introduces their utility function, identifying their affinities and the consequent externalities that arise. Section 13.4 defines the major social conflicts that are relevant to understand the evolution of human capital through

---

1. This kind of approach seems to emerge in dependency analysis such as those of Cardoso and Falletto (1970) and Bresser Pereira (2014).

this period, and Section 13.5 presents data on the progress of public investments in education and human capital stock over the period. As the combination of data in Section 13.5 and the utilities in Section 13.3 generates a complex analysis of the outcomes, I adopt the methodology introduced in Chapter 7: educated guesses for relative utilities arising from public investments in education extracted by the many social classes are made and the conclusions analyzed. Although this seems a nonscientific approach, it is only an analytical device to simplify exposition and give a more concrete idea of the expected consequences of the nontrivial, implicit system of equations that is created. Section 13.6 shows some statistics created by this method, and relies on them to present a general view of the class conflict consequences for the evolution of human capital building in Brazil over this period. Section 13.7 summarizes the major conclusions of the chapter.

13.2 MAJOR PROTAGONIST SOCIAL CLASSES WITHIN THIS PERIOD

To understand the evolution of public education in the period of Brazilian history named "search for social identity," it is worth noting that Brazil emerged from transformations in the early 20th century as a country where four major social classes could be identified, plus a state bureaucracy, which was considerable in the Brazilian scenario given the growing role of cities in political disputes, the level of urbanization of this social group, and their educational level, which was above the average of the whole population.[2]

The Brazilian elites were mainly composed of landlords involved in varied farming and livestock production, and urban company stakeholders mainly engaged in industry, trade, and services, such as financing. These elites are divided in two major social classes here. The traditional elites are composed of those whose origins were mainly in slave-owning families, which had a long history in Brazil. They were spread over the whole country and their ethnic origins were mainly Portuguese. They are represented henceforth as ro, which stands for rich and old.

The second social class composing the elites was formed by enriched immigrants of European and Japanese descent, who were overwhelmingly engaged in industry, trade, and urban services, such as financing, but who started from small businesses and made fortunes. Eventually they also spread to rural activities, such as farming and livestock, as well as mining. Most of them or their ancestors brought to Brazil mainly their skills and few resources. Before they progressed financially, they often shared neighborhoods with other immigrants who never became as economically successful as they did. They

---

2. For a detailed description and analysis of the social role of this social segment, see Bresser Pereira (2008, 2014, Chapter 6).

were mainly descendants of Italians, Portuguese, Spanish, and Germans, and had higher educational levels than the first social class within the elites. They are represented henceforth as rn, which stands for rich and new.

The lower social strata could also be divided in two major social classes. The first is the low-educated poor social strata, formed by the majority of the population whose ancestors had been in Brazil for generations, although they could have come from Africa as slaves. A small share had Portuguese origins, many from extramarital relationships. They were very low educated and skilled, as their ancestors were very low skilled[3] and had no access to any formal education. They formed the majority of the population of all regions, although their share in the total population was higher in the north, northeast, and the states of Minas Gerais and Rio de Janeiro. Henceforth they are represented as po, which stands for poor and old.

This po class was originally overwhelmingly engaged in rural activities, as Brazil was still predominantly a rural society in the early 1930s. They were peasants, rural workers, or both, as they often had their own small landholdings, and complemented their income by selling to landlords some of their available working hours. Members of this social class engaged in urban activities also had qualitatively similar time sharing, although in different activities and proportions. They often had their own petty businesses, but some of their working hours, at least over their lifetime, were spent employed by larger businesses.

The low income of this urban social segment generated an informal sector, which competed with larger formal businesses as a consequence of tax evasion and, mainly, the lack of any need for management skills because of the small size of these firms. As a consequence, larger competitors that had to use more sophisticated and expensive management skills to run their businesses could not match the prices of these small enterprises, which prospered in Brazilian cities, supplying markets with clothes, shoes, and many goods and services that in richer countries with better income distribution are supplied by larger firms. This is not a Brazilian phenomenon only: it existed in most developing countries over the 20th and even 21st centuries.

The other social class that could be included in the lower social strata is formed by poor European and Japanese immigrants who started moving to Brazil in the late 19th century. Of course, their descendants also fit within this social stratum. Although its members were not rich, they did not have standards of living as low as those of the previous social class. They had better qualifications, and many ascended socially to the upper class as they became successful businessmen. They lived in both rural and urban areas, and slowly captured a large share of the skilled positions in the labor market. They migrated persistently to the middle class, as they were more skilled

---

3. See Chapter 7 for a better discussion on the genesis of their low skills.

than the poor and old (po) social stratum. They had higher human capital and made greater demands for public investments in education, although at strategic school levels, as discussed later. They were mainly concentrated in south and southeast Brazil, although they spread over all regions. Henceforth they are represented as pn, which stands for poor and new.

13.3 SOCIAL AFFINITIES AMONG SOCIAL CLASSES

The individuals in each of these social classes had specificities in the externalities they got from the standard of living of the members of all social classes, as they had different social identities with these other Brazilians. A simple mathematical representation of their utilities can help understand this idea, before a discussion of their consequences for the development of Brazil since 1930. Eqs. (13.1)−(13.4) show the natural logarithm of the utility function for a representative consumer from each of these four social classes.

$$u_{pn}(k) = \lambda_k u_{pn}(c_k) + \lambda_{kpn} u_{pn}(c_{pn}) + \lambda_{kpo} u_{po}(c_{po}) + \lambda_{kro} u_{ro}(c_{ro}) + \lambda_{krn} u_{rn}(c_{rn})$$
(13.1)

$$u_{po}(m) = \lambda_m u_{po}(c_m) + \lambda_{mpn} u_{pn}(c_{pn}) + \lambda_{mpo} u_{po}(c_{po}) + \lambda_{mro} u_{ro}(c_{ro}) + \lambda_{mrn} u_{rn}(c_{rn})$$
(13.2)

$$u_{ro}(b) = \lambda_b u_{ro}(c_b) + \lambda_{bpn} u_{pn}(c_{pn}) + \lambda_{bpo} u_{po}(c_{po}) + \lambda_{bro} u_{ro}(c_{ro}) + \lambda_{brn} u_{rn}(c_{rn})$$
(13.3)

$$u_{rn}(a) = \lambda_a u_{rn}(c_a) + \lambda_{apn} u_{pn}(c_{pn}) + \lambda_{apo} u_{po}(c_{po}) + \lambda_{aro} u_{ro}(c_{ro}) + \lambda_{arn} u_{rn}(c_{rn})$$
(13.4)

where $u_{pn}(k)$ is the natural logarithm of the utility $U_{pn}(k)$ of a representative member of the class of pn, which is individually represented by k. $U_{pn}(k) \geq 1$, so $u_{pn}(k) \geq 0$. His/her own consumption index is given by c_k, which represents a present value of a future flow of consumption, properly defined from utility maximization for the expected consumption and individual income future flows considering the existing wealth stock of individual k.[4]

All the other utility functions included in Eq. (13.1) are defined in the same way as $u_{pn}(k)$, but the consumption index included is for the expected flows for a representative consumer of that particular social class. Hence, for example, $u_{po}(c_{po})$ and $u_{ro}(c_{ro})$ are the natural logarithms of the utility function of representative consumers of the social classes po and ro, respectively. The indexes c_{pn} and c_{ro} are defined in the same way as c_k. They are indexes representing the present value of a future flow of consumption, properly defined

---

4. This index c_k is defined as a positive real number.

from utility maximization for the expected consumption and individual income future flows considering the existing individual stocks of wealth of these representative consumers.

Furthermore, $U'_{ij}(c_{ij}) > 0$; $U''_{ij}(c_{ij}) < 0$; $U'_{ij}(c_{ij}) \rightarrow +\infty$ when $c_{ij} \rightarrow 0$; and $U'_{ij}(c_{ij}) \rightarrow 0$ when $c_{ij} \rightarrow \infty$, as usual, where $U'(.)$ and $U''(.)$ are the first and second derivatives of function $U(.)$ with respect to their only arguments, respectively. In these mathematical representations ij stands for all subscripts found in Eqs. (13.1)−(13.4). It is also assumed that all these first and second derivatives are continuous for $0 < c_{ij} < \infty$. From the fact that the utility functions defined in Eqs. (13.1)−(13.4) are for representative consumers of each social class, it is obvious that $c_k = c_{pn}$; $c_m = c_{po}$; $c_b = c_{ro}$; and $c_a = c_{rn}$.

The many λs are parameters, defined in real numbers, which indicate the proportional impact of the measured utility on the total utility of that particular consumer. λ_k, λ_m, λ_a, and λ_b measure the proportional impact of the utility obtained from own consumption on total utility. Therefore, $0 < \lambda_k$, λ_m, λ_a, and $\lambda_b \leq 1$. The other parameters λ with three subscripts represent the proportional impact that the individual utility of the representative consumer of the social class represented by the two last subscripts has on the individual represented by the first subscript. Thus, for example, λ_{mrn} is the elasticity of the utility of individual m with respect to the utility of a representative consumer of the rn social class.

By assumption, $1 > \lambda_{ijf} \geq 0$ for all i, j, and f, representing any of the subscripts found in Eqs. (13.1)−(13.4). Therefore, whenever there are externalities extracted from utility of others, they are positive. If $\lambda_{ijf} = 0$, there is no externality extracted by agent i from the representative agent jf. Furthermore, it is also reasonable to assume that $\lambda_i > \lambda_{ijf}$ for all i, j, and f. This means that individuals always value their own consumption more than they value consumption of others. Additionally, if an individual utility is $u_{jf}(i)$, then $\lambda_{ijf} \geq \lambda_{svd}$, where $s \neq i$ and $vd \neq jf$. This means that individuals always extract more externalities from consumption of individuals of her/his own social class. In a more general concept, individuals are assumed to have some class solidarity or class consciousness, in Marxian language.

Because of social identity and ethnic origins, it is assumed that $\lambda_{apn} \geq \lambda_{bpo}$. This means that the new bourgeoisie, which mainly originated from immigrants and their descendants who prospered, has more solidarity with their compatriots than the old elites had with the old poor Brazilians. It should be noted that the old elites had origins in a slavery environment in which segregation was strong. They grew up learning that different opportunities were a consequence of the color of one's skin. This made a large difference in their sensitivity to demands of other segments of society when compared to the views of the new elites.

Another important relationship is $\lambda_{apn} > \lambda_{apo}$. This arises from the fact that the new elite had more solidarity with the new poor, which had similar ethnic origins, than they had with the old poor, with whom they had no social identity.[5] Nevertheless, $\lambda_{bpn} > \lambda_{bpo}$. The old elites had more solidarity with all European and Japanese immigrants than they had with the old poor. This is an inheritance of slavery and the fact that Portugal has reasonable ethnic diversity. The perceived contradiction built in the slavery period opposed Brazilian natives, Africans, and their descendants on one side against Europeans and their legitimate descendants on the other. Hence the old elites felt they were closer to the immigrants than to the old poor. Another relevant relationship is $\lambda_{krn} > \lambda_{kpo}$. The European and Japanese immigrants, even when poor, tended to have more solidarity with their ethnically similar than their economically similar. This phenomenon weakened class organization in local conflicts.

These differences in preferences and sensitivity to social claims implied that when the social strength of the new elites increased relative to that of the old elites, the ability of the working class formed by immigrants to get greater benefits from public policies was enhanced, although the old poor were seen as a burden for these policies in national alliances. That is why some social policies were relegated to state and county governments, so their qualities were proportional to the share of local population with social strength and voice. Access to public education was among these decentralized policies. States with a higher share of immigrants in their population tended to have more friendly policies on public education. As the immigrants concentrated in specific regions, these differences led to huge regional disparity in Brazil.[6]

Other instruments of differentiation among social groups and classes, in addition to spatial policy heterogeneity, were used in Brazilian society in this period of high social diversity and low cohesion. Labor protection laws are good examples. Despite difficulties in differentiating on this subject, protection rules for urban workers were not fully extended to rural workers or those engaged in informal activities. Such differentiation was built in the origin of these laws and remained until recently.

There are other important relationships among the parameters in Eqs. (13.1)–(13.4) that are relevant to understand the evolution of the Brazilian economy after 1930:

$$\frac{\lambda_m}{\lambda_{mpo}} > \frac{\lambda_k}{\lambda_{kpn}} \quad \frac{\lambda_m}{\lambda_{mpo}} > \frac{\lambda_b}{\lambda_{bro}} \quad \frac{\lambda_m}{\lambda_{mpo}} > \frac{\lambda_a}{\lambda_{arn}}$$

---

5. After redemocratization of Brazil in the 1980s this relationship led to separatist movements in the south, a region mainly populated by European immigrants and their descendants, while Brazilian politics was too much influenced by the old Brazilians. As Rio de Janeiro and São Paulo are important cities and have many European immigrants and their descendants, as well as old Brazilians, the southern separatists certainly wanted to stay with them. The obvious expected disputes over these two cities weakened any separatist movement.

6. See Barros (2011, 2013).

These relationships mean that the poor and old social strata had less solidarity with their fellows in the same social class, and had the lowest class consciousness in Marxian language. This was a consequence of their social composition. They had higher ethnic and cultural diversity and their constant social demoralization made them more introspective, reducing the flourishing of cooperation. Thus despite their predominant share in Brazilian society, the po social class did not cooperate to enforce public policies that could benefit their interests to the extent that their numbers would suggest.

13.4 CLASS CONFLICTS IN THE PERIOD OF SEARCH FOR NATIONAL IDENTITY AND INCENTIVES FOR EDUCATIONAL POLICY

The major social conflicts within this period were among these four social classes with the identities and solidarities noted in the previous section. The state bureaucrats were left outside the major class identification because of their tendency to change their priorities over the years, so it is difficult to define any relevant utility function for them with well-established relationships for their parameters, with some obvious exceptions. Of course the members of this bureaucracy had their own demands, and their power was such that they managed to impose many of these in exchange for their support. Special retirement pensions, high salaries, and job stability are some of their accomplishments beyond those reached by other social groups. Furthermore, their conflict with other social classes was not straightforward and their alliances varied over the whole period.

Members of both elites (rn and ro) selfishly left education to be privately financed, especially for younger children. As the po class was the majority of the population in Brazil, their inclusion in publicly financed education would impose a heavy fiscal burden on the elites. It would cost them less to educate their children if they paid for private education and did not pay their share in the cost to provide this service to all other social classes. Thus their choice over the whole period was to leave education finance to families, with no involvement of the government. Nevertheless, while the majority of the population did not go through the necessary cycles (up to high school) to get to university, it was rational for them to support publicly financed universities, as this would reduce individual costs to attain this service for their descendants. Secondary education was in between these two extremes, with the funding method varying in different states and different periods. As incomes also varied, it was possible to have changes in this situation according to individual incomes in the same social class.

The pn class desired publicly financed education when they started to arrive in Brazil in the late 19th and early 20th centuries, but its members did not have the political power to impose this policy in their new country so soon after their arrival. When they became socially established in Brazil, they also started to reach higher income levels than the po class, as they had more human capital. Hence their interest in publicly financed basic education reduced, as the benefit became relatively low when compared to the costs involved, unless they were located in counties in which they formed a large share of the population.[7] This rationale was a motivation for their support for local governments to be in charge of basic education. Eventually, when they became a high share of the middle class, rationality brought them to support publicly financed universities, and to a lesser extent secondary schools, as their families formed a large share of those who would benefit at these two levels.

The po social class was the one that would gain most from publicly financed primary education. As its members had the lowest incomes, they would have the highest surplus when the benefits are compared to the tax burden that would be imposed on them. Thus their preference was for publicly financed primary education. While few individuals in this class reached the qualifications to claim access to higher education, especially universities, they would lose from public finance for these institutions, under a simple cost–benefit analysis. Hence this policy did not have the support of this social class, at least in the first half of the period under study. Their preference for publicly financed secondary education varied from period to period and depending on social particularities of localities.

It is worth noting that these preferences are for average individuals, and are not common to all. There were differences in preferences arising from particular circumstances. For example, if the decision concerns the share of GDP allocated to education for any social class, a probability density function such as that drawn in Fig. 13.1 might be found. Depending on the circumstances of individuals (income, number of children, etc.) and their solidarities with others, a person could have different preferences, as shown in this figure. Hence the comments on the relationships among preferences are for the average of each class.

13.5 RELEVANT FACTS ABOUT HUMAN CAPITAL EVOLUTION AFTER 1930

These basic incentives among social classes, as outlined in the previous sections, and the evolution of their relative political strength, identity, and organization over the period defined the dynamics of public education in Brazil in the years after 1930. Hence there were many oscillations in the public commitment to education over the period, although it was

---

7. Note that individuals have more solidarity with others of their own social class.

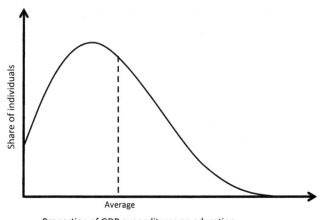

Proportion of GDP expenditures on education

FIGURE 13.1 Probability density function of the distribution of preferences for the share of GDP invested in publicly financed education.

underfinanced most of the time if an optimal long-term growth rate strategy is the target, given the relative political powers of the many social classes in the last 20 years. This section provides data on educational evolution and financing in Brazil since 1933, so the many equilibria among social classes can be identified.

Fig. 13.2 shows the evolution of average schooling years and human capital per capita since 1933. Data for average schooling were extracted from Maduro (2007), from 1933 to 2000, and INEP, from 2000 to 2013. The time series for human capital is generated by a method similar to that in Chapter 8. Firstly, the stock of physical capital is generated from the share of investments in GDP in Brazil from 1900 to 2013.[8] A depreciation rate of 7% is used over the whole period, and the stock of capital at the beginning of the period is set so there was no fall in the capital–output ratio in the first part of the 20th century, up to 1930. This initial level has an almost negligible impact on the relevant data, as only figures after 1933 are actually analyzed.

The next step is to estimate the domestic rate of return to capital, which was obtained from US series on asset returns. The series were the implicit rates extracted from the evolution of the yearly averages for the Dow Jones index from 1922 onwards and the rate of return to corporate bonds from 1939 to 2014.[9]

---

8. Taxa de investimento—preços correntes (% PIB)—Instituto Brasileiro de Geografia e Estatística, Sistema de Contas Nacionais Referência 2000 (IBGE/SCN, 2000 Anual). Extracted from IPEADATA.

9. They were both extracted from the Economic Report of the President, various years.

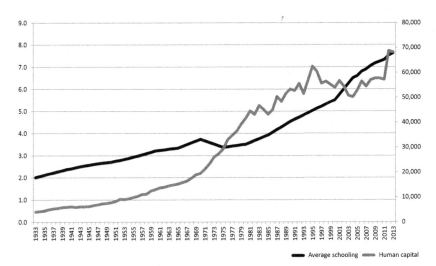

FIGURE 13.2 Human capital stock and schooling in Brazil, 1933–2013. Note: Schooling is measured in the left axis. See text for details on estimations of human capital. *Original data from Maduro Jr., P., 2007. Taxas de Matrícula e Gastos em Educação no Brasil. EPGE-FGV, Rio de Janeiro and INEP for schooling and own estimates for human capital.*

Both US return rates are transformed to Brazilian economy through the assumption of one-year forward arbitrage, so that:

$$(1 + r_{USt}) = \frac{E_t}{E_{t+1}} (1 + r_b) \frac{P_{t+1}}{P_t} \qquad (13.5)$$

where r_{US} is the rate of return in the US asset; E_t is the local currency per US dollar exchange rate; P_t is the Brazilian year average domestic consumer price index (IPC-FIPE); and r_b is the Brazilian equivalent rate of return.[10] With all other variables available, r_b is estimated from Eq. (13.5).

As the two US rates of returns are different for most years, it is necessary to combine them to obtain a unique Brazilian rate of return that could be used to estimate the stock of human capital. Hence, I estimated α for the following Cobb–Douglas production function:

$$Y_t = A_t K_t^{\alpha} (H_t L_t)^{1-\alpha} \qquad (13.6)$$

The first-order condition for profit maximization by all firms implies that:

$$(1 - \alpha_t) = \frac{w_t H_t L_t}{Y_t} \qquad (13.7)$$

---

10. E_{t+1} and P_{t+1} are the exchange rate and price index in the subsequent year. Note that the rational expectations hypothesis was introduced, as the actual future values were taken as the best representation of current expectations.

Data from PNAD-IBGE for average wages and employment and GDP is used to estimate the right-side proportions and, consequently, α_t from the left side. This data is available only from 1992 to 2013. With these figures for these years, r_t is estimated from the other first-order condition for profit maximization by firms, which implies that:

$$\alpha_t = \frac{r_t K_t}{Y_t} \qquad (13.8)$$

As α_t, Y_t, and K_t are already estimated, this equation could generate r_t in Brazil for the period 1992—2013.

A regression is run of this estimated r_t on the two domestically transformed rates of return obtained from Eq. (13.5). This regression generates the right weights to combine the two r_b for the Brazilian economy to generate one unique Brazilian rate of return before 1992, which is r_t in Eq. (13.8). Before 1939, only the transformed series from the Dow Jones is used.

With these estimated r_t, the estimated K_t, and the figures to Y_t (GDP), the series for α_t for the period 1933—91 is created. Eq. (13.7) is used to generate total labor income ($w_t H_t L_t$). Then I assume that:

$$H_t = \frac{w_i H_t L_t}{1 - \left(\frac{1}{1+r_t}\right)} \qquad (13.9)$$

or at any moment the stock of human capital per worker is the present value of all the future flow of income it generates, as seen in Chapter 4. This method relies on the implicit assumptions that human capital does not depreciate; it is embodied in individuals *ad infinitum*; and the current income it generates is the best forecast for its future values. Certainly these are strong assumptions, but the outcome is surely a good approximation. This series for H_t is shown in Fig. 13.2, together with that for schooling years.

The data in Fig. 13.2 indicates that human capital has risen over the whole period from 1933 to 2013. Both series, the average schooling years of the population and the stock of human capital per worker engaged in production, unveil the same long-term trend. This positive trend was also found in the share of GDP dedicated to education in Brazil over this period, as revealed by Fig. 12.3 of Chapter 12. Nevertheless, all three series unveil that there was no steady rise in per capita human capital or social effort to accumulate it over the whole period, but actually the long-term behavior had moments of higher and lower growth of the availability and effort to build this factor of production.

Furthermore, Fig. 13.3 shows that the starting point in the extension of public engagement in building human capital in 1933 was very modest. Less than 5% of the total population was enrolled at any public school level. This share reached 24% in 1999 and started falling thereafter, mainly because of the reduction of the share of young people in the total population. This long-term rise in enrollment as a share of population happened at all three levels,

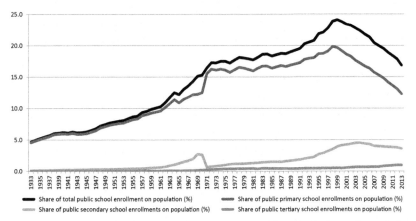

FIGURE 13.3 Brazilian share (%) of enrollments in public schools in total population, 1933−2013. Note: Radical movements between 1970 and 1971 were a consequence of a reform which changed the distribution of years between secondary and primary schools. *Original data from INEP for 2005−13 and Maduro Jr., P., 2007. Taxas de Matrícula e Gastos em Educação no Brasil. EPGE-FGV, Rio de Janeiro for the years before.*

primary, secondary, and tertiary. Thus this data confirms what was concluded from analysis of the data in Figs. 12.2 and 12.3 of Chapter 12. There was a long-term increase in educational effort over this period of Brazilian history. From now on the share of population enrolled in public education is referred to as the extension of the educational effort.

Other important time series for this period focus on the proportion of expenditure on education per student in the total per capita GDP and the share of GDP employed in public education by level. The former unveils the social effort to ensure quality of education for those participating in the public educational system, while the latter reveals the gross social effort for each level of schooling. Fig. 13.4 shows data for the former variable at the three educational levels, while Fig. 13.5 shows the series for the latter, including the aggregated expenditure, which is shown in Fig. 12.3 of Chapter 12. From now on the share of GDP employed in public education is referred to as the social effort toward public education or human capital building, while the proportion of public expenditure on education per student in the total per capita GDP is taken as the quality effort.

Fig. 13.4 shows how students at secondary and tertiary levels were much more valued by society than students at primary schools. Only after 2002, within the Lula term as Brazilian president, did primary schools become relatively more relevant than the other two levels. It could be said that this period was the first in Brazilian history in which secondary schools became an effective important frontier of education for the majority of the poor Brazilian population. The rise of the social effort on this educational level, parallel to that dedicated to primary schools, was also a consequence of the higher

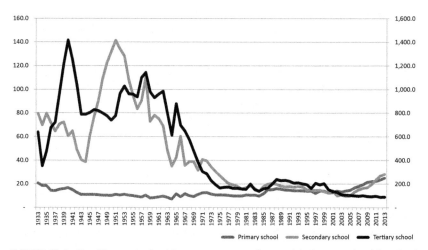

FIGURE 13.4   Brazilian proportion of government expenditure per student at each public school level to per capita GDP. Note: Values for tertiary education are in the right vertical axis. *Expenditures per student:Original data from INEP for 2005–13 and Maduro Jr., P., 2007. Taxas de Matrícula e Gastos em Educação no Brasil. EPGE-FGV, Rio de Janeiro for the years before. Population and GDP: IBGE, extracted from IPEADATA.*

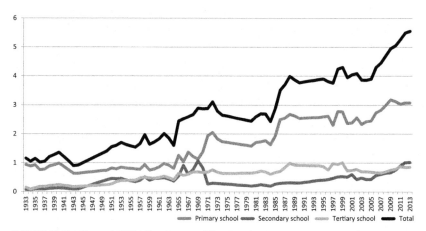

FIGURE 13.5   Share of GDP (%) spent on public education in Brazil by its three levels and total. *Original data from Maduro Jr., P., 2007. Taxas de Matrícula e Gastos em Educação no Brasil. EPGE-FGV, Rio de Janeiro for 1933–2000 and INEP thereafter.*

strength of the po social class in the social and political equilibrium. Fig. 13.5 shows that secondary education became socially more valued than tertiary education in absolute terms in the last years.

Figs. 13.4 and 13.5 add some more important information to Fig. 13.3. While the latter stresses the long-term increasing role of education in Brazilian society throughout the whole period of search for national identity, the former two figures show that there were fluctuations in the social effort on education at different schooling levels. Together, the two figures reveal that there were differences in the emphases on the distinct educational levels in these years. Despite the long-term increase in the social effort on education, there were periods in which social valuation of a particular level of education was above that of others. These differences arose from the relative political and ideological powers and direct gains of the various social classes from these relative changes, analyzed in the next section.

13.6 GENERAL VIEW OF CLASS CONFLICT CONSEQUENCES FOR THE EVOLUTION OF HUMAN CAPITAL

The data in the previous section indicates that there was a long-term trend to improve public investment in education over the whole period of the search for social identity. In addition, it shows that this long-term trend was not steady, but fluctuated, with periods in which these improvements were high and others in which they were lower. Furthermore, this long-term trend was not homogeneous for all performance indicators of public policy for education. In some periods improvements were more concentrated on the quality of particular schooling levels, while others had more focus on extension to a broader share of the population. All these differences depended mainly on the relative power of the many relevant social classes within each period. This could be either political or ideological power. Both stretch the gains of a social class, whether or not they coincide.

A first step to understand the role of each social class in the outcomes from education is to understand their gains and losses from the evolution of the many schooling performance indicators. Table 13.1 summarizes qualitative guesses at the impact of positive changes in such indicators on the balance of welfare for each social class. The positive impact comes directly from the benefits of such policies, while there are also negative impacts arising from the tax burden imposed by these policies. Opportunity costs that could be taken into account are not included in the welfare balances summarized in this table.

These guesses indicate that the po class is the only one that always gains from public investments in education, as its tax burden was low over the whole period and its expenditures on education were so low that all public investments improved its available resources, with negligible tax costs.[11] Hence it can be said that the po had long-term gains in its relative social strength over the whole period, despite some retreats. Often these gains were mainly captured through ideological advancements rather than political power.

---

11. Despite the high share of indirect taxes in the Brazilian public budget, a high share of these up to the 1960s was collected from international trade, and poor consumers had a high share of their consumption concentrated in informal sector goods and services and primary commodities, all facing very low tax burdens.

TABLE 13.1 Summary of Selfish Outcome for Each Social Class From Rises in Human Capital Building Indicators

		Poor and Old	Poor and New	Rich and Old	Rich and New	Bureaucracy
Social effort (share of GDP dedicated to education)	Total	Gain	Gain	Lose	Lose	?
	Primary	Gain more	Lose	Lose	Lose	Lose
	Secondary	Gain	Gain	Gain less	Gain less	Gain less
	Tertiary	Gain less	Gain more	Gain	Gain	Gain more
Quality priority (expenditure per student/per capita GDP)	Total	Gain	Gain	Lose	Lose	?
	Primary	Gain more	Lose	Lose	Loose	Lose
	Secondary	Gain	Gain	Gain less	Gain less	Gain less
	Tertiary	Gain less	Gain more	Gain	Gain	Gain more
Access (enrollment per population)	Total	Gain	Gain	Lose	Lose	Lose
	Primary	Gain more	Lose	Lose	Lose	Lose
	Secondary	Gain	Gain	Gain less	Gain less	Gain less
	Tertiary	Gain less	Gain more	Gain	Gain	Gain more

Elaborated by the author.

For example, the increasing fragility of racist ideas and the rise of policies such as that all children should have access to schooling are ideological advances for these social strata, which prospered even at times in which the political strength of the po class was falling.

At the other extreme, the rn and ro classes lose from public investments in primary education and have limited gains from secondary education. Nevertheless, both benefit reasonably well from tertiary education.[12] In spite of the long-term ascending political strength of the rn,[13] its benefits from public policies saw many reversals over this period, such as the relative fall of the emphasis on quality in tertiary education when compared to other schooling levels. The strong priority for social policies introduced by the 1988 Constitution is another example of its relative loss of ideological and political powers.

The ro face a long-term loss of political power and ideological strength. Persistent advances in agrarian reform policies and the rise in primary education public investments are examples of these losses. Nevertheless, its political strength, arising from its local political power and spatial distribution, helped to keep some of its social benefits and generated periodic gains, even if they were sometimes momentary. For example, it still has a lower tax burden than the rn class, because of its relative higher share of wealth in rental assets, such as land, buildings, warehouses, and houses, as well as its still strong involvement in wholesale trade activities and exporting primary commodities production.

The bureaucracy and the pn classes are in between the two extremes represented by the po on one side and the ro and rn on the other. They gain more from public investments in tertiary education, especially in the most recent years, but also have a positive benefit from secondary education. They both lose from further effort in primary education, as the tax burden was always higher than the benefits they obtain. The proportionally highly urban spatial distribution of these social classes gave an especial ability to press for their interests. The social mobilizations before the military coup of 1964 and those demanding democratization and direct presidential elections in the early 1980s are examples in which these classes were the major social players. Nonetheless, the major demands do not always correspond to their direct interests, as they were influenced by ideologies of other classes. Their ability to apply political pressure always increased political sensitivity to their particular interests. The inability of Brazilian governments to reduce the size of public sector employment and the proportion of public investments spent in middle-class neighborhoods are examples of their enduring political and ideological strength. Periods of Brazilian educational policies in which

---

12. It should be noted that there are implicit assumptions of some credit constraint and/or risk aversion in this hypothesis.
13. See Bresser Pereira (2014) for arguments supporting this hypothesis.

secondary and tertiary schools are the major beneficiaries show moments in which they manage to impose their agenda.

13.6.1 Identification of Subperiods in the Brazilian Search for Social Identity

Before proceeding to a presentation of fluctuations in the relative power of the social classes and specifically their influence on educational policy, it is worth dividing the period 1930–2014 into eight subperiods, listed here, which have more homogeneous social outcomes within them. These subperiods were identified basically from fluctuations or changes in long-term trends of the proportion of public investment in education to GDP, which appears in Fig. 13.5. The extremes of these periods were arbitrary selected, but they were made to coincide with important political events. This division helps identify the role of the relative strength of social classes in the determination of educational public policy.

1. *Vargas's authoritarian regime*, which goes from 1930 to 1945. This was a period with no democracy and a stagnant proportion of investments in education to GDP.
2. *Early democracy*, which extends from 1945 to 1964, when there was the military coup. There was a steady rise of the proportion of public investments in education to GDP.
3. *Military dictatorship*, which extends from 1964 to 1974, when the so-called Brazilian Miracle ended. There was a rise in the proportional investments in public education in this period.
4. *Military authoritarian regime*, extending from 1974 to 1984, when a civilian president was elected. Public investments in education fell within this period.
5. *Redemocratization*, which extends from 1984 to 1989, when there was election of the first president by popular ballot since 1989. There was a strong rise in the social effort toward education, as the ideology of social inclusion gained strength.
6. *Democratic settlement*, which lasted from 1990 to 2002, when Lula, a former union leader, was elected president. There was a very slight rise in the social effort toward education.
7. *Popular democracy* started in 2003, with the first mandate of President Lula, and ended with his last term in 2010. This period saw a steady rise in the share of public investments in education in GDP.
8. *Bureaucratic resurgence*, which started in 2011 and still commands Brazilian politics. It has a similar trend in total effort toward education, although with some changes in priorities in these investments, as the data in Fig. 13.5 indicates.

Taking these periods into account, simple means for the indicators of social effort on human capital accumulation, quality priority, and democratic access were calculated for the first and second halves of each period. When there were odd years within the period, the data for the middle year was discarded for means calculations. The indicators are percentage share of GDP spent by the public sector on education, as a measure of the social effort; percentage of expenditure per enrollment as a share of per capita GDP, as a proxy for quality priority; and enrollment in public schools per head of population, also measured as a percentage, as the measure for access priority.

Table 13.2 shows the means for each indicator in each subperiod. In addition to the totals of these indicators, data is given for the three schooling levels, primary, secondary, and tertiary, and for the first and second halves of the subperiod, respectively. Table 13.3 shows the proportional change between these two parts of the subperiods. Proportional changes were obtained as the first difference of the natural logarithms of the means for the two parts of the subperiod. If it is negative, it means there was a fall in the indicator within the period. The higher the number in Table 13.3 for the subperiod, the higher the proportional rise in the indicator. For example, Table 13.3 shows that the subperiods of the Vargas authoritarian regime and the military authoritarian regime are the two in which there were falls in the total social effort toward education. In the case of the first Vargas era, primary schooling was neglected, while secondary schooling lost social efforts in the military authoritarian regime. It should be noted that the falls in enrollment per population in the two last periods are a consequence of the changes in the population age composition. It is also worth noting that differences of years included within periods demand caution when comparing the numbers from different periods in Table 13.3. This table is built to help comparisons among indicators within the same period.

Table 13.3 shows that all indicators oscillate over the whole period between 1930 and 2013. In most subperiods there are both rising and falling indicators. There is no uniformity even within the classes of indicators, so sometimes there are rises for some schooling levels and falls for others. For example, in the period of democratic settlement (1990−2002) the social effort rose in secondary and total schooling, while it fell in primary and tertiary schooling. This kind of behavior makes the analysis of priorities in human capital building reasonably complex. Furthermore, the benefits obtained by distinct social classes from each educational indicator vary relatively and quantitatively, as noted before. Table 13.1 shows these differences. Hence any analysis of their behavior relying on social conflicts becomes even more complex than could be inferred simply from the variety of changes in the many indicators.

A complete analysis of the evolution of the public investments in education demands a set of hypotheses that, under the assumptions in Table 13.1, would explain the outcomes in Table 13.3. This is a difficult task and it would take a long time to justify such hypotheses, so this exercise is not pursued here. The alternative approach used here is to forward a general view of these outcomes.

TABLE 13.2 Performance Indicators of Social Effort (Share of GDP on Public Education), Quality Priority (Expenditures per Enrollment as a Share of per Capita GDP), and Access Priority (Enrollment in Public Schools per Inhabitant) Throughout the Subperiods

	Share of GDP (%) Dedicated to Education				Expenditures (%) per Enrollment in Public Schools as a Share of per Capita GDP				Enrollment per Population (%) in Public Schools			
	Primary	Secondary	Tertiary	Total	Primary	Secondary	Tertiary	Total	Primary	Secondary	Tertiary	Total
1930–45	0.87	0.09	0.16	1.11	16.83	72.63	638.79	20.88	5.19	0.12	0.02	5.34
	0.76	0.11	0.20	1.08	12.81	52.33	1013.61	17.45	5.94	0.22	0.02	6.18
1945–63	0.74	0.34	0.26	1.34	10.63	110.44	836.18	18.19	6.98	0.30	0.03	7.31
	0.85	0.43	0.47	1.76	9.14	80.31	976.70	17.77	9.29	0.57	0.05	9.90
1964–73	1.14	0.64	0.59	2.36	9.88	42.52	681.76	17.96	11.55	1.50	0.09	13.14
	1.66	0.55	0.70	2.91	11.33	37.12	336.78	17.91	14.54	1.52	0.22	16.28
1974–84	1.68	0.26	0.64	2.58	10.41	24.12	173.30	14.65	16.16	1.08	0.37	17.62
	1.68	0.22	0.67	2.57	10.26	16.10	160.50	14.13	16.42	1.37	0.42	18.21
1985–89	2.22	0.29	0.69	3.20	13.40	18.83	163.07	17.31	16.51	1.51	0.42	18.45
	2.66	0.32	0.96	3.93	15.82	18.97	232.86	20.84	16.78	1.66	0.41	18.86
1990–2002	2.57	0.36	0.91	3.84	14.41	17.18	210.79	18.86	17.81	2.13	0.43	20.37
	2.53	0.51	0.87	4.06	13.23	13.24	169.88	17.28	19.10	3.89	0.52	23.51
2003–10	2.49	0.48	0.69	3.98	14.68	10.83	104.58	18.06	16.98	4.43	0.66	22.07
	3.03	0.67	0.72	4.79	20.25	16.97	96.51	24.22	15.01	4.07	0.75	19.83
2011–14	3.06	0.98	0.86	5.44	23.58	26.19	90.91	30.78	13.01	3.74	0.95	17.70

Calculated by the author using data from Maduro Jr., P., 2007. Taxas de Matrícula e Gastos em Educação no Brasil. EPGE-FGV, Rio de Janeiro, IBGE, and INEP.

TABLE 13.3 Proportional Changes of Means of Indicators in the Second Half of the Period, When Compared to the First-Half Means

	Share of GDP (%) Dedicated to Education				Expenditures (%) per Enrollment in Public Schools as a Share of per Capita GDP				Enrollment per Population (%) in Public Schools			
	Primary	Secondary	Tertiary	Total	Primary	Secondary	Tertiary	Total	Primary	Secondary	Tertiary	Total
1930–45	−0.13	0.27	0.25	−0.03	−0.27	−0.33	0.46	−0.18	0.14	0.59	−0.20	0.15
1945–63	0.13	0.25	0.62	0.27	−0.15	−0.32	0.16	−0.02	0.29	0.64	0.48	0.30
1964–73	0.38	−0.15	0.17	0.21	0.14	−0.14	−0.71	−0.00	0.23	0.01	0.93	0.21
1974–84	0.00	−0.15	0.04	−0.00	−0.01	−0.40	−0.08	−0.04	0.02	0.24	0.12	0.03
1985–89	0.18	0.10	0.33	0.21	0.17	0.01	0.36	0.19	0.02	0.09	−0.03	0.02
1990–2002	−0.01	0.34	−0.05	0.06	−0.09	−0.26	−0.22	−0.09	0.07	0.60	0.18	0.14
2003–10	0.20	0.33	0.05	0.19	0.32	0.45	−0.08	0.29	−0.12	−0.08	0.13	−0.11
2011–14[a]	0.01	0.38	0.17	0.13	0.15	0.43	−0.06	0.24	−0.14	−0.09	0.23	−0.11

The proportional changes are calculated as the difference of the natural logarithms of the two means.
[a]Comparisons are with the second term of the Lula government, between 2007 and 2010.
Calculated by the author using data from Maduro Jr., P., 2007. Taxas de Matrícula e Gastos em Educação no Brasil. EPGE-FGV, Rio de Janeiro, IBGE, and INEP.

TABLE 13.4 Weights Associated With Each Concept in Table 13.1

Concept	Associated Number
Gain more	1.5
Gain	1.0
Gain less	0.5
Lose less	−0.5
Lose	−1.0

Author elaboration.

Further transformation of the data for each period was undertaken, combining the hypothesis in Table 13.1 with the outcomes of Table 13.3. Specifically, the five concepts appearing in Table 13.1 were associated with numbers. These associations appear in Table 13.4. The numbers for each particular social class were multiplied by the proportion between the natural logarithms appearing in Table 13.3 for each period. Thus each social class earned a number for each educational indicator appearing in Table 13.3 for each period.

To make the analysis simpler, an aggregate outcome was generated for each period for each social class. This was calculated as the sum of the previously mentioned multiplication through the lines of each table for each social class. Hence the aggregated statistics have sums for all the indicators for a given period for a specific social class. The sum only included the number referring to schooling levels, as the totals are already fully represented by the evolutions of the indicators at the three levels.

After these initial steps, the mean over the social classes for the statistics for each period was obtained. One more step generated final statistics unveiling the relative performance of each social class in each period, which was calculated subtracting the means over the classes from each individual value for a specific period for each social class. This value was divided by the standard deviation of each period obtained from the data for a given period for all social classes. The outputs of these calculations were the educational relative performances of each social class in each period, given their relative strength in the class struggle. It should be noted that these outputs come from political and ideological strengths and refer only to the educational output of these conflicts. Table 13.5 shows the outputs, and the last line gives averages for all periods for each social class.

All these calculation devices had as major goals to eliminate spurious weighting arising from unit definitions and to reduce the impact of arbitrary

TABLE 13.5 Indicators of Educational Relative Performance of Each Social Class

Period	Poor and Old	Poor and New	Rich and Old	Rich and New	Bureaucracy
1930–45	−0.6	1.2	−1.4	−0.2	1.1
1945–63	0.8	1.4	−1.4	−0.6	−0.1
1964–73	1.6	0.7	−0.8	−0.6	−0.9
1974–84	0.5	1.1	−1.9	−0.0	0.4
1985–89	1.3	1.2	−1.0	−0.8	−0.6
1990–2002	1.1	1.0	−1.5	−0.8	0.1
2003–10	1.5	0.8	−0.8	−1.0	−0.6
2011–14	0.3	1.6	−0.6	−1.5	0.1
Average	**0.8**	**1.1**	**−1.2**	**−0.7**	**−0.1**

Calculated by the author using data from Maduro Jr., P., 2007. Taxas de Matrícula e Gastos em Educação no Brasil. EPGE-FGV, Rio de Janeiro, IBGE, and INEP.

weights appearing in Table 13.4 for gains and losses represented in Table 13.3, through the deviations from means and standardization through division by standard deviations. These last two steps tried to reduce the impact of the length of periods on the statistics so analysis can be conducted comparing periods. It should be noted that there is still a reasonable degree of subjectivity in the outcomes, as the weights attributed to the concepts shown in Table 13.4 are completely arbitrary.

The first obvious conclusion arising from data in Table 13.5 is that there was a long-term fall in the power of the two rich social classes. The two poor social classes, in turn, had gains over almost all periods identified in the table. Thus the long-term evolution of educational indicators in Brazil in the 85 years between 1930 and 2014 unveils that its major determinant was the relative rise in political and/or ideological power of the two poorest classes. Despite the state control by Brazilian elites for most of this period, there was long-term progress in the power of the poorest social strata.

Brazilian bureaucracy has an unstable behavior. Sometimes it behaves like the rich classes, while in other periods it behaves similarly to the pn class, which is also composed mainly by urban segments. It can be seen that the developmental ideology of Roberto Simonsen, Celso Furtado, and many others, which prevailed in the periods of the Vargas authoritarian regime (1930–45), early democracy (1945–64), military authoritarian regime

(1974–84), democratic settlement (1990–2002), and bureaucratic resurgence (2011–14), always had the bureaucracy and the pn classes as its major beneficiaries,[14] at least in what concerns the evolution of education. This corroborates with the hypothesis that this is mainly a middle-class ideology.

Another interesting outcome of these exercises is to narrow the common hypothesis that the Vargas authoritarian regime brought the "masses" to the political stage in Brazil. This data shows that only the interests of the pn social class, which was composed mainly by urban Caucasian descendants, were really contemplated by educational policies. The majority of the poor population, mainly African and native descendants included in the po class, did not benefit from the educational policies. Thus the effect should be rather characterized as a restrictive political inclusion of the "masses."

A curiosity emerges from this data when the relative powers of the po and pn social classes are compared in Lula's (2003–10) and Dilma's (2011–14) terms as presidents. While there were relatively more gains for the po social class in Lula's terms, the reverse happened in Dilma's first term (2011–14). This becomes interesting when it is noted that Lula has origins in the po social class, while Dilma had her origins in the pn class. Each of these presidents biases educational policies for their own class, although they were in the same political alliance in power.

An additional comment is worth making. Data in Table 13.5 indicates a typical case in which *de facto* and *de jure* political powers depart from each other. The military coup of 1964 had as its major goal to avoid a socialist revolution and/or *de facto* control of political power by the po class and urban bureaucracy, perhaps including also some social segments of the pn class. As the ideological battle was mainly in the hands of the bureaucracy and small segments of the pn class, the governability solution found by the militaries was to foster the benefits of the po class through education. Hence although this class was excluded from *de facto* political power, it exercised strong *de jure* political power through the militaries in charge of the state in Brazil in the period 1964–73.

13.7 CONCLUSIONS

There was a long-term improvement in the educational effort in Brazil over the whole period of search for national identity in the years between 1930 and 2014. All indicators for human capital building shown in this chapter unveil this same long-term trend. Furthermore, this effort became increasingly inclusive, extending progressively to a higher share of the total population throughout the whole period under analysis.

---

14. The averages of the statistics in Table 13.5 over these periods for these two social classes are the only ones over the means for all periods.

Nonetheless, this long-term trend was not constant over the years. There were many fluctuations in most relevant indicators, unveiling that human capital building was more intense in some periods and slowed down in others. These fluctuations were not the same for all indicators introduced in this chapter, as they focus on different features of the human capital building process. An explanation for such differences in performance of the distinct indicators is that the consequences of changes in the many features they capture are not similar for all social classes. For example, the elites (rn and ro) benefit more from rises in the quality of tertiary education, while the po gain more from extended public primary and eventually secondary schooling access. Hence, changes in the equilibrium of political and ideological power among social classes led to the diverse performance of the many indicators.

Overall, it can be said that in spite of the oscillations in the performance of the human capital building indicators, there was a long-term rise in the power of the poor social classes, both new and old, to influence human capital building policies in Brazil over this period. As these classes together form the majority of the Brazilian population, their benefits from educational policies boosted Brazilian long-term development, reducing the human capital gap with the benchmark countries, or at least avoiding its widening.

The many political alliances that have governed Brazil since 1930 often resorted to promotion of public investments in education as a proposal to attract the political support of members of the po class, as they were the majority of the Brazilian population. Nevertheless, most of these appeals were not properly translated into policies, with little impact on the quality and extent of education. The low and only slowly rising political organization of the po as a social class restricted the demand for more robust educational policies.

This argument indicates that Brazilian low catch-up since 1930 is a consequence mainly of the fact that λ_{mpo} is low. The low class consciousness of the po class was a major determinant of the low investment in public education that could raise local human capital relative to that of benchmark countries and redefine the sectors and technologies of Brazilian production. This would raise productivity and per capita GDP of the country, reducing its relative backwardness. Ethnic diversity of the po social class was a major cause of this fact.

The data presented here, which is limited to educational statistics, challenges some old ideas on the relative political power of the many social classes in specific periods of recent Brazilian history. For example, the evidence here is that there was an initial fall in the political strength of the po social class in the Vargas authoritarian period (1930−45). Often workers are seen as benefiting from the initial populist era, as Vargas started to build labor rights within this period. This idea is apparently contradictory to what is found in the analysis of preferences of the social classes and the data for educational indicators.

Furthermore, it should be noted that a large share of the Brazilian poor population lived in rural areas and small towns whose economic welfare was very much connected to agricultural and livestock production. Policies protecting local industry harmed the welfare of these social segments. There is no reason to think that some labor benefits to urban workers offset the losses for small towns and rural workers arising from these exchange rate and import tariff policies, as from the poor performance of educational policies.

Chapter 14

Conclusion

Chapter Outline

14.1 INTRODUCTION

This book tries to explain Brazilian relative economic backwardness considering a set of benchmark countries, namely the United States, Canada, Australia, and New Zealand (the Western Offshoots); three countries located in the Southern European Periphery—Portugal, Spain, and Greece; and four in the Northern European Periphery—Sweden, Norway, Switzerland, and Finland. The choice of countries was determined by the desire to understand why Brazil did not succeed in becoming a developed country, thus only countries that had significantly more successful performance were included in the sample. Countries with circumstances excessively different from those of Brazil, such as South Korea, Israel, and Hong Kong, were not included in the comparison because these other differences could jeopardize the comparative effort.

The analysis began with the recent distinction between the proximate and the fundamental or ultimate causes of development, as underlined by North and Thomas (1973), Acemoglu et al. (2005, 2014), Spolaore and Wacziarg (2013), and Caselli (2005), to mention a few examples. While proximate causes highlight the economic mechanics of growth and development, the fundamental causes stress the determinants of these mechanics. This book focuses on both proximate and fundamental causes of Brazilian relative backwardness.

Unlike previous hypotheses put forth to explain Brazilian relative underdevelopment when compared to the benchmark countries, the explanation presented in this book starts from the hypothesis that modern endogenous growth theory is the basic set-up to understand proximate economic growth and development. Thus the book assumes that no serious deviation from the mainstream growth models is necessary to understand Brazilian development, as had been made by previous hypotheses, such as those forwarded by Furtado (1959) and Cardoso and Falletto (1970).

This simple theoretical perspective points to human capital accumulation and technical progress as the major engines of growth or proximate determinants of growth and development. However, the growth model that supports the view of economic dynamics underlying the hypothesis of this book works at a world level, hence most of the endogenous determinants of technical progress and human capital accumulation operate at a world scale. Local public policies can play some role in both enhancements, although they are particularly relevant in human capital accumulation when local relative performance is the object of analysis.

Accordingly, the role of technical progress has not been stressed: it applies to the whole world, because of its high costs of development and the fact that there are gains of scale when it spreads spatially and its output reaches a higher number of consumers.[1] Furthermore, the introduced simplifying assumption that there is full information with no transmission costs negates the relevance of technical progress for the development of a particular country that is not at the forefront of human knowledge, as was the Brazilian case throughout the whole period studied.

To understand relative development levels among countries or regions it is necessary to approach the economy from a world equilibrium, but with many goods and services and monopolistic competition. This model is only able to determine relative income among countries if there is an arbitrary initial human capital spatial distribution. Thus relative per capita gross domestic product (GDP) among nations and regions at any moment would evolve from this initial distribution. Physical capital moves through country frontiers to ensure arbitrage on the markets for factors of production.

Given these basic theoretical ideas, a special focus on the dynamics of human capital spatial availability is necessary. It is argued that a general hypothesis in line with those of perfect flows of factors of production, goods, and services is that the rates of growth of human capital for families around the world, if there is no government intervention, can be very close to each other. Thus initial differences in human capital availability tend to be reproduced over the centuries, although public investments in education and population movements across country borders could change this equilibrium.

Given these general theoretical standpoints, it is possible to propose a particular hypothesis to explain the proximate causes of Brazilian relative backwardness. Other theoretical developments, which are further from a

---

1. Rivera-Batiz and Romer (1991a,b) stress this relationship.

consensus than those summarized here, are necessary to advance an explanation for the fundamental causes of Brazilian relative backwardness, and a specific section of this conclusion is devoted to discussing these.

The next section presents a restatement of the major hypothesis explaining the proximate cause of Brazilian relative backwardness, and is a summary of Chapters 2−9. Section 3 summarizes the hypothesis to explain the fundamental causes of Brazilian relative backwardness, as presented in Chapters 11−13. Section 4 comments on the consequences of the hypotheses of this book for the necessary steps for Brazil to overcome its current backwardness.

14.2 RESTATEMENT OF THE MAJOR HYPOTHESIS

This book presents a simple hypothesis to explain Brazilian relative backwardness when compared to a set of countries, detailed in the previous section. Although the European countries included in the benchmark sample started from a much higher per capita GDP in 1500, when Brazil was officially occupied by the Portuguese, they also widened the gap with respect to Brazilian development, mainly in the 19th century. Chapter 2 gives a more detailed analysis of the data supporting this conclusion.

After identifying the main period of the Brazilian development delay, theoretical foundations of a hypothesis that could explain this delay are introduced in Chapter 3. They envisage a world economy with many countries that would generate multiple possible equilibria, depending on the original per capita spatial distribution of one factor of production, which was taken to be human capital as a consequence of simple conjectures on relative costs of migration and data on the two alternative migrations of human and physical capitals, presented in Chapter 5. The major conclusion of the model in Chapter 3 is that in a world with many goods and many factors of production there is no reason to have any arbitrage incentive for flows of factors of production across country borders after factor price equalization, even if the reached equilibrium would generate high per capita income disparities.

A corollary of this theoretical conclusion is that per capita GDP disparities between Brazil and any benchmark country could be mainly explained through the relative stocks of per capita human capital. This hypothesis is subjected to some analysis in Chapter 4. The conclusion is that human capital is the core explanation of these disparities, especially when the role of endogenous human capital accumulation in physical capital accumulation or international flows of this last factor of production is taken into account.[2]

Thus two questions arise. First, how does human capital move throughout history in specific countries? This question is split into two others. What is the tendency of human capital spatial distribution if families are left to

---

2. Barros (2014) further extends the potential impact of this relationship on the role of human capital in per capita GDP disparities.

accumulate it endogenously, from market incentives, supposing no government intervention? This problem is dealt with in Chapter 5. It shows that without government public investments in human capital there is a tendency for the disparities in the per capita stock of human capital to be reproduced over generations, not only among countries but also among families. Thus inequalities among countries can persist forever under this hypothesis, and there is no market mechanism that pushes for their reduction. The model in Chapter 5 advances this argument, as it shows that public investments in education change the stable rate of accumulation of human capital; consequently, even when the many parameters of the model are similar for the representative families in different countries, those with higher public investments in education tend to have a relatively higher growth of stock of human capital. Thus public policies for human capital accumulation in the 19th century may have been responsible for the widening of the gap between per capita incomes of Brazil and benchmark countries.

Before going into a deeper analysis of the process of human capital building in Brazil and the benchmark countries in the 19th century, a specific source of this accumulation is further analyzed. As Brazil is part of the so-called New World, which includes the European colonies whose occupation had lasted less than 400 years by the 19th century, it was the subject of a sizable population inflow, not only as a consequence of free decisions in Europe, but also as the outcome of enforced transport from Africa. These newcomers had different average stocks of human capital. Thus an exercise is undertaken in Chapter 6 to estimate how much of the human capital embodied in the immigrants could explain the differences in the growth of per capita GDP between 1820 and 1900 when comparing Brazil and the United States. The apparent share of this difference attributed to such population movements is high, reaching 95.7% of the total and offering some initial empirical support to the hypothesis developed.

Chapter 7 starts to focus on the disparities of income between Brazil and European benchmark countries. As these countries had a much higher per capita GDP than Brazil in the early 19th century, the initial concern is to explain such differences in development level between Brazil and Europe. It is shown that the per capita human capital of Brazil was already much lower in the early 19th century than that of European countries, because of the population composition. The high proportion of Africans, natives, and their descendants in the Brazilian population in 1800 accounted for this lower level of per capita human capital.

Given this Brazilian initial lower human capital availability in the early 19th century, Chapter 8 presents estimations of the relative evolution of this stock throughout that century, until 1930. Estimated times series data shows there was a widening of the existing gap for chosen European benchmark countries, especially from the second half of the 19th century. Hence the lower human capital hypothesis could also explain the gap built within this period. Brazil lagged behind because its human capital building in the 19th century was slow.

Chapter 9 starts with a presentation of long-term trends in the proportion of per capita GDP between Brazil and a set of developed countries. The long series indicate that there was stabilization or even a partial trend reversal in inequalities after turning points in the 20th century, which differ from country to country. The chapter builds a hypothesis for this change in the long-term trend. European immigration to Brazil throughout the second half of the 19th century and especially in the first half of the 20th century was a key determinant of this reversal, as it increased Brazilian per capita GDP. Nevertheless, stabilization of differences in educational policies in Brazil and European countries also played some role, especially in the second half of the 20th century.

Chapter 10 brings a transition from discussions of the proximate determinants of Brazilian relative backwardness to the fundamental ones. It presents a survey of previous hypotheses on the subject. The focus is mainly on the views of Latin American structuralists, especially Celso Furtado, dependency theory, represented by Fernando Henrique Cardoso, and an institutionalist view, with a particular focus on the hypothesis forwarded by Raymundo Faoro. While the structuralist hypothesis focuses mainly on proximate causes of development, stressing the loss of capital accumulation potential and productivity increase because of the primary commodities specialization of the Brazilian economy, dependency theory and institutionalists focus on fundamental causes of development. Political alliances among specific social classes enforcing primary commodities specialization were the major cause of Brazilian underdevelopment, according to the view put forth by dependency theory. Inadequate institutions built from the Portuguese colonial inheritance were the major causes of Brazil's failure to be a stage for the flourishing of vibrant capitalism, according to Faoro's standpoint.

14.2.1 Fundamental Causes of Brazilian Underdevelopment

Chapter 11 focuses specifically on the fundamental causes of Brazilian relative development backwardness. It draws on a Marxian hypothesis that social conflicts shape institutions, rather than the other way around, hence it starts from the inversion of the popular current institutionalist hypothesis. The ultimate engine of growth is the history of unceasing social conflicts among social groups, including social classes. The solutions of the social conflicts of today are only the starting point for the conflicts of tomorrow. This permanent evolution of conflicts shapes current institutions, but also generates their continuous evolution. Institutions are seen only as sources of transitory inertia for economic and social consequences of changes in the balance of power among social groups. They work only as frictions for movements among market equilibria. Hence they are something to which economists should give little attention.

From this theoretical standpoint, the hypothesis of this book is that the history of social conflicts in Brazil was such that there was not the necessary focus by public policies on education throughout the 19th and 20th centuries. Thus countries whose social conflicts had as one of their outputs some promotion of human capital accumulation through public policies jumped ahead of those that did not have this outcome. Brazilian conflicts and political hegemonies arising from them were such that this was not a major concern of public policies. The consequence was that the country lagged behind European countries and Western Offshoots. Chapter 12 focuses on the evolution of these conflicts and their consequences for public investments in education in Brazil in the four centuries before 1930. Chapter 13 gives a deeper analysis of the period after 1930.

14.3 SOME RELEVANCE OF THE CONCLUSIONS

The relevant part of the conclusions of this book for economic policies is quite simple: Brazilian relative backwardness will only be overcome through greater effort to provide more and better education to the population of the country. This view is shared by many people, even if they do not agree with most of the analysis forwarded here. As a consequence, there is already a greater effort in Brazilian society regarding education.

This policy, however, has to focus on the majority of the Brazilian population, unlike what has been seen over most of the recent history of the country. There are already relevant corrections of this adverse bias, although there is still a long way to go. As the share of GDP dedicated to public investments in education is already high, the major concern now is with the efficiency of policies. Corporate interests of the involved state bureaucracy, including current teachers, form the major obstacle to the necessary gain of efficiency at present.

Another consequence for policies arising from the analysis of this book is that all the developmental efforts promoted by Brazilian governments over the last century yielded very meager contributions to Brazilian development. Policies to promote specific sectors, such as import tariffs, subsidized credits, and differentiated tax regimes, have very low or no effective impact on development: their major consequence was to transfer income among individuals, mainly those in the business elites of the country. The worst consequence, but one that is also very common, is to enrich segments of the state bureaucracy, sometimes by offering corruption opportunities, but also by justifying their salaries through demands for controls by the public sector.

It is worth noting that some of these policies benefit social classes or segments disproportionately to their relative political power. Their interests were crystallized in ideologies such that even when they were politically weak, they still drew substantial benefits from these policies beyond any relative strength parameter. Current labor laws in Brazil are good examples. Their rigidity and bias toward casual individual gains of a few, at the expense of the majority of workers, benefit mainly judges, lawyers, and union leaders, all members of the state bureaucracy; but they harm all other social segments through their negative impact on the upward trend of wages and productivity. The promoted ideology of labor protection is so strong that it has been an important obstacle for Brazilian development, but is very difficult to overcome.

Overall and as a summing up of this book, it should be stated that countries are less important than smaller social units, such as families, communities, and social classes, in what concerns economic development. Thus national policies should be simpler and less distortive of market incentives. They should focus on ensuring equal access to education of similar quality for all citizens of a country, rather than restricting their contracting freedom. Brazil, in particular, needs a more market-oriented institutional framework with less corporate interests embodied, as well as a more inclusive educational policy with a focus on quality.

References

Abramitzky, R., Boustan, L., Eriksson, K., 2012. Europe's tired, poor, huddled masses: self-selection and economic outcomes in the age of mass migration. American Economic Review 102 (5), 1832—1856.

Acemoglu, D., Autor, D., 2013. Lectures in Labor Economics, Manus. Department of Economics, MIT, Cambridge, Mass.

Acemoglu, D., Johnson, S., 2005. Unbundling institutions. Journal of Political Economy 113 (5), 949—995.

Acemoglu, D., Robinson, J., 2012. Why Nations Fail. Crown Publishers, New York.

Acemoglu, D., Robinson, J., 2015. The rise and decline of general laws of capitalism. The Journal of Economic Perspectives 29 (1), 3—28.

Acemoglu, D., Johnson, S., Robinson, J., 2001. The colonial origins of comparative development: an empirical investigation. American Economic Review 91 (5), 1369—1401.

Acemoglu, D., Johnson, S., Robinson, J., 2002. Reversal of fortune: geography and institutions in the making of the modern world income distribution. Quarterly Journal of Economics 117 (4), 1231—1294.

Acemoglu, D., Johnson, S., Robinson, J., 2005. Institutions as a fundamental cause of long-run growth. In: Aghion, P., Durlauf, S.N. (Eds.), Handbook of Economic Growth, vol. 1A. Elsevier, North-Holland, Amsterdam and Boston, pp. 385—472.

Acemoglu, D., Robinson, J., Gallego, F., February 2014. Institutions, Human Capital and Development. NBER Working Paper, #19933.

Acemoglu, D., 2009. Introduction to Modern Economic Growth. Princeton University Press, Princeton.

Aghion, P., Howitt, P., 1998. Endogenous Growth Theory. MIT Press, Cambridge, Mass.

Alden, D., 1984. Late colonial Brazil, 1750—1808. In: Bethell, L. (Ed.), The Cambridge History of Latin America, Colonial Latin America, vol. 2. Cambridge University Press, Cambridge, UK.

Alexopoulos, J., Cavalcanti, T., 2010. Cheap goods and persistent inequality. Journal of Economic Theory 45 (3), 417—451.

Allen, R., 2001. The great divergence in European prices and wages from the middle ages to the first world war. Explorations in Economic History 38 (4), 411—447.

Almlund, M., Duckworth, A., Heckman, J., Kautz, T., 2011. Personality psychology and economics. In: Hanushek, E., Machin, S., Wößman, L. (Eds.), Handbook of the Economics of Education, vol. 4. Elsevier, Amsterdam.

Alston, L., Libecap, G., Miller, B., 1999. Titles, Conflict and Land Use: the Development of Property Rights and Land Reform on the Brazilian Amazon Frontier. The University of Michigan Press, Ann Arbor.

Arezki, R., Cherif, R., 2010. Development Accounting and the Rise of TFP. IMF Working Paper.

Arrow, K., 1994. Methodological individualism and social knowledge. American Economic Review 84 (2), 1—9.

Arthur, B., 1989. Competing technologies, increasing returns, and lock-in by historical events. Economic Journal 99 (394), 116—131.

Ashraf, Q., Galor, O., 2011. Dynamics and stagnation in the Malthusian Epoch. American Economic Review 101 (5), 2003—2041.

Ashraf, Q., Galor, O., 2013. The 'Out of Africa' hypothesis, human genetic diversity, and comparative economic development. American Economic Review 103 (1), 1—46.

Baer, W., 2008. The Brazilian Economy. Rienner, Bouder.

Barro, R., Lee, J.W., April 2013. Educational Attainment for Total Population, 1950—2010 available for download at: www.barrolee.com/data/yrsch.htm.

Barro, R., Sala-i-Martin, X., 1992. Convergence. Journal of Political Economy 100 (2), 223—251.

Barro, R., Sala-i-Martin, X., 2003. Economic Growth, second ed. McGraw-Hill, New York.

Barro, R., 2012. Convergence and Modernization Revisited. NBER Working Paper, #18295. National Bureau of Economic Research, Cambridge, Mass.

Barros, A., 2011. Desigualdades Regionais No Brasil. Elsevier, Rio de Janeiro.

Barros, A., 2013. Desigualdades regionais e crescimento. In: Veloso, F., Ferreira, P., Giambiagi, F., Pessoa, S. (Eds.), Desenvolvimento Econômico: Uma Perspectiva Brasileira. Campus-Elsevier, Rio de Janeiro.

Barros, A., 2014. Some Evidence on the Sources of Brazilian Relative Backwardness: An Alternative Development Account Method. Datamétrica, Recife unpublished manus.

Becker, G., Murphy, K., Tamura, R., 1990. Human capital, fertility and economic growth. Journal of Political Economy 98 (5), s12—s37.

Becker, G., 1960. An economic analysis of fertility. In: Universities-National Bureau (Ed.), Demographic and Economic Change in Developed Countries. Columbia University Press, New York.

Becker, G., 1964. Human Capital. NBER, New York.

Bethell, L., de Carvalho, J.M., 1989. 1822—1850. In: Bethell, L. (Ed.), Brazil: Empire and Republic, 1822—1930. Cambridge University Press, Cambridge, UK.

Bhattacharya, S., Deb, J., Kundu, T., 2015. Mobility and conflict. American Economic Journal: Microeconomics 7 (1), 281—319.

Bils, M., Klenow, P., 2000. Does schooling cause growth? American Economic Review 90 (5), 1160—1183.

Black, S., Devereux, P., 2010. Recent developments in intergenerational mobility. In: Ashenfelter, O., Card, D. (Eds.), Handbook of Labor Economics, vol. 4B. Elsevier, Amsterdam (Chapter 16).

Black, S., Devereux, P., Salvanes, K., 2005. Why the apple doesn't fall far: understanding inter-generational transmission of human capital. American Economic Review 95 (1), 437—449.

Bolt, J., van Zanden, J.L., 2013. The First Update of the Maddison Project: Re-estimating Growth Before 1820. Maddison Project Working Paper 4.

Bonelli, R., Pessoa, S., Matos, S., 2013. Padrões de crescimento industrial no Brasil. In: Veloso, F., Cavalcanti, P., Giambiagi, F., Pessoa, S. (Eds.), Desenvolvimento Econômico: Uma Perspectiva Brasileira. Campus, Rio de Janeiro.

Bordo, January 20—29, 2002. Globalization in historical perspective. Business Economics 37 (1).

Borjas, G., 1987. Self-selection and the earnings of immigrants. American Economic Review 77 (4), 531—553.

Borjas, G., 1991. Immigration and self-selection. In: Abowd, J.M., Freeman, R.B. (Eds.), Immigration, Trade, and the Labor Market. University of Chicago Press, Chicago, pp. 29—76.

Borjas, G., 2008. Labor outflows and labor inflows in Puerto Rico. Journal of Human Capital 2 (1), 32—68.

Bresser Pereira, L.C., 1964. Origens étnicas e sociais do empresário paulista. Revista de Administração de Empresas 3 (11).

Bresser Pereira, L.C., 1974. Empresários e Administradores no Brasil. Brasiliense, São Paulo.

Bresser Pereira, L.C., September, 1993. Empresários, Suas Origens e as Interpretações do Brasil. In: Paper presented in the I Congresso Brasileiro de História Econômica e à II Conferência Internacional de História de Empresas. Campinas-SP, Unicamp.

Bresser Pereira, L.C., 2008. Burocracia Pública Na Construção Do Brasil. FGV, Mimeo, São Paulo.

Bresser Pereira, L.C., 2014. A Construção Política do Brasil: Sociedade, Economia e Estado desde a Independência. Editora, São Paulo, p. 34.

Brezis, E., 1995. Foreign capital flows in the century of Britaiñs industrial revolution: new estimates, controlled conjectures. Economic History Review 48 (1), 46—67.

Broadberry, S., Campbell, B., Klein, A., Overton, M., van Leeuwen, B., 2011. Appendix for British Economic Growth, 1270—1870: An Output-based Approach. London School of Economics, Manus.

Broadberry, S., Campbell, B., Klein, A., Overton, M., van Leeuwen, B., 2012. British Economic Growth, 1270—1870: An Output Based Approach. Studies in Economics #1203. Department of Economics, University of Kent.

Buarque, S., 1936. Raízes Do Brasil. José Olympio, Rio de Janeiro.

Card, D., Krueger, A., 1992. Does school quality matter? Returns to education and the characteristics of public schools in the United States. The Journal of Political Economy 100 (1), 1—40.

Card, D., Krueger, A., 1996. Labor Market Effects of School Quality: Theory and Evidence. NBER Working Paper Series, #5450. NBER, Cambridge, Mass.

Cardoso, F.H., Faletto, E., 1970. Dependência e Desenvolvimento na América Latina: Ensaio de Interpretação Sociológica, seventh ed. Editora LTC, Rio de Janeiro.

Cardoso, F.H., 1964. Empresário Industrial e Desenvolvimento Econômico. Difusão Europeia do Livro, São Paulo.

Cardoso, F.H., 2013. Pensadores Que Inventaram O Brasil. Companhia das Letras, São Paulo.

Caselli, F., Coleman, W., 2013. On the theory of ethnic conflict. Journal of the European Economic Association 11 (S1), 161—192.

Caselli, F., 2005. Accounting for cross-country income differences. In: Aghion, P., Durlauf (Eds.), Handbook of Economic Growth. Elsevier, Amsterdam.

Chang, W., 1979. Some theorems on trade and general equilibrium with many goods and factors. Econometrica 47, 709—726.

Chiswick, B., Hatton, T., 2003. International migration and the integration of labor markets. In: Bordo, M., Taylor, A., Williamson, J. (Eds.), Globalization in Historical Perspective. University of Chicago Press, Chicago, pp. 65—120.

Chiswick, B., 1999. Are immigrants favorably self-selected? American Economic Review 89 (2), 181—185.

Chiswick, B., 2000. Are immigrants favorably self-selected? An economic analysis. In: Brettell, C., Hollifield, J. (Eds.), Migration Theory: Talking Across Disciplines. Routledge, New York, pp. 61—76.

Cury, C., 2001. Cidadania republicana e educação: governo provisório do marechal Deodoro e Congresso Constituinte de 1890—1891. DP&A, Rio de Janeiro.

Darendorf, R., 1959. Class and Class Conflict in Industrial Society. Stanford University Press, Stanford.

Daude, C., Fernández-Arias, E., 2010. On the Role of Productivity and Factor Accumulation in Economic Development. IDB Working Paper Series, IDB-WP-155. Inter-American Development Bank.

Dean, W., 1971. A industrialização de São Paulo (1980—1945). Difel/Edusp, São Paulo.

Diamond, J., 1997. Guns, Germs, and Steel: the Fates of Human Societies. W.W. Norton & Company, New York.

Dillingham, W., 1911. Statistical Review of Immigration 1820—1910. Government Printing Office, Washington.

Ding, N., Field, B., 2004. Natural Resource Abundance and Economic Growth. Working Paper, No. 2004-7. Department of Resource Economics, University of Massachusetts, Amherst, MA. Available for download at: http://www.umass.edu/resec/workingpapers.

Easterly, W.R., Levine, R., 2012. The European Origins of Economic Development. NBER Working Paper, # 18162. Cambridge, Mass.

Edvinsson, R., 2005. Growth, Accumulation, Crisis: With New Macroeconomic Data for Sweden. Almqvist & Wiksell International, Stockholm.

Edvinsson, R., 2013. Historical National Accounts for Sweden 1800—2000. Groningen University, Groningen.

Engerman, S., Sokoloff, K., 1997. Factor endowments, institutions, and differential paths of growth among new World economies: a view from economic historians of the United States. In: Haber, S. (Ed.), How Latin America Fell Behind. Stanford University Press, Stanford.

Engerman, S.L., Mariscal, E., Sokoloff, K.L., 2009. The evolution of schooling institutions in the Americas, 1800—1925. In: Eltis, D., Lewis, F., Sokoloff, K. (Eds.), Human Capital and Institutions: A Long Run View. Cambridge University Press, UK, New York, pp. 93—142.

Esteban, J., Ray, D., 2011. Linking conflict to inequality and polarization. American Economic Review 101 (4), 1345—1374.

Esteban, J., Mayoral, L., Ray, D., 2012. Ethnicity and conflict: an empirical study. American Economic Review 102 (4), 1310—1342.

Faoro, R., 2001. Os Donos Do Poder, third ed. Editora Globo, Rio de Janeiro.

Fausto, B., 1970. A Revolução de 1930-Historiografia e história. Brasiliense, São Paulo.

Feenstra, R.C., Inklaar, R., Timmer, M.P., 2013. The Next Generation of the Penn World Table available for download at: www.ggdc.net/pwt.

Feenstra, R., 2004. Advanced International Trade. Princeton University Press, Princeton.

Feliciano, C., 2005. Educational selectivity in U.S. immigration: how do immigrants compare to those left behind? Demography 42 (1), 131—152.

Ferreira, P.C., Pessoa, S., Veloso, F., 2013. On the evolution of total factor productivity in Latin America. Economic Inquiry 51 (1), 16—30.

Frank, A.G., 1967. Capitalism and Underdevelopment in Latin America. Monthly Review Press, New York.

Freyre, G., 1933. Casa Grande & Senzala. Maia & Schmidt, Rio de Janeiro.

Furtado, C., 1959. Formação Econômica Do Brasil. Fundo de Cultura, Rio de Janeiro.

Gibson, C., Jung, K., 2002. Historical Census Statistics on Population Totals by Race, 1790 to 1990, and by Hispanic Origin, 1970 to 1990. For The United States, Regions, Divisions and States, US Census Bureau, Working Paper #56.

Glaeser, E., 2011. Triumph of the City. Penguin Press, New York.

Gohn, M., 1995. História dos Movimentos e Lutas Sociais: A Construção da Cidadania dos Brasileiros. Loyola, São Paulo.

Goldin, C., Katz, L., 2008. The Race Between Education and Technology. Harvard University Press, Cambridge, Mass.

Goldsmith, R., 1986. Brasil 1850—1984: Desenvolvimento financeiro sob um século de inflação. São Paulo.

Gollin, D., 2002. Getting income shares right. Journal of Political Economy 110 (2), 458—474.

Gould, E.D., Moav, O., 2010. When Is 'Too Much' Inequality Not Enough? The Selection of Israeli Emigrants. http://www.ecore.be/Papers/1280145355.pdf.

Graff, H., 1987. The Legacies of Literacy: Continuities and Contradictions in Western Culture and Society. Indiana University Press, Indianapolis.

Gramsci, A., 1971. Selections From the Prison Notebooks. Lawrence & Wishart, London.

Grogger, J., Hanson, G., 2008. Income Maximization and the Selection and Sorting of International Migrants. NBER Working Paper, #13821. NBER, Cambridge, Mass.

Guimarães, A.P., 1977. Quatro séculos de latifúndio, fourth ed. Paz e Terra, Rio de Janeiro.

Hall, R., Jones, C., 1999. Why do some countries produce so much more output per worker than others? Quarterly Journal of Economics 114 (1), 83−116.

Harcourt, G., 1972. Some Cambridge Controversies in the Theory of Capital. Cambridge University Press, Cambridge, UK.

Hatton, T.J., Williamson, J.G., 1992. International Migration and World Development: A Historical Perspective. NBER working paper series on historical factors in long run growth, #41. NBER, Cambridge, Mass.

Hatton, T.J., Williamson, J.G., 1998. The Age of Mass Migration: Causes and Economic Impact. Oxford University Press, New York.

Heckman, J., Kautz, T., 2012. Hard Evidence on Soft Skills. NBER Working Paper, #18121. NBER, Cambridge, Mass.

Heckman, J.J., Humphries, J.E., Urzua, S., Veramendi, G., 2011. The Effects of Educational Choices on Labor Market, Health, and Social Outcomes (Unpublished manuscript). University of Chicago, Department of Economics.

Heckman, J., Stixrud, J., Urzua, S., 2006. The effects of cognitive and noncognitive abilities on labor market outcomes and social behavior. Journal of Labor Economics 24 (3), 411−482.

Hegel, G.F., 2001. The Philosophy of History, Kitchener. Batoche Books, Ontario, Canada originally published in German in 1837.

Hertz, T., Jayasundera, T., Piraino, P., Selcuk, S., Smith, N., Verashchagina, A., 2007. The inheritance of educational inequality: international comparisons and fifty-year trends. The B.E. Journal of Economic Analysis & Policy 7 (2), 1−46.

Hoffman, M., 2004. International capital mobility in the long run and the short run: can we still learn from saving-investment data? Journal of International Money and Finance 23, 113−131.

Houston, R.A., 2011. Literacy. In: European History Online (EGO). The Institute of European History (IEG). http://www.ieg-ego.eu/houstonr-2011.

Hsieh, C.-T., Klenow, P.J., 2010. Development accounting. American Economic Journal: Macroeconomics 2 (1), 207−223.

Ianni, O., 1975. O Colapso Do Populismo No Brasil, third ed. Civilização Brasileira, Rio de Janeiro.

IBGE, 1990. Estatísticas Históricas Do Brasil. IBGE, Rio de Janeiro.

Imlah, A., 1958. Economic Elements in the Pax Britannica. Studies in British Foreign Trade in the Nineteenth Century. Harvard University Press, Cambridge, Mass.

Jerome, H., 1926. Significant features of migration. In: Jerome, H. (Ed.), Migration and Business Cycles. NBER, Cambridge, Mass, pp. 29−53.

John, O.P., Srivastava, S., 1999. The big five trait taxonomy: history, measurement and theoretical perspectives. In: Pervin, L.A., John, O.P. (Eds.), Handbook of Personality: Theory and Research, Chapter 4. The Guilford Press, New York, pp. 102−138.

Jones, R., Scheinkman, J., 1977. The relevance of the two-sector production model in trade theory. Journal of Political Economy 85 (5), 909−935.

Jones, B., 2008. The Knowledge Trap: Human Capital and Development Reconsidered. NBER Working Paper, #14138. NBER, Cambridge, Mass.

Keeling, D., 1999. The transportation revolution and transatlantic migration, 1850–1914. In: Field, A.J., Clark, G., Sundstrom, W.A. (Eds.), Research in Economic History, vol. 19. JAI Press, Stamford, CT, pp. 39–74.

King, R.G., Levine, R., 1994. Capital fundamentalism, economic development, and economic growth. In: Carnegie-Rochester Conference Series on Public Policy 40, pp. 259–292.

Klenow, P.J., Rodríguez-Clare, A., 1997. The neoclassical revival in growth economics: has it gone too far? In: Bernanke, B., Rotemberg, J.J. (Eds.), NBER Macroeconomics Annual, vol. 12. MIT Press, Cambridge, MA, pp. 73–103.

Leamer, E., February 1995. The Heckscher-Ohlin Model in Theory and Practice. Princeton Studies in International Finance, #77. International Finance Section, Department of Economics, University of Princeton, Princeton.

Leff, N., 1982. Underdevelopment and Development in Brazil, 2 vols. George Allen & Unwin, London.

Leff, N., 1997. Economic development in Brazil, 1822–1913. In: Haber, S. (Ed.), How Latin America Fell behind. Stanford University Press, Stanford.

Lindert, P., Williamson, J., 2014. American Colonial Incomes, 1650–1774. NBER Working Paper, #19861. NBER, Cambridge, Mass.

Long, J., Ferrie, J., 2013. Intergenerational occupational mobility in Great Britain and the United States since 1850. American Economic Review 103 (4), 1109–1137.

Lovejoy, P., 2000. Transformation in Slavery: History of Slavery in Africa. Cambridge University Press, Cambridge, UK.

Lovejoy, P., 2011. African Contributions to Science, Technology and Development. UNESCO, The Slave Route Project, Manus, Ouidah, Benin.

Lucas, R., 1980. Methods and problems in business cycle theory. Journal of Money, Credit, and Banking 12 (4), 696–715.

Lucas, R., 1988. On the mechanics of economic development. Journal of Monetary Economics 22 (1), 3–42.

Maddison, A., 2001. The World Economy: A Millenial Perspective. OECD, Paris.

Maddison, A., 2011. Historical Statistics of the World Economy: 1-2008 AD. Maddison Project.

Maduro Jr., P., 2007. Taxas de Matrícula e Gastos em Educação no Brasil. EPGE-FGV, Rio de Janeiro.

Malthus, T., 1798. An Essay on the Principle of Population as It Affects the Future Improvement of Society.

Manta, F., Pereira, R., Vianna, R., Araújo, A., Gitaí, D., da Silva, D., Wolfgramm, E., Pontes, I., Aguiar, J., Moraes, M., Carvalho, E., Gusmão, L., 2013. Revisiting the genetic ancestry of Brazilians using autosomal AIM-Indels. PLoS One 8 (9), 1–11.

Marcílio, M., 1984. The population of colonial Brazil. In: Bethell, L. (Ed.), The Cambridge History of Latin America, Colonial Latin America, vol. 2. Cambridge University Press, Cambridge, UK.

Marx, K., Engels, F., 2004. Manifesto of the communist party. Marxists Internet Archive 1848.

Marx, K., 1867 (English translation, 1967). Capital, vol. I. International Publishers, New York.

Meyerink, K., Szucs, L., 1984. The Source: A Guidebook to American Genealogy. Ancestry, Provo, UT.

Milanovic, B., Lindert, P., Williamson, J., 2007. Measuring Ancient Inequality. NBER Working Paper, #13550. National Bureau of Economic Research, Cambridge, Mass.

Mincer, J., 1958. Investment in human capital and personal income distribution. Journal of Political Economy 66 (4), 281–302.

Mincer, J., 1974. Schooling, Experience, and Earnings. NBER Press, New York.

Mitchell, B., 1988. British Historical Statistics. Cambridge University Press.

Mortara, G., 1941. Estudos Sobre a Utilização do Censo Demográfico para a Reconstrução das Estatísticas do Movimento da População no Brasil. Revista Brasileira de Estatística, IBGE 2 (5), 39–89.

Moura, C., 1987. Os quilombos e a rebelião negra. Brasiliense, São Paulo.

Musacchio, A., Fritscher, A., Viarengo, M., 2014. Colonial institutions, trade shocks, and the diffusion of elementary education in Brazil, 1889–1930. The Journal of Economic History 74 (3), 730–766.

Nichols, A., Favreault, M., 2009. A Detailed Picture of Intergenerational Transmission of Human Capital, manus. Urban Insitute, Washignton, D.C.

North, D., Thomas, R., 1973. The Rise of the Western World: A New Economic History. Cambridge University Press, Cambridge, UK.

North, D., 1990. Institutions, Institutional Change, and Economic Performance. Cambridge University Press, New York.

Nunn, N., 2007. The Long-term Effects of Africa's Slave Trade. NBER Working Paper, #13367. NBER, Cambridge, Mass.

Obstfeld, M., Taylor, A., 2003. Globalization and capital markets. In: Bordo, M., Taylor, A., Williamson, J. (Eds.), Globalization in Historical Perspective. University of Chicago Press, Chicago.

Obstfeld, 2002. Globalization and capital mobility in historical perspective. Revista de Economia 9 (1), 5–19.

OECD, 2013. PISA 2012 Results: What Students Know and Can Do. OECD, Paris available for download at: www.oecd.org/pisa/keyfidings/pisa-2012-results.

Olsson, O., Hibbs, D., 2005. Biogeography and long-run economic development. European Economic Review 49 (4), 909–938.

ÓRourke, K., 2004. The Era of Free Migration: lessons for Today. IIIs Discussion Paper.

Piketty, T., 2014. Capital in the Twenty-first Century. Belknap, London.

Pinker, S., 1997. How the Mind Works. W.W. Norton, New York.

Prado Jr., C., 1945. História Econômica Do Brasil. Brasiliense, São Paulo.

Prebisch, R., 1949. El Dasarrollo Económico en America Latina y Algunos de sus Principales Problemas. Reproduced in Desarrollo Econômico, 26 (103), 479–502, 1986.

Prescott, E.C., 1998. Needed: a theory of total factor productivity. International Economic Review 39 (3), 525–551.

Putterman, L., Weil, D., 2010. Post-1500 population flows and the long run determinants of economic growth and inequality. Quarterly Journal of Economics 125 (4), 1627–1682.

Ranis, G., 1991. Towards a model of development. In: Krause, L.B., Kim, K. (Eds.), Liberalization in the Process of Economic Development. University of California Press, Berkeley, CA, pp. 59–101.

Redekop, B., 2009. Common Sense in Philosophical and Scientific Perspective. Christopher Newport University, Manus.

Reis, J., Gomes, F., 1996. Liberdade por um fio. História dos quilombos no Brasil. Cia. das Letras, São Paulo.

Ribeiro, D., 1995. O Povo Brasileiro: A formação e o sentido de Brasil. Companhia das Letras, São Paulo.

Rivera-Batiz, L., Romer, P., 1991a. International trade with endogenous technological change. European Economic Review 35 (4), 971–1001.

Rivera-Batiz, L., Romer, P., 1991b. Economic integration and endogenous growth. The Quarterly Journal of Economics 106 (2), 531–555.

Robinson, J., 1953−54. The production function and the theory of capital. Review of Economic Studies 21 (2), 81−106.

Rodrik, D., 2011. The Future of Economic Convergence. NBER Working Papers, #17400. National Bureau of Economic Research, Cambridge, Mass.

Roser, M., 2014. "Literacy," Our World in Data. Retrieved from: http://www.ourworldindata.org/data/education-knowledge/literacy.

Roy, A.D., 1951. Some thoughts on the distribution of earnings. Oxford Economic Papers New Series 3 (2), 135−146.

Sacerdote, B., 2002. The nature and nurture of economic outcomes. American Economic Review 92 (2), 344−348.

Sachs, J., Warner, A., 1995. Natural Resources Abundance and Economic Growth. NBER Working Paper #5398. NBER, Cambridge, Mass.

Samuelson, P., 1948. International trade and the equalization of factor-prices. Economic Journal 58, 163−184.

Samuelson, P., 1949. International factor price equalization once again. Economic Journal 59, 181−197.

Schmidt, F.L., Hunter, J., 2004. General mental ability in the world of work: occupational attainment and job performance. Journal of Personality and Social Psychology 86 (1), 162−173.

Schumpeter, J.A., 1934. The Theory of Economic Development: An Inquiry into Profits, Capital, Credit, Interest and the Business Cycle. Transaction Publishers, New Brunswick, NJ.

Sen, A., 1999. Development as Freedom. Oxford University Press, Oxford.

Simonsen, R., 1957. História Econômica Do Brasil. Companhia Editora Nacional, São Paulo.

Sjaastad, L.A., 1962. The costs and returns of human migration. Journal of Political Economy 70 (Suppl.), 80−93.

Skidmore, T., 1967. Politics in Brazil 1930−1964: An Experiment in Democracy. Oxford University Press, Oxford.

Solow, R., 1956. A contribution to the theory of economic growth. Quarterly Journal of Economics 70 (1), 65−94.

Spolaore, E., Wacziarg, R., 2013. How deep are the roots of economic development. Journal of Economic Literature 51 (2), 325−369.

Sraffa, P., 1960. Production of Commodities by Means of Commodities: Prelude to a Critique of Economic Theory. Cambridge University Press, Cambridge, UK.

Stiglitz, J., 1974. The Cambridge-Cambridge controversy in the theory of capital: a view from New Haven: a review article. Journal of Political Economy 82 (4), 893−903.

Takayama, A., 1982. On theorems of general competitive equilibrium of production and trade: a survey of recent developments in the theory of international trade. Keio Economic Studies 19, 1−38.

Taylor, A., 1996. International Capital Mobility in History: The Saving-investment Relationship. NBER Working Paper, #5743, Cambirdge, Mass.

The Conference Board, January 2014. Total Economy Database. http://www.conference-board.org/data/economydatabase/.

Thomas, R., Hills, S., Dimsdale, N., 2010. The UK recession in context — What do three centuries of data tell us? Bank of England Quarterly Bulletin Q4. Available at SSRN: http://ssrn.com/abstract=1730149.

Thornton, R., 2000. Population history of native North American. In: Haines, M., Steckel, R. (Eds.), Population History of North America. Cambridge University Press, Cambridge.

UNESCO, 2006. Education for All Global Monitoring Report 2006. UNESCO.

Villela, A., 2011. A bird's eye view of Brazilian industrialization. In: Baer, Fleischer (Eds.), The Economies of Argentina and Brazil: A Comparative Perspective. Edward Elgar, Northampton, Mass.

Weber, M., 1930. The Protestant Ethic and the Spirit of Capitalism. Routledge, London.

Weber, M., 1968. Economy and Society. University of California Press, Berkeley.

Wegge, S., 1999. To part or not to part: emigration and inheritance institutions in nineteenth-century Hesse-Cassel. Explorations in Economic History 36 (1), 30—55.

Wegge, S., 2002. Occupational self-selection of European emigrants: evidence from nineteenth-century Hesse-Cassel. European Review of Economic History 6 (3), 365—394.

Wegge, S., 2009. Do Migrant Origins Matter? Migrants Vs. Non-migrants: Self-selection of Migrants Out of the Home Population. Manuscript. College of Staten Island & Graduate Center, City University of New York.

Wegge, S., 2010. Who Migrated and Who Stayed Home? The Village Versus the Individual: Self-selection of Migrants Out of the Home Population in 19th Century Germany. Unpublished.

World Bank, 1997. Expanding the Measure of Wealth: Indicators of Environmentally Sustainable Development. World Bank, Washington.

World Bank, 2011. The Changing Wealth of Nations: Measuring Sustainable Development in the New Millennium. World Bank, Washington.

World Bank, 2013. World Economic Indicators. World Bank, Washington.

Xie, Y., Killewald, A., 2013. Intergenerational occupational mobility in Great Britain and the United States since 1850: comment. American Economic Review 103 (5), 2003—2020.

Index

'*Note:* Page numbers followed by "f" indicate figures and "t" indicate tables.'

Printed in the United States
By Bookmasters